I0457849

The Book of John
A Gospel of Endurance

Written by:
J. Scott

SPARKY BITES
PUBLISHING

A VACANT DOG IN A VICIOUS LOT

ISBNs:
Hardcover: 978-1-968023-04-1
Paperback: 978-1-968023-05-8
eBook: 978-1-968023-06-5
Audiobook: 978-1-968023-07-2

This is a work of narrative nonfiction inspired by true events. Names, locations, and certain details have been changed or fictionalized to protect privacy and support the story's structure. Composite characters and dramatized scenes have been used for clarity and emotional resonance, though the core truths remain faithful to the lived experiences.

This book is not intended to provide medical, psychological, or theological advice. Readers seeking such support should consult qualified professionals.

Any resemblance to actual persons, living or dead, is coincidental unless explicitly stated.

The views expressed are solely those of the author and do not represent any institutions mentioned or alluded to.

This book includes depictions of abuse and trauma. Reader discretion is advised.

First Edition, August 2025
Written by J. Scott
Cover Design by J. Scott
Narrative by J. Scott
Edited by J. Scott
For more information, visit sparkybitespublishing.com

Content Note:
This book includes depictions of domestic violence, physical abuse of a minor, suicidal ideation, and references that may imply sexual abuse. Reader discretion is advised. If you or someone you know is affected by these topics, support resources are listed at the end of the book.

To my father,
who walked through every fire with faith, who loved without conditions,
who showed me what it means to endure with grace.

And to every family member, nurse, doctor, friend, and stranger who stood
beside him when the road grew dark—
this story belongs to you, too. You were the quiet miracles. You helped carry
the light.

Table of Contents

Foreword

He was born in 1945, as one war was ending—and another one, the one inside him, was quietly beginning.

He never wanted to be a symbol. He just wanted to be a husband. A father. A man with a good pair of boots—and a Bible that didn't fall apart in the middle—especially not in the middle of a promise.

I didn't write this to prove anything. I wrote it so he'd be remembered. Not as a war story. Not as a diagnosis. But as a gospel. Not the kind written in Greek and studied under steeples—but the kind lived in pain and quiet faith. A gospel of endurance.

Some parts of this story may be hard to read—especially for those who knew my grandfather only as a gentle man in his later years. But this is the truth my father lived through. The pain wasn't the whole story, but it was part of it. And my hope is that, by seeing it through our eyes, you'll better understand the depth of my father's quiet strength—and what it cost him to become the man we came to love.

My father never passed that pain on with his hands—he broke the cycle. But we saw it in his eyes. In the weight he carried. In the grief of a son who was betrayed by the man meant to protect him. His suffering was generational, not physical—but it shaped everything.

So if you've come here looking for something clean or easy— something tied with a theological bow—you won't find it.

But if you've come looking for light in the dark… you're not alone.

Prologue: Refined by Fire

"It's necessary to go through the fire to be tempered and refined."

Those were my father's words.

Not poetic. Not theoretical. He meant it literally.

He didn't mean metaphorical fire.

He meant Vietnam—the sharp report of mortars splitting the sky, the heat of blood beneath your palms, the weight of someone else's last breath. He meant coming home with a whole body and a shattered memory.

He meant holding your wife's hand in the doctor's office, waiting to hear how much time you had left together.

Prologue: Refined by Fire

He meant sitting in a camper with your sons outside a VA hospital, calling a campground home while hope and healing stayed just out of reach.

He meant watching your little girl die—and still waking up the next morning because someone still needed you.

Fire, to him, was never just a metaphor.

But neither was redemption.

He learned something in those years that he didn't read in a book or hear in a sermon. He learned that refinement doesn't come before the flames. It comes through them.

And somehow, instead of letting it harden him, he let the fire hollow him. He let the fire take a part of him—so he could make room for others.

He told other vets: "Your hell isn't hotter than anyone else's."

Because when you realize you're not the only one burning, the smoke stops feeling like shelter.

You stop leaning on crutches that feel like comfort—but collapse under real weight.

You start walking through the fires. Not around. Not above.

Through.

He never asked to be anyone's example. He just refused to let the fire define the end of the story.

This book isn't about escape. It's about endurance. About being broken and still standing. About presence in the pain, and the sacredness of showing up when no one else does.

If the Gospel of John is about signs that point to God, then this is about a man who became one.

This isn't a biography. It's not a sermon either.

It's a map of the fires he walked through—and the people who learned, because of him, that you don't have to run from the heat to find hope.

He didn't quote scripture often. But when he did, it wasn't to impress—it was because it lived inside him.

He didn't use scripture to win debates.

He sang it like a song that never left him. Especially the words from the Gospel of John.

"The light shines in the darkness, and the darkness has not overcome it."

He believed that. Even when he couldn't see the light.

Especially then.

So maybe this isn't just *The Book of John*. Maybe it's a book for everyone who thinks God has gone quiet. For the brokenhearted. The doubting. The barely-holding-on.

You're not forgotten.

You're not disqualified.

Prologue: Refined by Fire

You're not alone in the fire.

Because sometimes, the miracle isn't escaping the flames.

Sometimes, the miracle is finding someone who walks through them with you—and realizing, somehow, you're still standing.

This is the fire.

And this... is what came through it.

I: Let There Be Pain

I wasn't there when the tomb split open. But I've seen stones roll away in quieter places—in the hush after a slammed door, in the stillness of a child's breath returning, in the moment a man decides to stay.

And once, in room 304.

I didn't ask for a miracle that day. But we don't get to direct the miracles—they come for reasons beyond us.

And even for someone who's seen them, who knows they're real... when it happens right in front of you, it still catches you off guard.

Because once you see it—once you feel it—it changes you.

It's hard to unsee.

I: Let There Be Pain

Maybe that's why it's on my mind now.

I'm here again—just in a different kind of room. Another place with too much fluorescent light. Another Thursday where I don't know how the story ends.

I keep thinking about what happened in that classroom. About how it all started.

About my dad—and how he's impacted lives he's never even met.

I just hope he knows.

I just hope he sees it.

So let me go back. Just for a moment.

Let me tell you what happened in room 304.

It was a Thursday in late March—March 28th, 2019.

Technically, it was mild for Wisconsin—upper forties, mostly cloudy, no real wind to speak of. But it didn't feel mild. The air still pressed against my chest like it hadn't decided what season it wanted to be.

The sky hung low, the way it does when something's about to happen. Spring in name only.

The fluorescent lights above gave everything a sickly, washed-out hue—more hospital than lecture hall. The walls, once cream, had faded to the color of old paper, and the air carried that thin, institutional chill—part air conditioning, part memory of too many exhausted bodies breathing the same recycled air. A clock ticked above the door, too loud in the quiet.

A girl behind me tapped her pen like a metronome. The radiator hissed and clicked, half-warming the room but fully interrupting any illusion of calm. My fingers ached from the cold—still stiff from the walk across campus—and the spiral-bound notebook beneath them was already warped from the pressure of the words I hadn't written yet.

The room looked like any other: scarred desks, slumped bodies, the dull glow of laptop screens reflecting in tired eyes. But underneath it all, something stirred. A tremble in the atmosphere. Like something was about to crack.

The syllabus claimed we'd discuss miracles—their role in shaping early Christianity. But I knew better. Not here. Not in a room like this.

Professor Wright had already made his stance clear. The smirks, the subtle dismissals, the intellectual scalpels disguised as critical thinking. I'd seen this pattern before: lay the premise, frame the faith, then dismantle it—methodically, surgically.

I wasn't here to argue. Just to listen. Take notes. Get the credit. Blend in. Let the kids whisper about the old guy in the corner—the salt in his beard, the gray at his temples, the sighs that came from real life, not bad sleep.

I caught them more than once. Diego nudging Bree, half-smirk in my direction. Boomer alert under a breath. A lingering glance. A seat avoided.

They didn't know what they didn't know. Yet. But they would.

Life teaches you.

I: Let There Be Pain

Death, loss, love, divorce, war. It all shows up eventually. And when it does, no philosophy textbook holds a candle to the memory of someone who showed up when you needed them.

There's knowing pain. And there's living it. Reading about miracles—and needing one.

I didn't know it yet, but everything I understood about faith—what it really looks like—started long before this class. Before I was born, even. Miracles don't arrive in shouts. They whisper. Until you can't ignore them anymore.

Maybe it was the fatigue from another sleepless night—class in the day, working at night, family, studies, life stacked so tightly there was no space between the layers. Some nights I fell asleep in the clothes I wore to class. Some mornings I woke up feeling like I never actually slept.

But that morning, something pressed heavier than usual. Maybe it was the flicker of tired light. Maybe it was the weight of a single breath I hadn't realized I was holding.

Maybe it was something else—something that whispered: Today you speak. Whether you want to or not, you will not stay silent today.

Faith doesn't just disappear in war or grief. Tragedy can break you—but it can also break you open. What kills it slowly is colder. Quieter.

Not fire. But doubt.

And in this classroom, faith wasn't being erased by suffering. It was being reasoned out of existence. Not by trauma, but by tenured voices eager to rewrite the divine into a footnote.

I saw it happening. In the rolled eyes. The scoffs traded behind laptop screens. Even in the way the faithful sat a little smaller each week—not ashamed, just exhausted.

When enough people tell you that what you believe is childish, irrational, obsolete—sometimes, you start to believe them.

And I'd had enough.

The room had already cooled with that sterile chill—the hum of laptops, the shuffle of backpacks, the crackle of a granola bar wrapper that sounded more like ceremony than hunger.

To my left, someone whispered a joke that died in a stifled laugh. A glance toward me, pretending I wouldn't notice.

I noticed. I always noticed.

Ahead, a guy in a hoodie scrolled his phone, one earbud in, absent even while present.

There was something detached about this room—like we were all floating through a lecture none of them had lived yet.

But I had.

I had buried friends. Watched a parent waste away. Stood outside an ICU, and felt the weight of flag-draped coffins as they fell into the earth—heavier still with the grief of those left behind.

They hadn't. Not yet.

One day, they would. Because life waits for no one. It bides its time—quiet, cruel, inevitable. And when it comes, it doesn't care what year you were born. War, death, the slow grief of lost friendships—it speaks every generation's name. And when it does, it sounds like someone you used to know.

That's when you learn the hard truth: Knowledge is not understanding. One is memorized. The other is earned—scar by scar.

That's why, when I saw the words on the whiteboard—big, bold, unapologetic—something shifted.

Professor Wright stepped forward. Marker in hand. Cap clenched between his teeth. It wasn't rushed—it was ritual. Each motion practiced. Precise. Calculated like everything about him. He didn't speak at first, just scrawled across the whiteboard in large, confident strokes:

MIRACLES ≠ EVIDENCE

The marker squeaked slightly as he wrote, and the silence that followed felt heavier than it should have. Like the air itself was listening.

Wright turned slowly, scanning the room not as if seeing students—but measuring them. One by one. Diego got a smirk. Bree, a nod. Reid, a longer pause. When his eyes landed on me, they didn't stay long—but they narrowed, just a little.

He enjoyed this part. The quiet before the strike.

"You'll find," he began, voice smooth, "that most things considered 'miraculous' are just interruptions in probability." He leaned against the desk—his posture casual, but his tone sharp enough to draw blood.

"Someone survives a crash. A diagnosis changes. A child is found. And what do we say?" He scanned again. "'A miracle.' Never mind the data. The mechanics. The odds that simply happened to tip in their favor."

He turned back to the board. "We want meaning. But wanting doesn't make it so."

A faint scoff came from Diego's side of the room. Not loud—just enough to punctuate.

Across from him, Aisha shifted in her chair. One hand reached for the tiny gold cross at her neck but stopped halfway.

Wright caught the motion. Said nothing.

He continued, "We're here to study religion. Not defend it. Not practice it. Analyze it. Dissect it. This class is not Sunday school. It's surgery."

He didn't raise his voice. He didn't need to.

The tension wasn't loud. It was measured. It was institutional. The kind that feels safe until it's not.

Kai rolled his eyes, just enough for Diego to notice. Lena tapped her pen twice, then folded her hands—defensive posture. And Bree? Bree smiled. The kind of smile people wear when they already know they're going to win.

Wright gestured toward the board again. "Faith," he said, "asks you to believe despite the evidence. Scholarship demands you do the opposite. If you're uncomfortable with that... you're in the wrong room."

There was no laughter. No challenge. Just the hum of fluorescent lights and the knowledge that this wasn't going to be a conversation—it was going to be a trial.

And for most of them, belief was already on the stand.

"Faith, by its nature, doesn't require proof. That's why it appeals to so many," Wright said. "But in here,"—he gestured to the room—"we deal in evidence. Things we can test. Observe. Repeat. That's the difference between belief and knowledge."

A few students nodded. Pens moved with obedient rhythm. Bree leaned forward, eyes gleaming, eager for the coming attack. Reid didn't move—just watched. The way a man watches a minefield.

Wright let the silence stretch. He enjoyed that moment—the power of it. He scanned the room like a man surveying his kingdom.

Diego leaned back in his chair, arms crossed, already smiling like he'd picked his side. "Yeah. Faith is just optimism with extra steps."

A couple of students chuckled. Bree nudged him slightly, smirking in approval.

"Faith can feel profound," Wright continued. "Even comforting. But that doesn't make it true. Faith tells us what we want to be true. Evidence tells us what actually is."

Bree clicked her pen twice, leaned back, and sighed. "Yeah. People want to believe something bigger is watching over them. Makes suffering easier to swallow."

She paused. Just for a second.

"Not that it actually changes anything."

Her voice sharpened again, but the hesitation lingered—small, almost imperceptible, but enough.

There it was again. *What actually is.* The phrase landed like a gavel. Final. Absolute.

I'd sat through weeks of this—slow erosion of belief, careful applause for doubt, the quiet disassembly of anything resembling faith. Every time I told myself: just get through it. Blend in. Let it pass.

But not today.

This was the moment I had prepared myself for. It arrived without fanfare. Just black ink on a whiteboard. But it may as well have been a spotlight.

I didn't feel anger. Not exactly. I felt something sharper. Something surgical. A blade pressing beneath the skin.

A holy ache.

I raised my hand.

Not a question.

A declaration disguised as one.

"Can I say something?" My voice was calm—but not uncertain.

Professor Wright looked at me. Really looked. He knew who I was—or at least what I represented. A student who sits quiet for weeks, then speaks with something that sounds more like conviction than curiosity.

"I'd like to speak," I said again, firmer this time. "Please."

A pause stretched between us—tight as piano wire.

Then he nodded.

"Go ahead."

That was the moment everything got still. Bree stopped writing. Diego's eyebrows shot up. Lena didn't blink.

"What about miracles?" I said. "Maybe they're not testable in a lab. But what if they're the very thing that *is* the evidence? For something bigger. Something we don't fully understand yet."

The silence that followed wasn't passive—it stretched, pulled, tense like a drawn bowstring. Bree shifted in her seat. Diego sighed. A few exchanged glances, waiting for Wright to land the blow.

He looked at me. Measured me. Then folded his arms.

"Let's be clear," he said. "Miracles aren't real."

His voice was low. But the words hit like a gavel.

"The Bible is full of them. Water into wine. Healing the blind. Raising the dead. But we don't see that anymore. If we ever did."

A few students chuckled.

Wright let the sound linger, almost tasting it.

"Though I suppose," he added with a smirk, "if we redefine 'miracle' to include beating traffic or finding your keys, then sure—maybe some of us live in a state of constant divine intervention."

Laughter again. Bree snorted. Diego clapped once, amused.

"Miracles," Wright continued, "require the suspension of natural law. They defy logic, data, replication—everything that gives us confidence in a claim. And yet, people still cling to them. Why?"

He paused. Then answered himself.

"Because people want to believe in something that makes suffering make sense."

That one hit. I saw Aisha flinch, just slightly. She fiddled with the cross around her neck.

Reid didn't move. Arms crossed. Jaw set.

Then Wright paced forward.

"Let's test it," Wright said. "Hands up if you've experienced something painful. Unfair. Something that left a scar—even if no one could see it."

Every hand went up.

"Now," he said, scanning the room, "how many of you were saved from that pain by a miracle?"

The hands stayed up for a beat. Then slowly, they dropped.

"Exactly," Wright said. "We don't see burning bushes. We don't see water turning into wine. We see pain. Chaos. Biology doing what biology does. That's the world we live in."

He let the silence stretch, then tilted his head slightly, mock curiosity in his eyes. "And if we don't see miracles anymore—if they've 'gone silent'"—he lifted his fingers in slow, deliberate air quotes—"then what exactly does that say about their so-called source?" He said it like the words tasted bad.

Kai leaned back slightly, exhaling through his nose. "We've had miracles in history before—Joan of Arc, Fatima, the Red Sea. But we also had mass hysteria. How do you separate the two?"

I: Let There Be Pain

A few students glanced toward him—Diego nodded slightly, considering.

Wright turned toward him, his expression unreadable. "That's the challenge, isn't it? We don't question mass hysteria—we document it. We study its effects, its psychology. But miracles? We elevate them. We carve them into history, call them sacred. Why?"

I watched the way the room shifted, the way Bree started scribbling again, how even Kai stopped tapping his pen.

"Maybe because miracles don't just change individual minds," I said. "They change trajectories. Joan of Arc didn't just see visions—she altered France's history. Fatima wasn't just mass hysteria—it left behind testimonies that transformed generations."

Wright's voice stayed soft, but the edge was unmistakable. "So if we don't see God, maybe that's because He isn't there. Maybe He never existed at all?"

I sat still, the words settling in my gut like cold stone. "Just because you don't see Him doesn't mean He isn't there," I said. "You don't see the wind, but you see the trees move. You don't see heat, but you feel the burn. You don't see gravity—but you trust the fall."

"Absence of visibility isn't absence of existence. It's just… bad lighting."

I let that settle, then added, "Same's true for design. You don't need to see the hand that built something to know it was built."

"If you walked into this building for the first time, would you assume the bricks stacked themselves?"

"Of course not," Wright said.

"Exactly. You don't need to see the architect to believe the building was designed. The intention is in the structure. Same goes for us."

A few students shifted. Wright didn't flinch.

Across the room, Gabe adjusted his watch, turning it slightly on his wrist. It wasn't a big movement—just a quiet shift, like something had landed differently than he expected.

He wasn't religious. Wasn't interested in theology. But this—this was design. And that made it harder to dismiss outright.

"You said good thinking means questioning assumptions—even our own," I said. "Back when we covered Buddhism, you talked about avidyā—that deep-rooted misperception of reality. You said it's like a spiritual blindfold. The cause of suffering is what we refuse to see."

I looked at him and added, with a slight shrug, "So what if the assumption that only the visible is real… is your 'blind spot'?"

He said nothing. I let the silence work for me.

"You used a marker to write on the board. But you didn't witness the creation of it—so what? The creator doesn't exist?"

Wright opened his mouth to speak—

"Of course not," I said, before he could answer. "You trust it had a maker because it has form. Function. Design. Just like your watch. Just like your suit."

I looked around the room now.

I: Let There Be Pain

"A sculpture didn't carve itself. A novel didn't write its own pages. Things that show intention don't show up by accident. They require a maker."

Wright's smile thinned. He turned back to the board with a sharp flick of his wrist—like brushing away something that wasn't there—and underlined evidence twice.

He didn't look at me when he spoke. "Design is easy to romanticize," he said. "But what about destruction?"

He stepped forward, voice low. "You know what we do have overwhelming evidence of?"

He didn't wait for permission to continue. "Suffering. War. Disease. Loss. Children buried before their parents. Good people dying while the wicked thrive."

He tapped the underline again. Harder. "Pain," he said, voice tight now, "isn't proof of God. It's proof of randomness. Chaos. Life without intervention."

For a second, no one said anything. The room felt sealed shut.

Then Lena's voice cut through the silence, quiet but steady. "Or maybe pain is the only thing that does make us pay attention."

Wright turned, lips twitching with interest. "Or maybe it just makes us invent meaning to cope."

Diego nodded, tapping his fingers lightly against the desk. "People aren't looking for miracles when they suffer. They're looking for meaning. That's just how the brain works—pattern recognition, cognitive bias, survival mechanisms."

He shrugged. "Pain doesn't prove divine intervention. It just proves the mind adapts under pressure."

I leaned in slightly. "But isn't it strange how we treat meaning like a side effect—something imagined to survive—when maybe it's the one thing we can't explain away?"

I glanced toward Wright. "You see something built with care, and you assume a designer. But when it comes to our own lives, our own stories... suddenly design is off the table?"

I let the pause stretch, then added, "That feels like a contradiction worth questioning."

Wright's expression tightened. He raised a hand—not to invite more, but to contain it. "Let's stay focused," he said, sharper now. "This is a class on religious studies, not personal metaphysics."

I didn't flinch. "I think this *is* the study of religion. We're talking about faith. About miracles. About why people believe—or don't. If someone can dismiss God just because they can't see Him or His work... how do they justify believing that life has no author at all? Isn't that its own kind of faith?"

A few students shifted. The silence wasn't skeptical anymore—it was searching.

"We don't just want answers," I said. "We want meaning. Especially when it hurts. That's what faith offers—meaning in the midst of pain. Not avoidance. Not escape. But purpose."

That's when someone in the second row leaned forward, voice low but cutting:

"If anything," he said, "thinking there's a purpose behind pain just makes it easier to accept. That doesn't make it true."

Wright let it hang—his hands folded, his expression unreadable.

I leaned forward in my seat. "My dad went through things as a kid that would've broken most people," I said. "Stuff I wouldn't wish on anyone. But that pain? It gave him the strength to survive Vietnam. A war that chewed men up and spit them out. And somehow—he made it."

Bree rolled her eyes. "So, suffering builds character? That's the defense of miracles?"

She leaned back in her chair, twirling her pen between her fingers. The smirk was still there—but something about it felt forced this time.

Then, quieter: "What if you're wrong?"

Not sharp. Not mocking. Just… different.

"What if there's nothing waiting for us? No meaning. Just… things happening, then stopping."

She shrugged quickly, shaking off whatever had just flickered across her face. "Just curious."

I watched her for a beat. She wasn't just asking.

"No," I said. "The pain wasn't the miracle. The survival was. The healing. The way one person makes it through hell and doesn't turn cold— but instead becomes someone who pulls others out."

Wright gave a tight smile. "That sounds inspiring. But it's still anecdotal."

I nodded slowly, shifting forward. "Maybe. But maybe the miracle was never something you could see. Maybe it's like the wind, or the heat. Or gravity. You don't see it—but you feel everything it moves."

I leaned in again.

"Maybe it was a bullet moving one millimeter to the right instead of the left. Or the wind picking up just in time to carry the scent of the enemy. Maybe it was the rain pouring down when he hadn't had water in two days. Maybe it was a landmine that didn't go off. Or a letter that showed up when he was ready to give up."

I looked across the room. Let the silence hold.

"The miracle doesn't have to be what you see. It could be something so small you'd never think twice about it—but it had an incredible impact. It saved someone. It changed them. It gave them just enough hope to stay."

Wright exhaled through his nose—slow, measured. He wasn't smiling anymore.

"Yeah," I said. "So is half of what makes us human."

And then something shifted.

Reid spoke for the first time all semester. His voice was deep, rough at the edges.

"My uncle used to say the same thing. That what nearly killed him ended up making him who he was. Didn't make the pain good. Just made it mean something."

Aisha nodded. Her hand hadn't left her cross. She didn't say anything. She didn't have to.

I: Let There Be Pain

Then Jamal, quiet in the back, looked up. His voice barely carried.

"Sometimes... people show up right when you need them. You don't know why. But they do."

That silence returned—but now it felt different. Heavier. Like the room was holding its breath.

Wright turned back to the board, stared at the words he had written, then at me. Something in his eyes had changed—just a flicker—but I caught it. Like the beginning of a crack in something long thought unbreakable.

He didn't respond. He just stared. And for a second—just a second—he hesitated. That was the beginning.

Not a revelation. Not a conversion. Just a pause. A small breath between certainty and silence. But in that breath, something opened.

You can't always see when something starts to shift—not until it moves.

And even then, it's easy to miss.

But I saw it. In his eyes. A door he'd kept bolted for years wasn't open yet—but maybe, just maybe, it wasn't locked anymore. And sometimes, that's all it takes.

I wasn't the light. But I'd seen it—reflected in my father's life, in moments too layered to be chance.

If this story had a beginning, it wasn't in that classroom. It was in the long shadow of his footsteps—long before I was born.

Like John once said of the Word—He was there in the beginning. Maybe so was this. The shaping. The stirring. The waiting.

I wasn't carrying the light. But I could point to it. And maybe... this was my turn.

What I just said—about being shaped, not just surviving—didn't start in any church or classroom. It didn't even start with faith.

It started much earlier, though I didn't tell them that part. Not the whole of it. I gave the class a story about my dad. Something simple. Something safe.

But what I was remembering... was different.

My dad never talked much about his childhood—especially not the years before the war. But sometimes, late at night, things would slip out. A detail here. A phrase there. Usually when he thought no one was really listening.

He once told me, almost offhand, "I was five. He asked for pliers. I gave him a wrench."

And then he went quiet.

I didn't know the whole story until much later. Even then, only in pieces. Trauma edits the memory. But what survived stuck like rust in the bone.

The sun was high, beating down on the patchy grass where my dad—barely five years old—tried to keep up with his older brothers. They were tossing a makeshift baseball back and forth, roughhousing the way boys do, all elbows and laughter and shouts. He'd found a stick, something vaguely bat-shaped, and held it in both hands as he ran toward them.

"Can I play?" he asked, eyes bright with hope.

One of them barely glanced at him. "Go away, you're too little."

The words stung. The others laughed—not cruelly, just offhand, the way older kids sometimes do without thinking. But it landed hard. His face fell, the stick lowering to his side.

He didn't argue. He never did. He just turned away slowly and wandered across the yard, kicking at the dirt with bare toes. His shoulders slumped, dragging disappointment behind him like a shadow.

That's when he saw the garage door cracked open. The smell of oil and rust drifted out, thick and metallic. My dad hesitated at the threshold. He knew what that space meant—what it held. It wasn't play. It wasn't safety. But it was something. Maybe a chance to be useful. Maybe to be seen.

He hovered, unsure.

Then came the voice.

"Get in here!"

Sharp. Commanding. Unmistakable.

He flinched but stepped inside.

The garage was hot with the smell of oil and rust. A tractor sat half-disassembled, engine open like a patient on the table. My grandfather—my dad's father—was crouched beside it, sweat running down his temples, shirt stuck to his back, grease on his forearms. He barked the order without looking.

"Hand me the pliers."

My dad—barefoot, legs dusty, eager to please—searched the mess of tools on the bench and grabbed the one that looked closest. A wrench.

He held it out, both hands gripping the cool metal like it might still be right.

He wasn't trying to defy. He wasn't being slow. He didn't know. He was five.

My grandfather turned and saw the wrench—and that was all it took.

The first hit came fast. A blur of motion. The wrench clattered to the floor, and before he could react, his father's knuckles cracked across his face, knocking him sideways. His small body hit the concrete with a sound that didn't belong in a home. The skin on his cheek split open on impact.

"You stupid little—"

He snatched the wrench off the floor.

The next blow landed with it—hard, metallic, brutal. It struck his back with a sickening thud, then again across his arm as he tried to shield himself. The sharp edge tore into his skin, ripping through the thin layer like paper. Blood bloomed instantly, dark against the dirt and oil-stained floor.

He tried to crawl away, but the wrench came down again, this time across his ribs. He screamed, the sound raw, animal—something primal forced out by terror and agony. Another strike. Another. Bone cracked. Not cleanly. Not completely. But enough to ache for weeks.

I: Let There Be Pain

His shirt, already thin, tore under the assault, giving way to welts and gashes. Strips of skin peeled back where metal bit too deep. One spot on his shoulder split so wide, the pink of exposed tissue showed beneath the torn flesh. He was slippery with blood now, hands leaving smeared prints on the floor as he tried to crawl, tried to disappear.

The garage echoed with the sound of it—steel hitting flesh, over and over. A wet, repetitive rhythm of pain that seemed to bounce off the walls and sink into the floor.

The screams weren't just sounds—they were signals. They reached the yard like a siren.

One of his brothers, the older of the two playing outside, dropped the ball mid-catch. "That's Johnny... that's Johnny yelling."

The younger one stood frozen. "We told him to leave... we told him to go."

They ran to the garage door but stopped just short of the threshold. The older brother's face twisted with guilt. "If we'd just let him play..."

Tears ran down his cheeks as he stared at the narrow crack in the door, afraid to push it open. The other brother wept openly, covering his ears.

Their sister clutched the doorframe, her knuckles white." Please stop," she whispered again and again." Please, please stop." But the wrench kept falling.

None of them moved closer. Not because they didn't want to—but because they knew. Getting too close meant risking the same. And none of them were brave enough—or maybe stupid enough—to take the blows for him.

So, they watched. They cried. And they remembered.

You think this is a game?" his father roared. "You wanna be stupid? Fine! I'll beat the stupid out of you."

And still, the blows came.

When it finally stopped, there was no apology. No mercy. Just silence. The wrench dropped to the floor with a final metallic clang.

My dad lay there, blood pooling under his elbow, one eye already swelling shut. His lip was split. His side heaved with shallow, stuttering breaths. His hand twitched once, as if he still meant to hand the tool over.

He was five. Just five. And already, he had learned what it meant to suffer. To bleed. To survive.

The blows stopped, but the memory didn't. Because he was five.

And five doesn't forget.

The garage was still. Too still. The kind of stillness that comes after a storm—where nothing feels real, and even the air seems afraid to move. Dust floated in the sunlight like it hadn't heard what just happened. The walls didn't speak. The floor didn't creak.

Even the tools were quiet—hanging in place, as if they'd turned their faces away.

He lay there, blinking against the light, tasting iron in the back of his throat. His ears rang. His face burned. Somewhere in the distance, he heard a door close. Or maybe that was just something inside him—shutting for good.

He didn't cry. Not because it didn't hurt, but because something in him had already learned: crying wouldn't fix it. Wouldn't stop it. Would only make it worse.

He wouldn't remember the details—not then. Not the number of strikes. Not the things that were said. Not even how long it lasted.

Trauma does that. It edits the story.

But he remembered the wrench. The way it felt in his hand. The shame of getting it wrong. The belief—ingrained from that day forward—that mistakes meant pain.

He didn't even know how young he'd been until one of his brothers told him years later. "You were five," they said. "Five."

And that was just one time. There were others. More tools. More fists. More moments where the air went still and the hurt came fast. That house had seven kids in it, and yet somehow, the punishment always found him.

I don't know why. Maybe no one does. But it was always him. Like something about him invited it—or maybe just couldn't escape it.

But somehow, he kept getting up. Not because he was strong. Not yet. That came later.

He got up because he had no choice. Because from the age of five, he learned what pain was. And more importantly, how to carry it.

And that was the beginning. Not of faith. Not of miracles. But of the long, winding road that would eventually lead him to both.

The shaping didn't start with a sign. It started with suffering. And over time, pain became the chisel that carved something stronger in him. Not obvious. Not immediate. But real.

I didn't know it then—but standing here now, I can see it clearly: Everything I believe about grace, about endurance, about what it means to survive... started there.

In a garage in 1950.

He didn't walk into that garage thinking he'd find pain—but he did. Just like we all do.

We walk into this world never expecting how much it hurts.

And if the old stories are right, sometimes the light doesn't come all at once. It slips in sideways, unnoticed at first. Not through signs in the sky—but through scars on the skin.

The Word became flesh. And flesh bleeds.

That moment—my dad holding out the wrong tool and being punished for it—wasn't just about cruelty. It was about misunderstanding. Misdirection.

He was a child offering what he had. And it still wasn't enough.

That's where it began. Not with belief. Not with grace. But with blood.

Before you can understand miracles, you have to understand what they stand against.

I: Let There Be Pain

And for my father, it started in a place without mercy.

A granola bar wrapper crackled somewhere behind me. The lights buzzed above like they always did—too loud, too cold.

"He never laid a hand on me," I said aloud. That wrench echoed through generations. It wasn't just blood. It wasn't just silence. It was the kind of pain that chokes belief before it's ever born.

If there was a God watching, He was either cruel, absent... or preparing something so incomprehensibly redemptive, we couldn't yet begin to see it.

My father never talked about that day. He never had to. It lived in the way he flinched at sudden sounds. In how he breathed differently when holding tools. In the silence that stretched between us—full of things he'd never say.

I was still a kid when I first heard the truth. Not from him. But from a conversation I was never meant to hear.

I don't remember where I was exactly—maybe in the hallway, maybe sitting on the basement stairs. But I remember their voices. My dad. Uncle Bob. Talking low, like they were afraid the past might hear them.

Uncle Bob was older. He'd told my dad to stay out of the garage that day. Said he was too small to help. He meant to protect him. But the beating still came.

And Uncle Bob carried that guilt for years.

"I told you to go," he said, his voice breaking. "I told you to go. You were five…"

They both cried. Quietly. Without shame.

And so did I.

Because that's how I learned. Not through a story. But through a memory too heavy to carry alone—finally shared between brothers.

The part that's stayed with me the most, though, is what never happened. My father never laid a finger on me. Not once. Not when I was mouthy. Not when I broke things. Not even when I made him so mad I could see it in the tension in his jaw.

He was beaten into silence—but somehow, that silence became a vow.

And if the Word became flesh…then it must've learned to bleed before it ever learned to speak.

The room held its breath.

Bree's pen, mid-air, hovered above her notebook. Her usual smirk had faded, replaced by a furrowed brow and a gaze that didn't meet mine. She scribbled something, then paused, the tip of her pen pressing into the paper, leaving a small ink blot.

Diego, who often wore skepticism like a badge, shifted in his seat. His arms, previously crossed in defiance, now rested on the desk. He stared at the floor, the rhythm of his bouncing leg the only movement betraying his internal turmoil.

I: Let There Be Pain

Aisha's fingers tightened around the gold cross at her neck. Her eyes glistened, and she blinked rapidly, as if trying to hold back a tide of emotions threatening to overflow.

Reid, ever the observer, leaned forward, elbows on his knees, hands clasped. His gaze was fixed on me, not with judgment, but with a depth of understanding that spoke of shared pain.

Kai, who often masked discomfort with humor, had his usual grin replaced by a contemplative expression. He tapped his fingers on the desk, a silent rhythm that seemed more for grounding than distraction.

Lena, seated near the window, looked out, her reflection faintly visible against the glass. She wiped a tear from her cheek, quickly, as if hoping no one noticed. Then, almost to herself, she whispered, "I didn't know it could be like that." Her voice was barely audible, but in the silence, it carried.

Professor Wright cleared his throat, the sound loud in the silent room. He opened his mouth to speak but hesitated, perhaps realizing that, for once, he didn't have the final word.

The silence that followed wasn't empty—it was filled with unspoken acknowledgments, shared vulnerabilities, and a collective reevaluation of beliefs.

In that stillness, something shifted—not just in the room, but in the air between us. Like a story had been told not for persuasion, but for participation.

And maybe that's where faith begins—not in answers, but in the honesty that invites someone else to say, "Me too."

II: The Parable We Live

The room was quiet. Not the kind of quiet that asks for attention—the kind that holds its breath.

I had just finished speaking. Not preaching. Not proving. Just... telling the truth as I knew it. As I lived it. And they didn't know what to do with that.

Until Kai broke the silence. "Didn't you say pain wasn't the miracle—but now it is?" Kai asked. "Feels like mental gymnastics to me."

A few students chuckled. Not many. Most were watching me—waiting for a response.

II: The Parable We Live

Kai only heard what he needed to reduce a wound to a slogan. It's easy to turn someone's pain into a point when you're far enough away from it.

I didn't speak right away. Not because I didn't have something to say. But because I had too much.

I stared at the whiteboard behind Professor Wright. The word *miracles* was still underlined. *Evidence,* he had written. Tangible, observable evidence. The kind we never had.

"No," I said finally. "Suffering isn't good. And trauma doesn't build character—not by itself. It can just as easily shatter it. But sometimes—sometimes the situations that cause pain pull something out of you that was already there, waiting. Perseverance. Insight. Courage."

Professor Wright turned slightly, arms crossed. "Or they invent meaning to survive it."

I leaned forward in my chair, elbows resting on the desk, heart thudding in my chest. "What if that's true?" I said. "What if meaning is invented? Does that make it less powerful?"

Wright tilted his head, curious.

"If someone's drowning," I continued, "and they cling to a story, a memory, a belief—something that pulls them up from the dark—does it really matter if that thing came from inside them or outside them? It still saved them."

Bree clicked her pen again. "Sounds like emotional crutches to me—appealing, sure, but hardly a valid framework for reality. The Stoics had a better grip on suffering—accept it, adapt, move forward. You don't need miracles for that."

He didn't say much—but when Bree spoke, I caught Ethan tilt his head slightly, like he was filing it away for later.

I wasn't sure what Ethan believed—but in that moment, it looked like something had shifted.

"Maybe," I said. "But some people don't just limp with those crutches. They carry others on them."

Her eyes flicked toward me. "That still assumes suffering needs external meaning. But what if meaning is just what we construct to avoid collapse?"

I studied her for a beat. "And what if that construction is the miracle?"

Her pen stilled.

"We keep acting like meaning is an illusion—something fragile we invent to cope. But maybe meaning is the very thing that keeps us alive when we shouldn't be. Maybe survival isn't just biology—it's belief that something beyond the pain still matters."

Reid, still quiet, added, "And what if it's not about crutches at all? What if it's about seeing things that were always there, but we were too blind or bitter to notice?"

Wright smiled faintly. "So now pain opens your eyes?"

"No," I said. "Pain can blind you. But surviving it—choosing something different after it—that's what opens your eyes."

I looked down at my notebook, then back at the board.

"You know," I said, flipping back a few pages, "last week you gave that whole lecture on literary structures in ancient texts. Remember? You said stories—especially in religious traditions—often carry more weight than direct statements."

Wright arched a brow, intrigued.

"I wrote it down," I continued. "You said, 'The parable is the preferred method of uncomfortable truth.'"

A few heads turned.

"And it stuck with me," I said. "Because some of the most powerful truths in scripture came through stories—not arguments. Even Jesus used parables to explain things people didn't want to hear."

I let the silence breathe.

"Sometimes," I said, "the only way to talk about God... is to talk about people."

Wright raised an eyebrow. "So you're saying your dad's life is a parable?"

I nodded. "Maybe not in the traditional sense. But what if every scar tells a story? What if every small choice to do better than what came before you—that's the parable we live?"

Bree rested her cheek on her fist, unimpressed. "That sounds poetic. But it doesn't prove anything."

"It's not about proof," I said. "It's about resonance. You don't look at a parable and say, 'That happened.' You say, 'That's true.' There's a difference."

Wright pushed away from the board slightly. "Let me ask you something." he said, addressing the class. "If your beliefs are handed down through pain, what makes them valid? Isn't that just trauma recycling itself through tradition?"

Kai leaned back in his chair, arms crossed. "Belief's just mental math. You add comfort, subtract fear, and call the remainder faith."

A murmur rippled through the room.

I answered before I had time to hesitate. "It's only recycled if you pass it on blindly. But if you examine it—wrestle with it—it becomes something forged, not inherited."

Bree jumped in again. "But how do you know you're not just fooling yourself? Believing in some divine purpose just so the pain has meaning?"

"I don't," I said. "Not always. But isn't that true of most things we believe? That love matters. That people can change. That truth exists. None of that is measurable. But we live and die by it."

Wright crossed his arms. "But the scientific method doesn't ask for meaning. It asks for repeatable outcomes. You're asking us to accept miracles that can't be tested. That makes them personal. Not evidence."

"Exactly," I said. "Personal. But that doesn't make them less real. My dad's survival wasn't a statistic. It was a man refusing to become what broke him. If that's not miraculous, I don't know what is."

A girl in the second row lifted her hand slightly. "What if... what if the miracle isn't the event? What if it's the endurance?"

I nodded. "Maybe it is. Maybe miracles aren't magic tricks. Maybe they're proof of love doing the impossible."

"Can you give an example?" someone near the back asked. Reid, I think. Quiet voice. Honest curiosity.

"My dad," I said.

A pause.

"He grew up in a house where pain was currency. You didn't earn love—you dodged anger. And if you were lucky, you didn't make it worse."

I saw Wright's eyebrow twitch, but he didn't speak.

One summer, when he was eleven, he worked every day on his Uncle Earl's farm.

Earl treated him with respect. Didn't yell. Taught him how to split logs, run the tractor, and—most of all—bale hay. Not just dragging bales off the bailer, but climbing rickety wooden stacks, one sweaty bale at a time, until the wagon looked like a leaning tower of golden bricks.

Bree crossed her arms, sharp as ever. "So what—you want us to believe suffering is sacred now?"

Her voice was flat, but her eyes were tight. "You keep dressing it up, but it still sounds like wishful thinking."

The smirk was still there—but this time, it looked more like a shield.

I felt my throat tighten. I could've stayed quiet. Let the story do the talking.

But some things need witnesses.

"No," I said. "It didn't get okay. Not for a long time."

Wright stepped in. "Then where's the miracle?"

I looked at him. Really looked. Not as a professor. Just as a man.

"The miracle," I said, "was that he didn't become the thing that hurt him. That he found a different way. That he loved his sons—even when no one showed him how."

That wasn't just survival.

That was a parable. The kind people don't tell, but the kind you live.

Someone shifted in their chair. A pencil dropped and rolled.

There was a beat of stillness.

Then Ethan spoke.

"Can I just say something?" His voice was quieter than usual—no slick tone, no posturing.

"I think it takes more strength to stay open than to shut down. Like… when you've been through stuff, it's easy to get cold. Bitter. But what you're describing?" He shook his head. "That takes work. That's discipline."

He looked down at his notebook, tapping the edge.

"I've got people in my family who gave up. Just quit trying. But your dad didn't. That's not weakness. That's… legacy."

Across the room, someone else cleared their throat. I didn't recognize her name—but I remembered her voice from a few weeks back. Kendra, maybe?

"My mom always said we inherit pain like recipes," she said. "And most of us pass it on without checking the ingredients. But your dad… he rewrote the recipe."

A few heads nodded.

Even Bree didn't speak this time.

"But we're not talking about love," she said finally. "We're talking about evidence. For God." Her tone was still sharp, but something underneath it had softened. "You want us to believe in divine intervention because your dad had trauma and didn't become a psycho?"

I opened my mouth. Closed it. For a second, my dad's story sat between us, naked and outnumbered.

Reid spoke again. "My uncle took his life last year," he said quietly. "I still think about the day he hugged me goodbye and said, 'Be good, kid.' I didn't know it was a goodbye." He swallowed. "If someone had been there—like your dad—maybe he'd still be here."

The room didn't move. No one shifted. No one scribbled a note or glanced at the clock.

Even Wright's arms dropped from his chest.

Bree looked down. Maybe writing. Maybe not.

No one breathed too loud. The air had thickened—heavy with something rawer than debate.

Professor Wright turned slowly back to the board. His voice, when it returned, had dropped a register.

"We're not here to settle theology," he said, quieter now. "We're here to examine how belief systems form. And why some endure."

I nodded.

"Maybe they endure," I said, "because they're not just built on logic. They're built on stories. On scars. On people refusing to give up when every reason said they should."

No one argued. Not Wright. Not the students. Even silence seemed to lean in.

I looked at Reid.

His eyes were still down. Shoulders heavy.

"My dad had someone too," I said, voice low. "An uncle—just like your uncle, who clearly meant so much to you."

Reid looked up. Just for a moment.

"A quiet man who didn't speak in sermons—but showed up in sweat and work and the kind of dignity that doesn't need an audience. A man who gave my dad the first taste of what it felt like to be safe."

It started with the weight of hay in his hands.

The first day, the sun baked the fields in long waves, cicadas buzzing a high constant above the engine's hum.

He was ten. Skinny. Determined.

Eisenhower was president, Elvis was on the radio, and Earl's old pickup still had a Truman for Farmers bumper sticker half peeled on the tailgate. Out here, it felt like time moved slower—days measured in sweat and calluses, not clocks.

Dust clung to his sweat-soaked shirt. His arms itched from the hay, and the rope handles had left raw red lines across his palms.

He was shirtless by noon, pants dark with sweat, boots caked in dirt. Every time the bailer kicked out another rectangle, he rushed to grab it, hoisting it over his head to the growing stack behind him. Higher.

Always higher.

The hay scraped his chest and arms. Chaff clung to his skin, itching along the base of his neck. His shoulders ached like fire.

But he didn't complain.

Earl watched from the driver's seat, cap low, cigarette clinging to the edge of his mouth. Every so often, he'd glance over and nod—not just a gesture, but a message. Approval. Respect.

"You keep going like that," Earl called, "you'll outwork me by next summer."

My dad grinned through the dust. "Maybe I will."

At noon, they sat in the shade of the tractor. Earl handed him a ham sandwich wrapped in wax paper and a bottle of warm soda. They didn't talk much. Just ate. The kind of silence that doesn't need filling.

Halfway through the sandwich, Earl pointed toward the ridge.

"You see that line of oaks?" he asked.

My dad nodded.

"Storm rolled through there last year. Tore everything up. Barns. Fences. But that big one in the center? Still standing. Roots go deep."

He didn't say anything more. But it stuck.

They worked until dusk. The tractor sputtered to a stop, and silence crept over the field—broken only by a birdcall and the ticking of cooling metal.

Earl wiped his hands. "You can stay the night if you want. Got a cot out back. No point dragging yourself home this late."

My dad hesitated. Then nodded.

The thought of avoiding his father's house—just for one night—was a miracle of its own.

He slept like the dead.

No yelling. No boots stomping the hall. No flinching awake at the sound of a slammed door. Just crickets. A fan ticking softly. And a cracked window breathing in the cool night air.

He woke before sunrise—not because he had to, but because he was ready.

Earl was already out on the porch, boots up, sipping black coffee from a dented tin mug.

"You're up early," he said.

"Couldn't sleep anymore," my dad replied, rubbing his eyes.

Earl grinned. "That's what honest work'll do to you. Makes rest real."

They worked the field again. This time, it was easier. His body remembered. The hay still scratched, but he moved smoother. Stronger.

By late afternoon, the sky had turned gold and lavender. Earl opened the red cooler, pulled out two bottles.

"You work like a man," he said, handing one to him. "You drink like a man."

My dad blinked. "Really?"

"Just one. A shorty. Don't tell your old man I said so."

The bottle was cold. The taste bitter. He didn't like it. But he liked how it felt. Like something earned. Like a rite.

Somewhere on the porch, a radio crackled to life—the tail end of a Milwaukee Braves broadcast drifting through the static. Eddie Mathews was up to bat.

Earl cocked his head toward the sound. "That's your guy, ain't it?"

Dad smiled, lifting the bottle like a quiet salute. "Yeah. That's my guy."

They listened as the announcer ran through the lineup. Mathews in the box, Aaron on deck. Warren Spahn had gone eight innings strong the night before—seventeen wins on the season and still going. Joe Adcock had cracked one into the stands that morning. Del Crandall was hitting like he had something to prove. Logan at short, Bruton tracking down everything in center.

It wasn't just a game.

It was a rhythm. A roster of names that felt like hope. Like a country holding its breath and swinging for something bigger.

Earl glanced sideways. "Think they'll go all the way this year?"

Dad tried to play it cool, but the question hit deep. Earl hadn't asked like a man talking to a kid. He'd asked like an equal.

"I think they might," Dad said, sitting a little straighter. "Mathews is due."

They sat on the porch as the sun slipped behind the barn. Just a boy, a man, the sound of a ballgame on the breeze, and the slow miracle of being seen.

Earl tapped the rim of his tin mug and said, almost to himself, "You don't gotta earn worth, boy. You just gotta remember it."

He walked home with a slight wobble in his step, the gravel road cooling beneath his boots, twilight brushing dust from his skin like a benediction.

The bottle Earl had given him still sat warm in his stomach, more bitter than buzz—but it wasn't the beer that made him feel different. It was the work. The sunburn on his arms. The soreness in his shoulders. The quiet pride of being trusted.

And for a flicker of a moment—just one—he thought maybe that was enough. Maybe he could get through the door, keep his head down, and no one would notice. Wash up. Change clothes. Slip into bed before his father even looked his way.

If he moved quick enough—quiet enough—he could pass for invisible.

The porch steps creaked under his boots. The screen door gave its usual high-pitched whine as he eased it open. The main door was worse— sticking slightly at the top, pulling loose at the bottom like it had been slammed one too many times.

It groaned open.

From the living room: "Get in here."

His father's voice—sharp. Slurred. Waiting.

He froze. The air shifted. Even the walls seemed to brace themselves.

The voice had that edge. Not a bark. Not a shout. That low, dangerous slur of a man balancing between anger and control—and wanting an excuse to lose it.

He turned toward the bathroom. Just a few more feet. Just make it to the door.

Too late.

Boots against floorboards. A chair scraping back. The sound of knuckles cracking—on purpose.

Then the heavy steps. Measured. Deliberate. Each one a sentence that didn't need words.

He didn't get a chance to explain. Didn't get to lie, or hide, or beg.

Just a hand—thick, calloused, fast—grabbing the collar of his shirt and yanking him sideways.

And just like that, the air he'd filled with dreams of safety was gone.

"You think I don't smell it on you?"

He tried to speak. The first blow caught his ribs. The second cracked against his temple.

"You drinking now?"

Another blow.

"You think you're a man?"

He hit the wall. Fell. Boots stomped forward.

Then fists. Again. One-two. Then more. The world tilted sideways. Blood in his mouth. From his nose. Warm. Thick. He didn't scream—but he cried out when the belt came next.

The belt wasn't discipline. It was performance. The ritual of power.

Crack. Crack. Crack.

His breath hitched in ragged gasps.

He curled tighter. A boot caught his ribs. Something inside shifted. Broke.

Down the hallway, a plate clinked into the sink. A cupboard opened. Closed. Silence.

A sob choked out from one of the younger kids—but it was muffled quickly.

Still the beating didn't stop.

"You think you're grown?" his father snarled. "You think you can drink like a man?"

Another blow.

But somewhere between the second rib-crack and the belt's first crack... he spat blood, lifted his head just enough, and muttered— *"That all you got?"*

Not loud. Not defiant. Just... tired. But unbroken.

He didn't say it to win. He said it to live. To remind himself there was still a self left inside the skin. And maybe, just maybe, that mattered more than the bruises.

The next blow came harder.

Something shifted in the room—not in the light, or the air, but in the man doing the beating. That line—that quiet refusal—wasn't just an insult. It was rebellion. And rebellion, to a man like him, was a threat. A mirror too honest to look at.

The blow landed with the rage of a man who'd spent years teaching fear as discipline—only to discover that fear had limits.

He wasn't hitting a boy anymore. He was hitting something he couldn't scare.

And that made him furious.

He snarled something unintelligible—half curse, half spit—then swung again. Not with precision. Not even with control. Just violence.

Clumsy, scattered, frenzied. Like he was trying to pound the defiance out of the floorboards themselves.

But it didn't work.

Because the boy didn't scream.

Didn't beg.

Didn't break.

And maybe that's why—after a few more blows, chest heaving, drunk on his own failure—he pulled back. Not because he was finished. Because he was afraid. Afraid of what it meant that the beating wasn't enough.

Then, just like that, it ended. The door slammed. The house went still.

He lay in a heap. Shirt torn. Skin on fire. Blood pooled under his cheek. One eye swollen shut.

The rug beneath him scratched at his skin like burlap. He could feel the pattern of the weave pressing into the side of his face, grounding him in the moment like it wanted him to remember every fiber of it.

Overhead, a spider moved across the ceiling. Slow. Unbothered. Its legs skated across the plaster like it had nowhere urgent to be. Like this was just another Tuesday night.

And maybe that's what hurt the most—how ordinary the aftermath felt. Like pain didn't even warrant ceremony.

That moment—burned into memory—wasn't just pain. It was a decision. I will never be this.

He didn't know what that meant yet. Didn't know how you unlearn rage or how many years it would take to feel anything but numb. But the vow had already formed, clenched somewhere behind his teeth, even as the blood leaked through them.

In the hours that followed, the house creaked with a guilty quiet.

Not the kind that offered peace. The kind that dared you to make a sound.

He lay in bed, the cotton sheets catching on his cuts like sandpaper. Every movement stung. Every breath felt like it scraped the inside of his ribs. His vision blurred—part swelling, part tears he refused to let fall.

Skin purpling with bruises that would bloom for days.

But what stuck with him most wasn't the pain.

It was the silence.

Not stillness. Not calm.

This silence had sharp edges.

It filled every corner of the house like fog, like smoke from a fire no one wanted to admit had happened. No footsteps. No apologies. Just the low hum of normalcy acting like it hadn't been shattered an hour before.

His father read the paper like it was any other night. His siblings shuffled down the hallway like ghosts. No one said his name.

And that silence—more than the fists, more than the bruises— taught him something.

Violence screams. But shame... whispers.

And it was whispering in every room.

The next morning, the house moved like nothing had happened.

The sun rose, like it always did, casting soft gold through the kitchen windows as if the light hadn't seen what the night had done. His mother stood at the sink, washing dishes in slow, mechanical motions. The rhythm of porcelain tapping porcelain. The hum of water running too long.

His siblings tiptoed past him like ghosts—heads down, voices swallowed. No one asked what happened. No one acknowledged the bruises blooming across his face or the way he winced with each step. No one dared.

He sat at the table, still sore, his shirt hanging loose over the cuts on his back. The chair felt harder than usual. His father sat across from him, reading the paper, the same hands that had beat him now calmly flipping to the comics. A sip of coffee. A cleared throat. No recognition. Just silence.

His mother placed a plate in front of him—eggs, toast, overcooked sausage. No words. No eye contact. But as she passed, her hand brushed his shoulder. Light. Barely there. But it was something. A signal. A tether.

He ate slowly, chewing past the ache in his jaw. Each swallow felt like a choice. Stay. Endure. Breathe.

That night, the house folded into itself early. No television. No conversation. The little ones tucked into their beds with forced smiles and fast prayers. The hallway darkened. No voices. Just the creak of floorboards, the soft groan of a settling house.

Then—the door.

It opened with a slow creak.

His mother stepped in. A chipped ceramic bowl in one hand. A warm cloth in the other. She didn't turn on the light.

She knelt beside the bed. Close. Not rushed. Her knees touched the hardwood. The cloth dipped into the water, wrung out gently, then brought to his face.

"I'm so sorry," she whispered, her voice nearly drowned in the stillness.

He didn't speak. Didn't move. Just breathed.

"I should've stopped him," she said, her voice catching. "I should've stood in the way. But I couldn't—not with all of you to protect."

She dabbed the cloth gently along his cheek, careful around the cut near his eye. The water was warm. Her hands were shaking.

He blinked once. His voice rasped out, low and hoarse. "Why does he hate me so much?"

She stared at the bowl for a long moment. "Because I love you so much."

The words didn't make sense. Not then. Not completely. But she said them like scripture. Like she'd rehearsed them for years.

"You're strong, Johnny," she said. "Stronger than he'll ever be. The moment you stood on your own two feet, he saw it. And it scared him."

She brushed his hair back from his face. The tenderness nearly undid him.

"Don't become him," she whispered. "No matter what. Promise me that."

He remained silent. But the promise settled deep, anchoring somewhere beneath the bruises. A quiet vow with no ceremony—just breath and blood and the sound of her voice.

"I love you," she said, her hand still resting against his temple. "Even when I'm too afraid to show it. I always will."

She kissed his forehead—soft and trembling—and held there for just a moment longer than she had to.

Then she picked up the bowl, folded the cloth inside, and left the room.

He didn't cry.

Not then.

But in the dark, he lay awake, staring at the ceiling where the spider had been, feeling the echo of her touch still warming the skin she'd cleaned. The smell of soap lingered. The tremble in her hands stayed with him.

And somehow—that night—that was the first time he felt safe.

Not because the house had changed. But because something in him had.

That was the night he stopped expecting love from his father.

And maybe that's what made the love he gave us so rare.

It wasn't inherited.

It was forged in fire.

The classroom was quiet again.

Not the awkward kind—just still.

Like everyone was waiting to exhale.

Wright didn't respond at first. Then he took a breath, clipped and slow.

"Do you know what a miracle is?" he asked.

"I think I do," I said.

"But do you really? Or do you just want to believe it badly enough?"

I looked at him.

"Are you asking if the miracle actually happened, or if we're just desperate enough to need it to?"

Wright tilted his head. "I'm saying miracles are parting seas. Raising the dead. Water into wine. Not a guy handing your dad a beer. You're dressing up coincidence like it's divine intervention."

A couple students shifted in their chairs.

"It's possible," I said. "I won't pretend it's not."

Wright exhaled, leaning back slightly. His fingers tapped absently against the edge of the desk.

"I'm asking if it's possible you're mistaking coincidence for meaning."

"Sure, it is," I said.

He raised an eyebrow, like he'd won.

"But it's also possible," I added, "that you're mistaking silence for absence. Or pain for proof that no one's listening."

A couple students murmured. Someone whispered, "Damn." Wright held up his hand. "That's enough."

But I wasn't done.

"I'm not trying to win an argument," I said. "But I do think it's fair to say there are more kinds of evidence than the kind you can see under a microscope. There's memory. Meaning. There's survival when you shouldn't have survived. There's mercy when it doesn't make sense. There's peace in the middle of something that should break you. And sometimes there's a voice, a single word, that reaches you when no one else can."

I looked down. "You say it's evolution. I say it was formation. Forging. That farmer—his uncle—didn't rescue him. But he reminded my dad he had worth. That mattered. That stuck. Even when the pain came back."

No one spoke for a moment.

Then Wright cleared his throat. "Still not evidence."

"Maybe not the kind you recognize," I said. "But it's a pattern. A direction. If every one of us is just the result of chaos, then nothing means anything.

"But if those moments build into something—something bigger— then maybe it's not just survival. Maybe it's preparation."

II: The Parable We Live

I paused, letting the silence settle around us again. Then added, quieter:

"My dad still watches baseball. It's the Brewers now. Not the Braves. But something about that sound—the pop of the glove, the crack of the bat—it still calms him. Still centers him. Like it's not just a game. It's a rhythm that never left."

No one responded. But they didn't need to.

And in that stillness, I felt something shift.

A few of them looked at me differently—like the Brewers cap I always wear meant something now. Like the jacket they'd seen a hundred times wasn't just school gear, but something older.

They didn't know I still have that glove. The Eddie Mathews model. The one my dad saved for when he was ten—sweating through hayfields, earning his first pay. It's in a shadow box now, in my home office.

He didn't have much to give back then. But somehow, that glove made it.

III: Not Every Miracle Bleeds

The class was silent again. Not stunned like before. More... unsettled. Like something sacred had brushed the edges of the room and then slipped out before they could decide what to do with it.

The wrench. The belt. The hayfield.

It all hung there—raw, unedited. Not wrapped in philosophy or theology. Just pain, carried forward.

Wright exhaled, slow and measured, his gaze flicking toward the board. For the first time, he didn't counter—didn't challenge. He just stood there, arms still crossed, thumb tapping idly against his forearm, as if recalibrating. Assessing. The rhythm of a man who knew he'd lost a battle but wasn't ready to concede the war.

III: Not Every Miracle Bleeds

Finally, someone whispered, "That story about the wrench... I'll never forget that."

Another voice added, "And the farm. That man—Earl—he sounds like the kind of person who saves people without realizing it."

I nodded. "He did. Just by showing up."

A beat.

Someone in the second row leaned forward. "But that's just it, right? The miracle was because of the pain. If your dad had a good family, none of that would've felt miraculous."

Bree jumped back in. "Yeah. It's not a miracle. It's just... contrast. Suffering sets the stage, so anything less than terrible feels divine."

Diego snapped his fingers. "Exactly. It's like... you go through hell, and then you call a glass of cold water a miracle. But is it? Or are you just thirsty?"

Laughter rippled—not mocking, but thoughtful.

Ethan shrugged. "But if you're dying of thirst, a glass of water *is* a miracle. Context doesn't make it less real. It makes it matter."

Lena nodded. "And sometimes, being seen in the middle of suffering feels holier than a thousand sermons."

Bree raised a brow. "But are we just redefining miracle to mean 'feels good in a hard moment'? Because if we stretch the word too far, doesn't it lose its meaning?"

I looked at Bree. Her question wasn't cruel—it was real. Honest.

The kind of question you only ask when you've seen hope disappoint too many times.

I let the silence settle for a second.

Then Aisha spoke, softer. "Maybe the word doesn't need to be narrower. Maybe we're just scared to admit that small things might carry sacred weight."

Reid crossed his arms but leaned in. "I think the problem is we keep trying to define it like it's math. But life isn't math. It's music. And sometimes the most important notes are the quiet ones."

Even Wright raised an eyebrow at that. He gave the faintest nod. Then used the moment to step forward again, his voice even and clear.

"That's the heart of the psychology behind miracles," he said. "It's not about divine intervention. It's about narrative structure. Meaning-making."

He turned to the board and wrote in clean, bold letters:

JOHN 20:16 — 'Jesus said to her, "Mary."'

Then he faced us again.

"Mary recognizes him—not through spectacle, but through something simpler. He says her name. She looks up, and says, 'Rabboni!'— 'Teacher.' That's it. She saw him."

He paused.

"That moment didn't need thunder or drama. It needed intimacy. It came after Jesus was gone. Supposedly gone forever. And then—he said her name. Just her name. And she knew."

He tapped the verse again, slower this time.

"Not a sermon. Not a miracle in the sky. Just one word. Her name. And everything shifted."

A few students nodded.

Wright pressed on. "You see it again and again in John. Not always parting seas or raising the dead. But moments—finding a coin in the dark, unexpected comfort in despair. People don't recognize miracles because they expect loud. They don't hear them because they don't know the voice."

He paused again—longer this time. Then, almost to himself:

"Maybe I've been listening for the wrong volume."

Lena raised a hand slowly. "So, you're saying people *recognize* miracles when they need them most?"

Wright nodded. "That's one theory. It's not malicious. It's survival. But just because something comforts you—that doesn't mean it's false."

Ethan, now leaning forward with his elbows on his knees, added, "But couldn't the opposite be true too? Couldn't comfort be a kind of proof? I mean... why do we assume only pain reveals truth? Why not joy?"

Wright didn't respond. But the pause gave space.

Aisha spoke next, barely above a whisper. "Maybe miracles aren't about timing. Maybe they're about recognition. Maybe it's not that they only happen in pain—it's just that pain wakes us up enough to see them."

Bree let out a short sigh. "Or maybe we're just desperate to believe in something more when we're low. That doesn't make it real—it just makes it *necessary*."

Reid scratched his jaw. "But doesn't that kind of necessity say something? If we *need* it that badly—meaning, connection, something sacred—maybe that need points to something real. Not imaginary. Just... hidden."

There was a pause. The kind that doesn't stall the conversation—it *stretches* it.

Even the students who hadn't spoken looked more awake now. Like the ground under their feet had shifted and they weren't sure yet whether it was safe to stand or start running.

Wright looked at me again. "So maybe the question isn't whether miracles exist. Maybe it's why we only find them in places we wish we could forget."

That hit harder than I expected. But I didn't flinch.

Instead, I leaned forward.

"Everyone keeps expecting miracles to smack you in the face. Big, obvious, undeniable. But sometimes they don't look like that."

A pause. I let the air stretch.

Wright rapped his marker against the word **MIRACLE** on the board. "Define a miracle," he said.

Bree raised her hand. "An event that violates natural law," she said, "typically attributed to divine intervention."

Wright nodded. "Textbook. Anyone else?"

A few more chimed in—some quoting religious texts, others referencing probability.

III: Not Every Miracle Bleeds

I stayed quiet. So did Diego.

Then Wright said: "How do we *know* something's miraculous? Is it because it saves us from something bad? Is that the only time we say it's 'miraculous?'"

Gabe, who rarely spoke, didn't raise his hand—but his voice came low, almost under his breath: "If you can't measure it, it's just a story."

Wright glanced over, eyebrow raised—but didn't challenge it. Just nodded, like he was taking note.

"Not every miracle bleeds," I said. "Not every miracle waits for tragedy to show up."

He raised an eyebrow, curious.

"Sometimes," I said, "a miracle looks like a moment you barely notice. Something small. Something quiet. Something you don't even realize was holy until years later."

"Like what?" Bree asked, skeptical but genuinely curious.

I smiled.

"Like a stupid little girl who swore she was gonna marry you."

He was fourteen. And hard. Not just tough—hard. Edges sharp enough to cut. Small for his age, but scrappy. Fought older boys and didn't lose. Not because he was stronger. Because he didn't stop.

Pain didn't register the same for him. He bled the way other kids sweated—easy, automatic, expected. Anger wasn't a response. It was the baseline.

He carried himself like someone always waiting for the next hit. Like if you stayed braced, it couldn't surprise you.

That day, he was at a softball game. His school versus another from a few towns over. Not much to do except show up, shout, and act unimpressed.

The sun baked the gravel lot behind the field, heat rising in slow waves that shimmered just above the asphalt.

He wasn't playing. Just hovering on the sidelines with the other guys—arms crossed, mouth quick, eyes sharp. Posture built for survival, not attention.

A few girls had come from the other school—little sisters, cousins, tagalongs. They clumped together by the snack shack, slurping melted snow cones and kicking gravel.

All except one.

She was maybe seven. Too small to matter, too confident to care. Walked like the whole world was hers—but not in a loud way. In a quiet, settled way.

That's what struck him first.

She didn't fidget. Didn't perform. She just sat. Alone. Still.

A ball popped into a glove somewhere behind the dugout. The crowd murmured, half-distracted.

Somewhere near the shack, a scratchy speaker played *That'll Be the Day*—Buddy Holly's voice bouncing across the dusty field, all swagger and warning.

He wasn't listening. Not really. But later, the irony would stick.

When a smaller kid nearby tripped and spilled juice all over himself, she was the only one who got up. No theatrics. No "look at me." Just a napkin and a smile.

He barely noticed her. But she noticed him. Watched him the way some kids watch dogs behind fences—curious, a little cautious, but not afraid.

After the third inning, she walked straight up to him. No hesitation. No introduction. Planted her feet in front of the bench and said, loud enough for half the row to hear:

"You're John."

He blinked. "Who's askin'?"

She pointed to herself. "Me."

He gave her a look. The kind that made grown men think twice. "What do you want, little girl?"

"I'm gonna marry you."

He stared. "What?"

She nodded. "I already told my friends."

Behind him, one of the boys snorted. He shook his head and muttered, "Yeah. That'll be the day."

He didn't even notice the song. Just scoffed and looked away—like the world couldn't touch him if he didn't look back.

He looked around. Mistake. Laughter started behind him. One of the older boys elbowed his friend. "Hey Johnny—better get a ring on it."

Another chimed in: "She's lockin' it down, man. I respect that."

She didn't flinch. Just smiled like she'd already won.

"I like your face," she said.

His face turned red. Heat rose into his ears. He stood up, muttered, "Go away," and walked off—fast.

But she followed him.

All the way behind the bleachers. Past the back fence. To the dusty strip between the gravel lot and the tall grass where he leaned on the rail, trying to disappear.

She didn't talk. Just stood nearby. Quiet. Watching him like she'd already claimed him and was making sure he didn't run off.

Eventually, her friends called her back. She didn't protest. Just left. But she never looked away. Not until she turned the corner, and even then—just barely.

He didn't ask her name. Didn't think to. But the image of her stuck—defiant and smiling, shoelaces untied, hands on her hips like she knew something he didn't.

She wasn't afraid of him. That's what stayed.

She didn't mock him. Didn't try to fix him. She saw him. And she stayed.

That stupid, fearless little girl.

III: Not Every Miracle Bleeds

He tried to forget her. He really did. But some moments don't leave just because you want them to. They settle in. They wait.

Years passed before he ever spoke of her again. And even then, it came out casually. As if the story didn't matter. But it did.

Because it was the first time in a long, long while… someone had looked at him like he wasn't broken.

I let the weight of it rest there for a moment. No strings. No romance. No long-term outcome. Just a boy who didn't know how to be loved… and a little girl who did it anyway.

Because sometimes the miracle isn't what it leads to. Sometimes the miracle *is* that it happened at all.

That someone saw you—and didn't flinch.

That someone spoke to you—and meant it.

That someone offered affection without fear, agenda, or hesitation.

And it stuck. Not because it changed his life. But because—for the first time—he saw the possibility that it could.

He'd never call her a miracle out loud. He was too stubborn. Too scarred. But he remembered. And when he told the story years later—half-laughing, half-embarrassed—he smiled like it was a secret he'd never stopped carrying.

A moment that shouldn't have mattered.

But it did.

And maybe that's the point.

Not every miracle bleeds.

Some just wave at you from across a field and say, "I see you."

Bree shifted in her seat, arms still crossed. Not combative now—just wary. "So what—you're saying being seen is enough to call it a miracle?"

Ethan didn't hesitate. "Sometimes, yeah." He looked down at his desk, like he wasn't sure he wanted to have said it out loud.

Reid added, "Especially when it's the first time someone ever did."

I nodded. "Exactly."

I leaned in, eyes moving across the room.

"How many times have you seen someone who looks like they're carrying something heavy—maybe a bad day, maybe more—and you just say hi, or ask how they're doing... and something changes in their face? A flicker. A light."

A few students looked up, stilled by the shift.

"Or maybe there's a kid who's picked on constantly. Always overlooked. And one person—just one—sees them. Smiles. Sits next to them. That doesn't just change their day. Sometimes it changes their whole life."

I let that breathe.

III: Not Every Miracle Bleeds

"You don't know what people are carrying. You don't know the moment when your kindness lands in the exact place it's needed. And when it does… maybe that's not random."

Silence.

Then Lena spoke—quietly, almost like the words surprised her on the way out.

"I had a teacher like that. Didn't fix anything. Didn't even know I was breaking. But I think she saved me anyway."

No one interrupted.

Because some truths don't need defense.

They just need space to land.

I looked around the room. Let it settle.

"Who knows," I said quietly. "Maybe that person grows up to be a leader. Or a teacher. Or a pastor. Someone who carries that miracle forward… and becomes the reason someone else keeps going."

And then—

Bree.

Her voice cut through, low and sudden.

"Or a rapist."

The air shifted.

The room froze—not from offense, but from something colder. Older.

She didn't smirk this time. Didn't cross her arms or toss her hair. She just stared at the desk in front of her.

Silent.█

No one breathed. The word didn't echo—it landed. Heavy. Final. And for the first time since the class began... she looked small.

Not weak.

Wounded.

No one moved. Even Wright didn't speak.

It wasn't the kind of silence that begged for someone to fill it. It was the kind that says: something true just slipped out—and we all heard it.

I didn't push. Not then. Because sometimes the miracle isn't saying the right thing. It's knowing when to let someone finally be seen.

Then—almost too late—Bree gave a short, breathy laugh.

"Relax," she said, brushing invisible dust from the desk. "It was just a joke."

But no one laughed.

Not because we were judging her. Because we knew. It wasn't.

Still, no one said a word. Not even her. She leaned back, eyes on the ceiling, like she was trying to reel something back that had already left her hands.

Aisha wiped one eye. Reid leaned back, arms crossed, but no longer defensive. And Lena—now silent again—looked away, hand near her mouth, like she hadn't meant to show how much it hit her.

III: Not Every Miracle Bleeds

But Wright?

Wright stayed still.

Then finally, he stepped forward. Not aggressive. But steady. Surgical. Eyes sharp. Arms folded.

"Let me ask you something," he said, voice quiet now. Dangerously even. "You're making these stories carry a lot of weight. You're framing them as miracles. But they're also selective. Anecdotal. Emotionally charged."

He turned to the board. Erased the word evidence. Wrote TESTIMONY. Paused. Then erased that too and, with deliberate slowness, wrote EVIDENCE again.

"I don't doubt that these moments are powerful," he said. "But can we really call something a miracle when it depends on memory and hindsight? Especially when we only name it miraculous after it fits the ending we want?"

He turned toward me again.

"If a little girl following a boy around is a miracle... then what isn't?"

The question didn't come with malice. It came with precision.

A few students nodded—Ethan, even Bree. Not as a challenge, but like they were genuinely trying to sort it out.

Ethan tilted his head. "It's not that the story isn't beautiful. It is. But he's right. You called it a miracle because it ended well. What if it hadn't?"

Bree leaned in—not flippant now, but measured. "What if she'd forgotten? Or he'd married someone else? Would you still call it divine—or just coincidence?"

Wright didn't pile on. He didn't have to. He let the silence carry the weight.

And I sat in it—for just a moment—long enough to feel the pressure beneath the questions.

Because this wasn't about belief.

This was about what you do when someone looks at your miracle... and calls it editing.

When they take what was sacred... and call it survival fiction.

So I looked at Wright. At Bree. At Ethan. At all of them.

And then I said—softly—"You know, it wasn't love at first sight."

A few heads turned.

"It wasn't a sign from heaven or some cosmic certainty. It was just a face. A moment. But for him—it was the first time in years something shifted."

A pause.

"Sometimes," I said, "it's not the miracle that needs defending. It's the person."

The class stilled again.

III: Not Every Miracle Bleeds

"And maybe seeing someone—really seeing them, without flinching—that's enough to shift something. Not erase the pain. Not redeem it. But to remind them that pain isn't the only truth."

Aisha nodded slowly. "And maybe... it's the kind of miracle that doesn't announce itself. It just waits. Until someone's ready to name it."

Ethan added, "Or carry it forward."

I looked at him. "Exactly."

I let the words settle.

"Maybe we think miracles are supposed to be loud because the world is loud," I said. "But some of them... some of them whisper. Maybe you only hear them when you're finally listening for the right volume."

Then, from the corner of the room—the smallest smile from Bree.

Not wide. Not fake. But real. Like she wasn't ready to speak—but maybe... finally ready to stay.

And that was enough.

Somewhere in the quiet, the air conditioner kicked on. A low hum filled the room.

It didn't break the silence—it held it.

The board still held the word EVIDENCE.

But for a moment, no one cared what it said.

Because the miracle, it seemed, was still happening.

IV: The Wounds That Stay

By the time the conversation resumed, something had shifted. Not in volume—there was no shouting, no chaos—but in tone.

The warmth of the last story had cooled. The room had recalibrated itself. The smiles faded, replaced by frowns of thought, suspicion, and something heavier: a return to intellectual defense.

Professor Wright stood at the front of the room like he always did—confident, composed, surgical.

But now, there was a new edge.

"Enough stories," he said quietly. "Let's step back. Look wider."

He turned slowly toward the board and, without a word, wrote:

HAITI. HIROSHIMA. HOLOCAUST. COVID.

Four words. Four wounds.

He underlined each one. Then turned back to us.

"If there is a loving, powerful God, then how do you explain these?"

Silence.

Lena looked down. Diego didn't smirk. Even Bree, cocky as ever, stayed still.

Wright's voice lowered—not angry, just cold steel wrapped in velvet.

"Miracles are convenient when you're telling stories about your parents. But real history isn't sentimental. Real suffering doesn't care about anecdotes."

Bree's eyebrows pulled together. Not in outright disagreement. Just... something else.

She opened her mouth—then stopped.

For half a second, her fingers tightened around her pen. A flicker of hesitation. Then, just as quickly, she exhaled, flicked the pen open, and nodded. "Yeah. Exactly."

Wright walked slowly across the front of the room.

"Do you really believe a God who lets children starve in refugee camps, or burn in missile fire, or gasp for air in ICU wards... is sitting on a throne waiting for us to thank Him?"

Bree exhaled sharply, almost too quickly. "Or pray for parking spaces."

A few chuckled—but not with joy.

Wright nodded. "Exactly."

Then he gestured across the room.

"If God exists, then He's either unwilling to stop evil—or unable to. Which means He's either indifferent... or weak."

He let it sit like poison in the air.

That was when I spoke.

Quiet. But clear.

"Are you assuming blessings are in short supply because God is making bad things happen... or just because He allows them?"

Wright raised a brow. "What's the difference?"

I leaned forward.

"This is going to get philosophical, but that's where you're already taking us, isn't it?"

He said nothing. Which meant I had room.

"I had a conversation with someone once. He told me this world was godless. That bad things happen *because* God doesn't exist. I offered him a blessing."

"And?"

IV: The Wounds That Stay

"He told me to keep it. Said I should save it for someone else. Someone suffering in this 'godless world.'"

A few heads turned. Lena blinked. Reid leaned back.

"But that's the thing," I said. "He assumed blessings were like water in a drought. That there's not enough. That pain means God's not showing up. That every scar is proof of absence."

I sat back slightly.

"But what if it's the opposite?"

Wright tilted his head. "You're suggesting God allows suffering to... what? Test us?"

"No," I said. "Not to test us. But to let love and evil be real. You can't choose the good if there's no freedom to choose wrong."

Ethan shifted. "So God just... sits back and watches us destroy each other?"

"No. He *lets* us. There's a difference. He didn't make us puppets. He made us with choice. That was the point. Love that's forced isn't love."

Wright stepped forward. "So He let Eve fall?"

"Yes."

"Let Satan tempt?"

"Yes."

He folded his arms. "And that's a good God?"

I met his gaze.

"It's a *just* God. One who knew that love without choice isn't love—it's control. And He created us to be stewards of this world. We chose something else."

Bree rolled her eyes. "So... every war, every cancer, every child ripped from their mother—that's on us?"

"I don't know," I said honestly. "But maybe it's not about blame. Maybe it's about what kind of world God *wanted*—and what we've done with it."

That's when Liam spoke.

First time all semester.

A cough. Gravelly. From the back.

"Blame doesn't help anyone," he said. "But neither does pretending this world is simple."

Wright blinked. A few students turned.

Liam sat back, arms folded. "My dad died of cancer last year. Out of nowhere. Didn't drink. Didn't smoke. Just woke up coughing one morning, and six months later... gone."

The room shifted—but no one spoke.

The quiet returned—but it wasn't cold this time. It was waiting."

Lena glanced up from her notebook. She'd been jotting something—not about theology, but maybe about us. Her expression was soft, unreadable, but not detached.

"I don't know if I believe any of it," she said, her voice calm, measured. "But that doesn't mean it's not true for them."

She didn't say it to challenge.

She said it like someone who was finally learning to listen.

No one responded.

But no one pushed back either.

Kai's fingers hovered near his notebook, but he never wrote anything. There was no calculation for this. No metric for survival.

Diego drummed his fingers against the desk once—then stopped. For the first time, he wasn't sure if there was a clever response.

Bree exhaled sharply. Her pen hovered over the page—but she never wrote anything.

Liam looked down at his desk, then back up. "I didn't blame God. Not because I didn't hurt. But because I knew better than to think God was supposed to be my shield from every bad thing. I don't think that's how it works."

He looked at Wright directly.

"If God's real—and I think maybe He is—then He didn't come to stop the pain. He came to stand in it with us."

Silence again—but it was different now.

Liam turned to me, nodded once.

"I don't know if I believe everything he believes," he said, gesturing toward me. "But I know he's not wrong."

I held his gaze. Didn't speak.

Didn't need to.

Something had shifted.

Not everyone saw it. But I did.

From that moment on, no one blinked when I said the word *war*. Because the next words I spoke didn't come from books. They came from something buried deeper.

There are some things you can't explain with logic.

Only with what's left after it.

Like the first time my father stepped off that plane.

It was 1966. LBJ was president. And my father was 21—already battle-tested, though no uniform had touched his back. He didn't need boot camp to learn pain. His training ground was a garage floor. His drill instructor was his father's rage.

But the draft didn't care about your scars. He got the letter in early '65. *"Congratulations,"* it said, *"your friends and neighbors have selected you to serve your country."*

He read it twice.

Then muttered, "Well, fuck my friends and neighbors."

But he didn't run. Didn't burn the letter. Didn't fake a limp or flee to Canada. He just packed a bag and reported for duty—because doing the hard thing was the only thing he'd ever known how to do.

Boot camp didn't break him.

It tried.

IV: The Wounds That Stay

But he was already broken in all the ways that made him useful. He could take orders. He didn't flinch. He didn't complain. He hit hard and didn't ask questions. The Army noticed. Offered him a shot at officer school.

He turned it down.

"I'm not leading anyone," he said. "I'll pull my weight. That's it."

Then the orders came. Vietnam. No debate. No delay.

He flew west, stopping in Hawaii—but never saw a beach. Just the inside of an airport, humid and loud, where soldiers were shuffled like freight. A layover between the known world and the one that ate you alive.

The next plane was quieter. Tighter. No one made eye contact. Just duffels and dog tags and the kind of silence that screams if you stay in it too long.

My dad sat near the middle of the transport, his gear at his feet, boots planted like roots. Hands gripping the frayed canvas of his bag like it might keep him from coming apart.

He didn't pray. Didn't breathe deep. Didn't blink much.

He just sat there—tight-jawed, 21, and already tired of hope.

And when they landed in Vietnam—rain slamming the tarmac like angry palms, sky the color of old bruises—he didn't flinch. Others did. One kid near the window whispered "Jesus," like it might summon safety. Another gripped the seat in front of him so tight his knuckles turned pale beneath the grime. But my father? He just stared ahead.

This wasn't new.

Just louder.

He'd seen fists fly in rooms with no windows. Had watched his mother vanish into silence, her voice left behind in the sink next to the broken plates. Violence had always been part of the air he breathed. This was just... a different kind of storm.

And the smell. That was what hit hardest. Diesel. Burnt rubber. Rotting foliage. And beneath it, something human. The scent of fire on skin. Not fresh. Not recent. Just something soaked deep into the soil—something that had been waiting.

That's how it started. Not with bullets.

Not with blood. With silence.

He stood with his gear slung over one shoulder, boots touching foreign soil, not with reverence—but with a readiness that felt more like resignation. One by one, the new arrivals filed out. Their uniforms still stiff, their expressions still hopeful—or at least pretending to be.

Then they saw the line of soldiers waiting at the edge of the runway.

Not to greet them.

Just to watch.

A few leaned against crates. Some crouched near the landing gear, smoking. None of them smiled. None of them spoke.

Something about them was wrong.

They were just... there.

Not wounded, exactly. But... worn. Fabric clung to their limbs, soaked through. One man's shirt was missing a sleeve. Another had boots duct-taped at the sole. A third had no helmet, just a mop of tangled hair that had stopped being cared for weeks ago.

But it wasn't their uniforms that stopped my dad.

It was their eyes.

Flat.

Vacant.

Not like they were looking at him—but through him. Through the plane. Through the sky.

Like whatever used to fill those men had bled out somewhere in the underbrush.

They weren't men anymore.

They were ghosts still wearing skin.

He didn't know—he couldn't have known—that he'd look just like that in a few weeks. That someone else, fresh off a flight, would look at him and whisper a silent prayer not to end up the same.

But that was the price of breathing here.

You learned to go hollow before the jungle could do it for you.

And some other kid would step off a plane and think, God help me—I hope I never look like that.

He didn't have long to adjust. They threw him into jungle detail within days.

No easing in. No orientation.

You learned by watching. Or you didn't learn at all.

The jungle had a rhythm—but it didn't share it easily. You could taste decay in the humid air before you saw the moss cloaking the trees. Insects buzzed like tiny engines. Every rustle might be wind—or boots. Every bird call echoed like a signal. The ground underfoot was a nauseous sponge, sucking at boots with every step. And every breath carried sweat, mud, and the weight of dread that this might be your last.

My father paid attention. He moved like silence had weight— hesitant footsteps on reeking underbrush. Even when mortar screamed overhead, he didn't flinch. They started calling him "Bulletproof." Not because he was untouched. But because he never showed it.

He walked through mortar fire like weather—inescapable and accepted.

When others went down—when screams cut through gunfire like torn fabric—my dad wrapped tourniquets with hands that didn't shake and kept firing. Silent. Steady. Unshakeable.

War transformed people. It didn't turn boys into men. It turned men into machines. And the ones who survived?

They burned. Quietly.

My dad burned. Slow, smoldering, hidden deep.

He learned the weight of gear, the ache of sweat-drenched fatigues, the rhythm of patrols measured by the hiss of bugs and the creak of leaf-littered paths. He counted footsteps, noted unnatural silent patches in the canopy, and memorized every hollow echo in the trees. He learned how to breathe so softly that even the jungle didn't notice. How to shoot without flinching. How to carry on after doing—and not doing—things that stayed in the bones.

The monsoon rains pounded the fields at night, turning the world into rust-colored mud. Meals came as glop from mess kits, oily and cold. His letters home grew shorter. Stripped of jokes. Void of hope. He stopped talking about what came next—no mentions of plans, of home, of after. Like somewhere deep down, he'd started to understand there might not be an after.

"Still here," he'd write. "Tell Mom I'm okay. Don't let Jimmy touch my baseball glove."

He wrote less each time; his handwriting shrank, ink blotting. The waits between letters stretched into static-stuck days.

But the hardest lesson? How to look at broken men—and at his own fracturing self—and feel nothing.

That's when the stare he'd feared on the tarmac became his own. He didn't flinch. Didn't blink. Didn't call out for help. He moved like someone who'd already decided which parts of himself mattered—and which ones he would leave behind.

But he wasn't untouched. He burned. Quietly. Deep. And the cracks showed only later—when civilian life returned, but the silence did not.

Nights were the worst. When the rain finally stopped, the jungle went silent—so quiet that memory found space to speak. In the hush, he saw her again—his sister barefoot in the grass. His mother's face when the orders came. And his father's low, steel-cold voice:

"Don't you dare come back weak."

That was the poison injection—cold, final.

He hadn't believed in God for a long time.

But out here—deep in the stink and the dark, hearing his own heartbeat in the mud—he found himself angry, demanding:

If You're real—explain this.

Because if there was a God, then this was cruelty.

And if there wasn't... then everything was worse.

One day, after patrol, he passed a man kneeling beside a half-zipped body bag.

The man wasn't crying. Wasn't shaking. He was just... still. Eyes locked open like he hadn't blinked in hours. Like maybe blinking would make it real.

The patch on his chest read *Graves Registration*—but the grunts called them something else.

Body snatchers.

They were the ones who came after the smoke cleared. After the screaming stopped. After the medics had done what they could, and all that was left were names to match and forms to file. They moved like shadows through aftermath—tagging limbs, piecing torsos back together, zipping what was left into green plastic.

This one—this man—looked like he hadn't stood upright in days. His shoulders sagged like the weight of death had settled there for good. Blood streaked the sleeves of his fatigues, but he didn't seem to notice. One glove was missing. The other hung limp from his wrist, as if even his hands had forgotten their function.

A clipboard lay in the dirt beside him, its metal clamp still holding a crumpled set of casualty tags. One was already half-filled out. *Unknown. Partial remains. Probable KIA.*

My dad slowed as he passed.

He didn't know what he expected to feel. Pity, maybe. Or revulsion. But instead, what settled in his chest was something colder. Familiar.

Recognition.

Because that man—he wasn't broken. Not exactly. He was *absent*. Like his soul had slipped out quietly during some previous cleanup and hadn't made it back yet.

The jungle behind them buzzed with the last rattles of a distant skirmish. Gunfire like hiccups. Distant enough to be dismissed. Close enough to matter.

The man didn't flinch.

Didn't look up.

Didn't even seem to hear it.

He just stared into the open mouth of the body bag like he was waiting for it to speak.

My father stopped a moment longer. Something about the posture—about the sheer stillness of it—pressed into him. Like watching a candle that's already burned itself out but hasn't collapsed yet.

He wanted to say something.

He didn't.

There were no words for that kind of fatigue. No blessing that could reassemble what war had taken apart.

So he kept walking.

Later that night, someone in his squad mentioned the body snatcher had been out there for days—three, maybe four. Part of Operation Junction City. A meat-grinder of a mission that left more questions than corpses. Whole squads went missing. Others came back carrying helmets full of dog tags.

The dead didn't line up neatly. They were pieces. Parts. Scattered among root systems and burnt-out foxholes like shrapnel that couldn't be recovered.

"They match what they can," the guy said around the fire. "Guess at the rest."

Someone else added, quieter, "Ghost work."

That was what they called it when the job had already swallowed the man doing it.

Ghost work.

IV: The Wounds That Stay

That night, my dad didn't sleep. He sat outside his tent, cleaning his rifle even though it didn't need it. Listening to the rain. Watching the trees sway like they were trying to forget something too.

He kept seeing the man. The eyes. The posture.

He realized what scared him most wasn't the death. It was the silence around it. The way that man didn't scream or cuss or fold. He just... absorbed it. Like a sponge.

And then?

Kept going.

Years later—decades—my dad would mention him in passing. Never with detail. Just a memory tucked into the edge of a conversation.

"Graves guy," he once said over coffee, voice soft. "Sat by the bag like it had asked him a question."

He never learned the man's name. Never asked.

But sometimes, he'd stop in the middle of a sentence. Like something behind his eyes had tugged too hard. And you'd know—he was back there. Just for a second.

Looking at a man with empty eyes and blood on his hands, and wondering how much a soul could carry before it started to crack.

That image never left him.

Because it wasn't a horror story.

It was a mirror.

By then, the monsoons had passed. The air turned sharp and dry, the jungle settling into a kind of cruel stillness. The ground, once a swamp of leeches and mud, cracked beneath every step. The trees didn't rustle anymore—they creaked. Like old bones that had been asked to bear too much.

Time didn't stretch long—it stretched wide. Like a river in flood. Wide enough to lose track of who was new, who was gone, and who was still pretending not to break.

It was 1967 now—the war at full throttle: U.S. troop levels climbing past 400,000, jungles alive with helicopters and tension, villages evacuated under Operation Cedar Falls.

His boots were more duct tape than leather. The soles peeled like old wallpaper. His uniform had faded to a shade that didn't match any issued color. The fabric was stiff from salt and sweat and stories he didn't want to remember.

His eyes had gone flat. The kind of flat that doesn't come from fear, but from seeing too much of it. The kind that stops scanning the treeline because it already knows where the danger is—it's in your gut, in your hands, in the way the trigger finger never quite relaxes, even in sleep.

He'd made it this far. Longer than most.

A week ago, he'd bought his short-timer's stick off a guy rotating out—Morris, who'd spent 18 months in-country and earned two Purple Hearts. Two bucks and a can of Dole fruit cocktail—bought from the PX— exchanged hands under a torn H-bar tarp at Firebase Echo.

The stick wasn't fancy—just a piece of dark bamboo, weathered and scarred with notches. Fourteen marks counting off days. Someone else's countdown etched into it. It didn't matter. You didn't carry it for what it looked like. You carried it for what it meant.

Morris had said: "Treat it like a good-luck charm. Or a lie. Either way, hold tight."

My dad lashed it to his pack. Didn't say much. Just nodded.

Because that's what hope looked like out there—a stick, passed from man to man, like a prayer without a name.

Near the mess tent, a battered transistor radio sputtered into life, its signal flickering between clarity and static.

A familiar tune rose through the static—soft, slow, almost sacred. It spoke of seasons, of time for war and time for peace.

The melody floated through the smoke and sweat like it didn't belong there.

Maybe that's why it stayed.

Which is why, when the sergeant called for one more recon—a simple sweep along Hill 823, they said, nothing big—my dad didn't argue. Didn't protest. Didn't announce he had eleven days left.

He just stood. Grabbed his gear. Shouldered the stick. And walked back into the jungle.

They moved light that day—six men and four M16s, no extra gear, no backup.

The heat clung like a second skin. Sweat pooled at the small of your back, ran down your legs in rivulets. Every breath tasted like copper and rot. Every step crackled through the brittle leaf litter.

And then—somewhere in his head, like a needle dropped onto vinyl—it started.

Not a song. Not exactly. More like a rhythm he'd known forever.

A whisper about time. About the way everything had its season. A time to come into the world. A time to leave it.

A time to destroy. A time to rebuild.

The words weren't real—just echoes. Memory fragments. Maybe scripture. Maybe something he'd heard on the radio back home, sung by a voice that didn't belong anywhere near a jungle.

He'd heard others mumble it too, like a prayer for the disillusioned. Not to believe—but to keep breathing.

That rhythm stayed with him as he moved—one step, then another, through heat and silence and the terrible stillness of waiting.

Because maybe this was his time to walk.

Then his boot caught on a root.

A crow burst from the trees, wings slicing the silence.

And then—it happened.

The crack of rifle fire. Sharp. Close. A mine behind them—pop—then screaming. Trees exploded bark like shrapnel. Bullets ripped through the canopy like lightning made of lead.

My dad dropped fast, the training automatic now. Dirt in his mouth. Hands on his M60. Scanning. Searching. Waiting.

IV: The Wounds That Stay

They never saw the shooters. Just glimpses—ghosts between branches.

Muzzle flashes like angry fireflies. Screams. Someone shouting orders—swallowed whole by the chaos.

Half the squad hit the ground.

One man didn't move.

Another tried to crawl, dragging a leg that wasn't connected the way it used to be.

Simmons—his tentmate—took shrapnel. A chunk of it. Right through the thigh. Screamed once. Then nothing. My dad got to him first.

Belt off. Tourniquet tight. Press. *Press*.

Simmons was bleeding fast. Too fast.

But Dad didn't blink. Didn't panic.

Just kept moving.

The firefight lasted twenty minutes. Maybe less. But it felt like forever. Like time had stopped to watch.

When the gunfire stopped, it didn't feel like survival. It felt like something had finished bleeding out.

The jungle held its breath. Smoke curled through the underbrush. Trees bent low with bullet wounds. A parrot shrieked once in the distance—loud, desperate, confused.

Dad sat there, knees in the mud, Simmons leaning against a tree beside him, pale but still breathing. The blood soaked through the tourniquet. His face was white as ash.

He spat something—maybe blood, maybe a tooth—and leaned his head back.

"Hey, Bulletproof," he rasped.

My dad turned slightly. Didn't say anything.

"...you ever think it's a miracle we're still breathing?"

There was no sarcasm in his voice. No joke riding underneath. Just the plain question of a man who had almost died and didn't know what to do with the fact that he hadn't.

My dad didn't answer right away.

He looked down at his hands—slick with blood that wasn't all his—and then at the Pig, its steel still warm from fire.

Finally, he said: "I don't believe in miracles."

Not cold. Not angry. Just flat. Like he'd run out of room for wonder.

Simmons didn't push.

He just looked up through the shredded canopy, sunlight filtering in like it didn't know better.

"Yeah," he said. "Maybe not. But I think they believe in *you.*"

That was it. No follow-up. No smirk. Just that.

And for the first time in weeks—maybe *months*—my dad didn't know what to say.

He came home a few weeks later.

Not with fanfare. Not with music or medals. Just a seat on a military plane packed with too many ghosts and not enough air.

The wheels touched down in California.

No one clapped. No one cheered. No one met them on the tarmac with signs or banners or tears of relief.

They got off the plane the way they'd gotten on—quiet, stiff, carrying more weight than their duffels.

A staff sergeant handed each man a cup of cold coffee and a voucher for a connecting flight.

That was it.

No debrief. No counselor. No one asked what they saw, what they lost, what they brought home in their blood.

He didn't kiss the ground. Didn't cry. Just walked into the terminal with his stick strapped to his pack and the silence of the jungle still in his bones.

And that's when he saw them—just beyond the security gate, clustered near the exit.

Protesters.

College kids, mostly. Signs held high: **"Baby Killer." "End the War." "No Blood for Pride."**

He stepped through the last set of sliding doors and into their line of sight.

One of them—barely twenty—broke from the group, walked right up, and spat.

Right on his boot.

He didn't move. Didn't yell. Didn't flinch. He just stood there, the spit sliding down cracked leather, and realized: He'd survived the jungle.

But home... Home was something else entirely.

No one asked who he lost. No one asked what he saw. No one even looked up.

There was a payphone by the gate. He didn't call anyone.

Not because he didn't want to—but because he didn't know what he'd say.

What do you tell a mother when she asks, *"Did you kill anyone?"*

What do you tell a brother who says, *"I kept your room the same"?*

What do you tell yourself, when the man in the mirror still wears combat boots?

He got on his connecting flight and stared out the window the whole time. Not watching the sky—just watching the reflection. Trying to decide which parts of him made it home.

He arrived in Wisconsin just after sunrise. The summer light was already stretching across the tarmac, golden and relentless.

IV: The Wounds That Stay

The airport air was thick with humidity, and the breeze carried the smell of cut grass and jet fuel. He walked through the terminal in his fatigues. A few people looked away. One man, passing with a newspaper under his arm, veered slightly closer, spat near his boots, and muttered, "Baby killer."

It hit his left boot. Just like the protester at Travis, who'd nailed the right.

Two steps into civilian life. Two boots marked like shame. One by someone shouting. One by someone whispering.

My father didn't respond. Not because he agreed. But because his anger didn't live in his voice anymore. It lived in his ribs. That was the fracture. The moment belief didn't break—but froze.

Because sometimes, faith doesn't shatter. It calcifies. And you carry it like bone.

And with each step away from the war, something stayed wrapped around his ankles.

Not memory—something heavier. Quieter. The kind of weight you don't notice until your bones start to bend.

Because the war didn't end when the fighting did.

It came home with him. In the shaking hands. The sudden rage. The silence that stretched too long in the middle of a conversation. In the way he sat facing every exit. In the way he flinched at nothing—and everything.

But also in something deeper. Something invisible. He came home carrying more than memories. More than trauma.

He came home with a cough.

Just a tickle at first. A dryness that wouldn't quit. The kind of thing you ignore. Because you're tough. Because you're twenty-three and breathing.

Then came the fatigue. The joint pain. The fog that settled behind his eyes like dust on old glass.

And still, he said nothing.

Because that's what men like him did. They survived. They outlasted. They waited for the storm to pass—and didn't realize it had moved inside.

It would be years before he understood. Years before someone said the words: Agent Orange. Pulmonary fibrosis. Cancer.

By then, he was married. Had kids. A job. A life he'd tried to build with the shaky hands of a man who never stopped bracing for the next explosion.

But the jungle wasn't done with him.

It had just learned how to wait.

The hum of the fluorescent lights felt sharper now, cutting through the silence.

I looked up from the desk. The room was still.

Not out of politeness. Out of gravity.

IV: The Wounds That Stay

Because even the students who hadn't lived through anything close to war understood, somehow, that something had just passed through the room.

Something that didn't need to be argued. Just held.

Ethan was the first to speak. His voice wasn't loud. "You think the war didn't break him... because the abuse already had?"

"No," I said. "The abuse didn't break him. It carved him into someone who knew how to survive. That's not the same thing."

Reid leaned forward. "So the pain made him stronger?"

"No," I said again. "It made him harder. Strong would've meant he could bend and come back. But hard things... they crack."

Aisha nodded slowly. "But he didn't. Crack."

"Not on the outside," I said. "But inside? There were places even God had to knock twice to get into."

That quieted the room again.

Bree, of all people, spoke next—voice subdued, but steady. "So survival wasn't the miracle?"

I shook my head. "Not by itself."

"What was?" she asked.

I thought about it. About the silence. The slow-burn ache of what came after.

"The miracle was that he came home... and didn't become the war. That he carried the jungle inside him and still managed to build a life where laughter lived again. That he had every reason to become a weapon—and instead, he chose to be a father."

Wright stood at the board, arms folded. Watching all of it. Measuring the room. But saying nothing.

Because this wasn't about theology anymore.

It was about scars—and what you do with them.

It was about carrying something that should've broken you... and choosing to be more than what tried to undo you.

It was about building something beautiful in a world that keeps handing you rubble.

And for the first time all semester, nobody needed to win the point.

Nobody needed to be right.

They just needed to sit in it.

Because sometimes, the greatest miracle isn't surviving the fire. It's coming out the other side... and choosing to be soft. To hold someone. To love anyway.

To still believe.

And maybe the ones who carry ghosts quietly... are the ones still making room for miracles.

V: The First of His Signs

The silence lingered, thick and unspoken, like the room itself had just remembered how fragile people could be. For a long breath, no one moved.

Then Professor Wright unfolded his arms—shaking off the weight like dust from an old coat. "We've spent a lot of time on suffering," he began, his voice steady but thoughtful. "On pain as proof of survival. But what about love?"

The room shifted. Not uncomfortable, but cautious. Bree scoffed under her breath, barely loud enough to register. Diego leaned forward, interested. Gabe and Ethan exchanged glances but didn't move.

The conversation had been on trauma—things seen, scars earned, fires endured.

Love didn't fit the pattern.

At least, not obviously.

Wright pressed further. "Is love miraculous, or just biological? A social construct designed for survival? Or something more?"

Bree spoke up without hesitation. "Love isn't a miracle. It's chemistry. Hormones and evolutionary instinct. Attraction, reproduction, adaptation." Her voice was sharp, efficient, the same tone she used when dissecting faith like an equation. "It's not divine. It's just biology doing what it does."

Diego frowned slightly, tapping his fingers against the desk. "But isn't that what we said about survival? That it's just adaptation? And yet, we called it miraculous when someone made it through war and didn't turn bitter." He turned slightly, now directing his words toward Bree, toward the room as a whole. "So why is love—sticking with someone, choosing them despite everything—not just as miraculous?"

Professor Wright nodded, intrigued. "That's the question, isn't it?" He turned back toward the board and wrote in clean, deliberate strokes:

MIRACLES: ENDURANCE VS. LOVE.

Ethan finally spoke up. "What about love at first sight?" He leaned back slightly, arms crossed, considering his own words as he said them. "Isn't that just coincidence?"

A few chuckles. A few smirks. Someone near the back muttered, "Yeah, Disney magic," but didn't push further.

That's when I stepped in. The moment had arrived—the one I'd been waiting for. I sat up slightly, glanced around the room, then spoke—not loudly, but intentionally.

"I know a man who met the love of his life twice," I said. "Once as a boy. Once as a man. And neither time was coincidence."

The air shifted. Not dramatically. Just enough. Wright raised an eyebrow, watching me. Bree stilled slightly, her pen hovering over her notebook like she wasn't sure whether to jot this down or ignore it completely. Gabe leaned in.

"And the first time he met her?" I continued, a slow smile tugging at my lips. "He didn't even know it yet."

Professor Wright didn't look away. He was measuring me now, waiting.

"Twice?" he repeated, voice even. "So are you saying love—real love—is preordained?"

The word hung there. Preordained. A step beyond fate. A suggestion that love itself might be something designed, orchestrated—not just stumbled into by accident.

Bree scoffed softly, shaking her head. "Now we're calling romance divine intervention?" She didn't say it cruelly, just bluntly—like someone who had learned long ago that love wasn't magic.

I didn't react—not yet. Instead, I leaned into the weight of the discussion, letting it stretch before answering.

V: The First of His Signs

"Not every love story is miraculous," I said carefully. "Not every first glance is divine. But sometimes, when you look back… you realize certain moments weren't accidents. They were signs."

A murmur moved through the classroom. Signs. That sounded familiar.

Diego tapped his pen thoughtfully. "That's actually kind of close to what John's Gospel does, right?"

Wright turned slightly. "Explain."

Diego shrugged, more confident now. "In John, miracles aren't just events. They're signs—things pointing toward something bigger than themselves. Water into wine wasn't just about wine. It was about abundance. Healing the blind wasn't just about vision—it was about revelation."

I nodded. "Exactly."

Professor Wright arched an eyebrow, intrigued. "So you're saying love at first sight—if it's real—isn't just attraction. It's… revelation?"

"Sometimes." I let that hang. Then: "Sometimes, love is the first miracle someone ever experiences. And the only one they never recognize until it's already shaped their entire life."

That made Bree pause—just briefly.

Gabe spoke up, slow, thoughtful. "So if love is a miracle… is heartbreak proof against it?"

Wright leaned back, arms still crossed. "Good question. If something divine exists, shouldn't it be immune to breaking?"

And that's when I smiled slightly—because the answer was already waiting in the next part of the story.

"Not every miracle is permanent," I said softly. "Sometimes they arrive just long enough to change everything. Sometimes they leave scars. But that doesn't mean they weren't real." The classroom was still.

The conversation had reached its turning point.

It was February 29th, 1968. A leap year. One extra day in a world that already felt like it was running out of time.

The country was unraveling—marches in the streets, body bags in the news, cities bracing for more fire. But in a small dance hall just outside town, a different kind of tension hummed beneath the floorboards.

My dad was home. Technically. But pieces of him hadn't made the trip back. Some were still buried under red clay halfway around the world. Others, sealed off behind the silence he wore like armor.

That night, he had plans. A safe date. A girl he knew casually—kind, quiet, liked walks and didn't ask questions. He wasn't in love. He wasn't even curious. But she was easy to be around. Predictable. That felt manageable.

Then his buddies dragged him somewhere else.

Locals knew it before the signs did. A roadhouse halfway between cheese curds and chaos, its neon letters buzzed overhead—crooked, blinking, defiant—just barely spelling "Brat Stop." Part barn, part dancehall, it smelled of bratwurst, spilled Schlitz, cigarette ash, and hairspray. Inside, the music rattled tabletops and hearts alike.

V: The First of His Signs

Boots scuffed across the floor like they'd been chasing something all week. This was where laughter echoed louder than regrets, and maybe—on the right night—a glance across the room was enough to rewrite a life.

He wasn't planning to stay. One drink. Maybe a song.

Then he saw her.

Across the floor. Not dancing. Just standing near the back, one arm loosely crossed over her stomach, the other holding a cigarette between her fingers like she'd just lit it—or was about to. Her expression was easy. Self-contained. Like the noise didn't touch her.

He noticed her hand twitch toward her pocket. Reaching for a match or lighter. He waited.

And when she slid the cigarette between her lips and went fishing for fire, he crossed the room.

No pickup line. No introduction. Just a lighter, flicked to life in his palm.

She leaned in without hesitation. Lit the cigarette. Took a drag. Then looked at him—not startled. Not coy. Just… amused.

"You always light smokes for girls you haven't met?" she asked.

He shrugged. "Only on Thursdays."

She laughed. Loud. Real. And that was it.

That's when the music shifted. A familiar voice floated through the room—Sonny and Cher, syrupy and hopeful. The kind of song that dared to believe in something. "*I Got You Babe.*"

He held out a hand.

She raised an eyebrow. "You dance?"

"Not well," he said.

She took his hand anyway.

They danced to one song. Then another. Then Daydream Believer came on, and she lip-synced every word like it was gospel—eyes closed, swaying like she meant every line.

Then came Fire.

The guitar hit first—sharp and swaggering. Then the voice, wild and uncontained, like it had torn straight through the speakers and set the room alight.

It was louder, meaner, unapologetically alive.

She moved like she'd been waiting for something to break loose. He stayed close, found her rhythm, matched her turn for turn like they'd been dancing that way for years.

After a while, they left the dance early to grab a bite to eat. But on the way, he stopped.

"There's something I've gotta do first," he said.

They pulled over at a gas station with a phone booth out front. He stepped inside. Dropped a dime.

The girl he was supposed to meet answered on the second ring.

"Hey," he said. Voice flat but steady. "I met someone else."

No explanation. No apology.

Then he hung up.

V: The First of His Signs

He slid back into the car. She didn't ask what the call was about. Maybe she already knew.

They drove until they found a late-night diner with burnt coffee and cracked red booths. Sat across from each other, sharing fries and stories. She asked where he went to school and he told her where he went to high school.

She shook her head. "No. Not high school. Grade school."

He blinked. "Drought School."

She stared. Then grinned so wide it almost cracked something.

"I knew that was you!"

He paused. Confused. "What?"

"The softball game. I told all my friends I was gonna marry this boy I saw. Little guy. Angry face. Split knuckle. You."

"I was going to Neeland school before my family moved to Ogema."

He stared at her. "That was you?"

She nodded. "Told them right then. I was gonna marry you someday."

He didn't know what to say.

Because what do you say to someone who saw you before the war, before the silence, before the hard edges—before the world did its worst—and still said, *I choose that one.*

He tried to laugh it off. But something caught in his throat. Some part of him, long rusted shut, moved an inch.

She didn't press. Just smiled like she'd known this all along. Like fate wasn't some thunderclap, but a slow burn with good memory.

They saw each other nearly every day after that.

Coffee refills turned into slow walks. Slow walks turned into long drives. Long drives turned into conversations that stayed long after the engine died.

He found himself telling her things he hadn't said out loud. Not to anyone. Not since he came home.

About the jungle. The heat. The noise. The quiet.

About the names he couldn't remember, and the faces he couldn't forget. About the way his hands sometimes shook, even when there was nothing left to fear.

She didn't flinch. Didn't try to fix it. Just listened. And made him laugh. It was like warmth sneaking in through cracks he didn't know he had.

A few weeks later, she started talking about rings. Not as a question. Not as a maybe.

As a statement.

Like: You're mine. You just don't know it yet.

She brought it up on a Tuesday. Over pancakes. Said it like she was talking about the weather.

"You ever think about getting married?"

He froze.

Not because he hadn't thought about it. But because it scared him how easily she said *we* without ever saying the word.

So he panicked.

Said he needed space. Said it was too fast. Said she deserved someone more whole.

She didn't cry. Just looked at him for a long moment. Then said, "Okay."

That was it.

He walked away. Told himself it was the right thing. That he was protecting her. That maybe if he got far enough, the war wouldn't follow.

It lasted one night.

The next morning, he stood at her door—unshaven, sleepless, holding a cup of gas station coffee and the weight of a decision he already regretted.

She opened the door.

He didn't give a speech. Just looked at her, small and tired, and said: "I made a mistake."

She nodded. "I know."

Then stepped aside to let him in.

They didn't talk about it again. Didn't need to. The decision had already been made.

It wasn't made at the altar. It was made years before—on a dusty softball field, when she pointed to a boy with a busted knuckle and said, *"That one."*

It was made again at the dance hall, in the way he waited for her to pull out a cigarette just so he could be the one to light it.

In the phone booth, where he hung up on someone else because suddenly, safety wasn't enough.

At a diner, across from a girl who didn't ask him to forget the war—only to survive it with her.

So when the wedding came, it didn't feel rushed.

It felt inevitable.

June 1st, 1968. A Saturday.

The country was burning—protests in the streets, tension in the air—but for a few sacred hours, something soft cut through.

Grandpa Komarek, her father, paid for it all.

Hauled chairs. Called in favors. Turned a rented VFW hall into something that felt like hope. Streamers hung from the rafters. The smell of polish still clung to the floorboards. Three hundred people came—family, neighbors, church friends, even a few who weren't sure why they were there, just that it mattered.

The groomsmen wore powder blue suits—standard for the time. The bride wore culottes and a short veil. No fanfare. No flash. Just the simple grace of a woman who knew what she wanted.

V: The First of His Signs

The pastor stood at the altar—a kind man, sharing a name with the groom, which made a few of the guests smile quietly when he introduced himself. But no one made a joke. It didn't feel like a coincidence—it felt like something more, like the right person was standing in the right place, saying the right words.

The pastor delivered a ceremony that was brief but real. No theatrics. No frills. Just two people making promises they couldn't yet explain.

Afterward, the tables filled with food—potluck warmth on paper plates. Ham, rolls, Jell-O salad. Coffee in metal urns. Wine in jelly jars. A local band played polkas and slow dances. And when "In the Mood" started, the floor shook with laughter and shoes and something like joy.

People danced like they hadn't had a reason to in years.

And when the band attempted *"Can't Take My Eyes Off You,"* they butchered it—off-key horns, missed notes, lyrics half-mumbled. But somehow, that made it perfect. The kind of moment you don't forget. Not because it was flawless—but because it was real.

Somewhere between the first toast and the last bite of cake, someone said it felt like a Midwest Cana. Because that's how miracles come sometimes—not in thunder, but in noise. Not in fire, but in music.

A soldier became a husband.

And a man who didn't believe in miracles stood at the altar, steady, watching the girl who never forgot him walk down the aisle like she always knew he'd make it home.

Maybe that's what faith is.

Not certainty.

Just showing up anyway.

I let the thought settle before I spoke.

"He chose her," I said. "And he kept choosing her. Long enough to walk through fire twice and still hold hands."

That landed. No one laughed. No one scoffed.

The mood had shifted. Bree twirled a strand of hair absently, lips pressed tight. Diego had stopped clicking his pen. Even Wright hadn't reached for his water glass in minutes.

I could feel them settling into it. Into the warmth of something that, for once, didn't end in fire. For once, the story had a middle—and that middle was music and cheap perfume and pancakes on a Tuesday morning.

Reid finally spoke. "So wait—he really just... dumped the other girl? No second thoughts?"

"He made the call from a gas station parking lot. Said, 'I met someone else.' Then hung up. That was it."

"Cold," Diego muttered.

"Clear," Aisha countered.

"But is that a miracle?" Professor Wright asked, leaning forward. His tone wasn't dismissive—it was calculated. He was regrouping. "Or is it just... human chemistry? War vet comes home, meets someone who doesn't flinch, and his brain releases enough serotonin to make him think it's fate."

He folded his hands. "We're social creatures. Pattern-seeking mammals with abandonment issues. Love feels sacred because our biology's desperate for security. That doesn't make it divine."

A few heads nodded. Others stayed still.

"And even if it *feels* miraculous," he added, "why does that count as proof? What's the standard here—emotional resonance?"

"You're saying love is just a reaction?" I asked.

"I'm saying we assign meaning to coincidences because we're afraid of chaos."

"Maybe," I said. "Or maybe… we call it chaos when we don't like the pattern."

Reid made a sound—almost a chuckle, but softer.

Wright tilted his head, unfazed. "Let me put it this way: If two people meet, connect, and live out their lives together, is that any more supernatural than two atoms colliding in a vacuum and forming a new compound?"

"I don't think atoms buy each other coffee," Aisha said.

Wright smiled, but only slightly.

Then Bree spoke.

"I don't believe in love," she said flatly.

She didn't blink. Didn't hedge. The words landed like she'd rehearsed them. But this wasn't theater. It was memory.

Heads turned.

She stared ahead, eyes distant, voice dry. "People stay together because it's easy. Or because they're afraid. Or because one of them doesn't know how to leave. That's not God. That's convenience."

She didn't blink. Didn't fidget. Her tone wasn't dramatic—it was surgical. Too calm to be performative. Too practiced not to be personal.

A few seconds passed.

"I'm sorry," Aisha said, gently.

Bree ignored her.

"People call it a miracle when someone stays," she said. "But they never talk about the people who should've left and didn't. Or the ones who prayed for someone and got nothing. Or the ones who believed and got hurt anyway."

She shrugged. "You can romanticize it if you want. But I've seen what love looks like up close. It doesn't save anyone."

I didn't argue. Not right away.

She wasn't trying to debate. She was bleeding slowly, methodically. Daring someone to say they understood.

"I think you're right," I said.

That got her attention. Her eyes flicked to mine, suspicious.

"I don't think love is a miracle because it feels good. I think it's a miracle because it doesn't always leave when it should."

Bree tilted her head slightly.

"My dad," I said, "should've left. He'd been taught to leave. Taught to bury things. Taught that softness gets you hit. And yet—he stayed. He didn't run from her. He didn't flinch. She chose him. He chose her. And he kept choosing her."

I met her eyes.

"Some people don't get that," I said. "And that's not fair. But that doesn't make it less real when it happens."

Bree didn't answer. But she didn't look away either.

"Maybe that's the problem," Diego cut in, his voice more curious than mocking. "The fact that it only happens sometimes. Like it's some divine lottery. How is that fair?"

"It's not," I said. "That's why it's grace."

He frowned. "That sounds like theological sleight of hand."

"It's not a trick," I said. "It's just… not a transaction."

Lena stirred in her seat. "So love isn't a promise. It's a surprise?"

"No," I said. "It's a promise someone keeps when they don't have to."

Bree looked down at her desk. Said nothing.

Ethan cleared his throat. "Okay, but seriously. Why does that mean God's real? Couldn't it just be… resilience?"

"Sure," I said. "But maybe those aren't opposites."

He made a small face but didn't press.

I looked around the room. The mood was different now. Not broken. Just bruised.

"There's a verse," I said quietly. "John chapter two. The wedding in Cana. They run out of wine. Jesus tells the servants to fill the jars with water. They do. Fill them all the way to the brim. Then the water becomes wine."

Aisha smiled faintly.

"Most people miss this," I continued, "but the wine didn't show up when the cups were empty. It showed up when they were already full. When they thought they couldn't take anymore."

Wright raised an eyebrow. "So suffering invites grace?"

"No," I said. "But maybe it makes us thirsty enough to notice it."

I didn't wait for the response.

"I think that's what love did for my dad. It didn't erase the war. It didn't make him whole. But it gave him something… real enough to stand on. Maybe something human—something holy."

I paused.

"And out of that ground—something new grew."

Then: "And then we were born."

It was almost a whisper.

Bree didn't speak. She didn't look away either. Her hand stayed still. And this time, she didn't reach for her pen.

I let the silence settle again—breathe-length, memory-length—then spoke.

V: The First of His Signs

"My brother first. Kevin. His lungs barely worked. The doctors weren't sure he'd make it through the first week. But he did."

I paused.

"Then me. Legs so twisted the soles of my feet pointed backward. They had me in braces before I could crawl. Said I might never walk without them."

I glanced around the room—no one interrupted.

"They say I was strong from the start," I went on. "Not big—but wiry. Determined. The kind of baby who didn't just kick—launched. My legs never stopped. Side to side. Over and over. Like I was trying to sprint my way out of the crib before I even knew how to crawl."

A few heads tilted. Quiet. Curious.

"One crib didn't last a week. Snapped a slat clean through from all the twisting. Another one cracked near the base. Warped from me pushing and pulling, trying to break out of whatever box they put me in."

I gave a half-smile. "My parents used to say I was born halfway out the door."

That drew a small laugh. Soft. Real.

"But it wasn't just motion for motion's sake. It was more than that. A restlessness. Like my body already knew life was coming fast—and I didn't want to miss any of it."

The room stayed quiet.

Not tense. Not judgmental.

Just quiet.

The kind that happens when people stop seeing the surface—and start listening for what's underneath.

That's when some heads turned.

Not in mockery. In something closer to guilt.

Like they were seeing me for the first time.

A few glanced down—at my legs, at my boots—like they expected to spot something obvious. Something bent.

But there was nothing to stare at.

The braces were gone. Long gone. The damage had healed into habit. Invisible now. But never undone.

And for once, their eyes stayed on me.

Not for show.

For understanding.

I cleared my throat. "And my sister, Nicki…"

The name hung there. Soft but undeniable.

"July 21st, 1972. She was born with complications. Couldn't sit up on her own. Couldn't talk. But she smiled like she'd been practicing for years."

Aisha's eyes widened. Not with shock. With recognition.

Then she pressed a hand to her lips.

We were looking for a sign. But maybe the sign was her.

"She was the miracle," I said.

V: The First of His Signs

I waited.

Then I added, soft as breath: "But sometimes the miracle doesn't stay."

Silence. Temporary, fragile—like a whisper you almost missed.

But this time... they heard it.

VI: That You May Believe

Silence stretched like a held breath. The kind you don't mean to keep holding.

They didn't know what I meant yet. Not really. They just felt the temperature drop after I said her name. After I said the miracle didn't stay.

Wright moved first.

Not a shift in tone—not yet. Just a slow, careful breath as he straightened his shoulders and let his voice find its footing again.

"So let's press that a little," he said. "You called her a miracle. But what exactly are we saying that means?"

I said nothing yet. Just watched him as he tried to pull the room back toward analysis.

"I'm asking seriously," he added. "Was it her birth that was miraculous? The timing? The response of your family? Because if a miracle can mean all of those things—or any of them—then it starts to mean nothing at all."

Some of the students glanced my way. Some stayed on Wright.

"I'm not being flippant," he said. "But if you're saying miracles are simply moments we *feel deeply*, then how do we distinguish them from ordinary experience? From chemical response? From sentimentality?"

He didn't say it harshly. But he was tightening the rope.

Bree didn't look up when she said it: "So basically you're saying he made it all up?"

Wright turned, unphased. "I'm saying emotional intensity is not the same as evidence."

"You ever had something happen that felt like it cracked the air?" she asked. "Like it meant something—before your brain had time to explain it away?"

He didn't answer. Which said enough.

"I'm just saying," Bree muttered, "maybe some things don't have to be proven to matter."

That surprised me—not what she said, but that it came from her.

She caught me looking. "Don't misunderstand. I'm not buying into anything yet."

"Didn't think you were," I said.

"But you said she was a miracle," Bree said. "And then you said she didn't stay. So... what does that mean?"

Now all the eyes were back on me.

Reid leaned forward slightly, elbows on the desk.

Aisha tilted her head, brows drawn in quiet concern.

I didn't answer right away.

"It means," I said finally, "that sometimes a miracle isn't the fix. It's the presence."

Wright's jaw moved. He didn't interrupt.

"She was born fragile," I said. "But she changed people. My dad most of all. And not in the easy ways."

The room stayed quiet.

"She couldn't talk," I continued. "She couldn't walk. But she'd laugh. Like—*really* laugh. Like she knew something we didn't."

I caught Aisha's glance. She wasn't writing anything down. Just listening, hands still.

"She was born in July. 1972. About three years after my dad came back from Vietnam."

There was a shift at that. Small. But Diego sat up straighter.

"Three kids," I said. "Kevin, me, then Nicki. All within four years."

"And you all had health issues?" Aisha asked, gently.

I nodded.

Aisha's voice was almost a whisper. "You said your dad was in Vietnam?"

"Yeah. '66 to early '68. Infantry."

She didn't blink. "Was he exposed?"

I nodded. "He didn't talk about it much back then. But the way they sprayed it—Agent Orange—the stuff they sprayed from planes. He couldn't have avoided it if he tried. It was in the water. The air. They called it vegetation control, but it was really just defoliation at scale."

Aisha's eyes softened. "Dioxin poisoning can stay in the bloodstream for years. Decades, even."

"Yeah," I said. "And sometimes it doesn't affect the soldier. Sometimes it shows up in the next generation."

Lena shifted in her seat. "Wait—so you think that's what caused everything? Your brother's lung problems, your legs?"

I exhaled slowly. "I don't know what caused it," I said. "The doctors never confirmed it. But they didn't rule it out, either."

Reid cleared his throat. "Do you think your dad believed it?"

"Eventually," I said. "But not at first. For a long time, I think he just assumed the universe was trying to break him again."

That landed harder than I expected.

No one scribbled notes. Even Diego didn't try to poke a hole in it.

Then Aisha spoke—quiet, but clear. "And your sister? Nicki?"

I looked up.

"Nicki was different," I said. "Even from us. Her body just... didn't follow the rules. Muscles too tight to function. Spine too soft to support. But she had these eyes—like she could see straight through people. She'd look at you like she knew you were pretending. Then she'd smile anyway."

No one moved.

"She wasn't easy," I said. "Feeding her took time. She'd choke on water. Spit up formula. She didn't sleep through the night. There were seizures."

Bree's face had changed—not softened, but focused. Like she was storing the story for later.

"And through all of it," I said, "my dad—this man who'd been trained to kill, taught not to feel—he became someone else. He sat beside her crib at night. He wiped drool from her chin. He sang songs he hadn't sung in decades."

I let that echo a moment.

"I'm not saying that makes it a miracle," I added. "But I am saying... something holy happened in that space."

Stillness again.

Wright didn't speak, but he didn't need to. The question was already there, humming underneath the silence:

So what happened to her?

I didn't answer it. Not yet.

I glanced at Aisha. "You said Agent Orange affects development?"

She nodded. "Neurological damage. Organ malformations. There are dozens of known links. And probably more they haven't admitted."

I hadn't meant to say more. But something in the way Aisha looked at me—soft, not pitying—loosened something.

"Yeah," I said. "I think my dad suspected. But he didn't say it."

"Guilt?" Reid asked.

"Probably. But more than that—I think he couldn't bear the idea that the war didn't just haunt him. It followed him home. It lived in his kids."

A few eyes dropped.

"So what happened?" Lena asked, voice quiet.

I looked down at my desk, not because I didn't want to answer—but because I remembered exactly where it began.

"That's a good question," I said. "This one started in July of '72... when the air felt too hot, the hospital lights were too bright, and my dad didn't know how much one room could change a person."

The radio played *Bill Withers'* "Lean on Me," low and steady, threading through the silence like a promise. It wrapped itself around the room like a hand on a shoulder.

The melody wove between beeping monitors and hushed voices, a quiet reminder that no one gets through alone.

It was too soon.

The air felt wrong. Too warm. Too sterile.

My mom remembered the lights in the delivery room casting everything in a sick yellow hue—like jaundiced sunlight through stained glass. My dad remembered the cold in his hands—how tightly he gripped hers, how she winced, how he loosened.

But he didn't let go.

Somewhere in the corner, the radio crackled again.

The song hadn't finished. It just kept going—like it knew something they didn't.

The labor wasn't long—but it was urgent.

Compressed.

Like the whole room had been thrown into fast-forward. Movements were precise. Voices clipped.

Later, my mom would say it felt like everyone was avoiding a word they didn't want to speak.

Nicki didn't cry at first. That's what no one forgets.

There was a beat—just a breath—but it stretched like a hallway with no end.

A silence so loud it became a presence.

Then—finally—a sound. Not a scream. Not even a cry. Just a gasp. A shallow drag of air into a body already tired from the fight.

My dad said he knew right then. Before the doctors spoke. Before the tests, the diagnoses, the late-night calls from specialists.

He just knew.

The radio kept playing—something newer now. A softer voice. A brighter tone.

A song about seeing clearly. About skies turning blue.

He heard it, but it felt cruel.

Like someone had queued up the wrong track for the wrong moment.

The doctors didn't say much.

They moved quickly—suctioned her mouth, tapped her back, shone lights into eyes that didn't respond the way they should.

My mom lay in the bed, eyes wide, arms empty, listening for a cry that never came.

Tiny. Silent. Beautiful.

But wrong in a way no one could name—yet.

Later, it had a name. Cerebral Palsy. **Severe.** The kind that changes everything before anyone can explain what's happening.

She couldn't lift her head well. Couldn't sit up without help. Her tiny limbs would seize without warning—muscles clenching like wires wound too tight. She didn't walk. Didn't talk. Not in words. But she made sounds—soft, melodic little hums when she was content. A fluttering kind of music that didn't come from her mouth so much as from her spirit.

She rarely cried. Even with all the pain, all the seizures, all the stiffness that bent her small frame—her default wasn't distress. It was endurance. But when she did cry, it wasn't loud. It was deep. A kind of low, aching sound, like something inside her was trying to surface but didn't know how.

She didn't have tear ducts—one more thing that hadn't formed right. So when she cried, there were no tears. Mom and Dad had to moisten her eyes by hand, gently wiping them to keep them from drying out.

It made the crying harder to witness somehow—grief without tears, pain without release.

And then—again and again, with a grace all her own—she smiled.

Not always when expected. Not always on cue. But when it came, it wasn't just a facial expression. It was revelation. It was light cracking through something old and cold. It was proof that joy could live in a body that didn't work. A body the world would call broken.

The doctors taught my parents how to feed her. She couldn't swallow properly. Every meal was a hazard. They had to jiggle her throat gently after each spoonful, coaxing food downward. A slight delay, and she could choke.

She slept on her back. Always. She could roll, barely, but if she rolled too far—if she ended up face-down—she couldn't lift her head to breathe. Her muscles would freeze. Panic would take over.

My mom stopped sleeping for nearly a year. She stayed half-awake through every night, listening for silence. Because silence could mean the worst.

My dad built things to help. Wedges, braces, soft foam contraptions meant to keep her safe. He was quiet about it. Just... did the work. As if trying to fix something with his hands could make up for everything he couldn't fix in his blood.

And still—Nicki smiled.

Even when her legs trembled, when her tiny hands curled tight against her will. Even when her eyes fluttered from seizures. Even when she was choking on a bottle at 2 a.m.—she smiled.

And my dad—this man who'd been forged in combat, who had hardened himself to endure loss and silence and blood—he melted. Slowly. Fully.

He would hold her at night, rub her back with his calloused hands, whisper things she couldn't understand... but maybe did.

He told my mom once, "She's better than I ever was, and she can't even walk."

That's how much she meant to him.

She wasn't just a daughter. She was a doorway. A thing that cracked him open in a way the war never could. She reached him not with words, but with being. With presence. With whatever it was she carried in those trembling hands.

Then came that night.

July 4th. 1974.

It was the first time my parents had left the house together since Nicki was born. Friends had invited them to a cookout. Fireworks. A little music. A rare moment to breathe. They almost didn't go.

But everyone insisted. The nurse—a woman they trusted—said, "Go. She'll be fine. I've got this."

She had experience. Had cared for special needs kids. She knew the routine. She fed her. Jiggled her throat to help the food go down. Watched her fall asleep.

Then she laid her down. On her back. Just like always.

She checked on her later—still on her back. Still breathing. Everything was quiet.

But sometime after that... Nicki rolled.

Not far. Just enough. Just enough to make the world stop.

Even the night held its breath.

No one heard her struggle.

No rustle. No cry. Just the hush of a room that had already let go.

The nurse was in the kitchen, rinsing a bottle. Somewhere outside, a dog barked. Then a cheer as a firework burst skyward—bright and crackling.

Inside, stillness.

Nicki's body had betrayed her silently. Not with flailing or alarms. Just... stillness.

There was no dramatic gasp. No violent seizure. Just a tiny body whose muscles refused to lift the head. Whose lungs tried, and failed, and gave up. Quietly. Softly.

VI: That You May Believe

Outside, the sky bloomed in reds and golds. Fireworks cracked and thundered.

Inside, she slipped away.

By the time the nurse returned, it was already too late.

Nicki was gone.

She was not yet two years old.

When the call came, the nurse didn't wait. She dialed the number with shaking hands and said only one word before my parents knew to run.

My dad drove like a madman. My mom screamed the entire way home, already knowing.

When they arrived, the nurse was waiting at the door, sobbing, incoherent. Inside, Nicki's blanket was folded back. Her body had already been moved.

My dad didn't yell. Didn't throw anything. Didn't speak.

He just walked past the nurse. Walked into the room. Sat on the floor. And held the photo—the only photo they had of her smiling.

Later that night, he went outside and screamed at God.

Not with questions.

With hate.

He cursed the sky. Cursed every story of angels, of grace, of a Father who loves His children.

Because what kind of God lets that happen?

What kind of miracle lets the miracle die?

And then—he screamed.

"You call Yourself a fucking *Father*?"

His voice tore into the night like something feral. Raw. Uncontained.

"You let her *suffer*. You let her *rot*. You watched. You fucking watched!"

His fists slammed the porch rail—once, twice, then again—until the wood cracked and his knuckles split open. Blood streaked the railing like punctuation.

Behind him, the house was hollow with sobs.

Outside, laughter rose down the block. Sparklers hissed. Music played from someone's garage. Fireworks thudded in the sky—red, white, gold—mocking the silence of the crib inside.

And still he roared.

"You don't get to call that love! You don't get to call that *grace*!"

He pounded the rail again—until the sound of flesh on wood was the only thing louder than the booming sky.

His knees gave out. He collapsed to the floorboards, clutching the photo to his chest like it was the only thing keeping his ribs from splitting open.

"If this is mercy," he choked, "then fuck mercy. And fuck You for promising it. For making me believe in it. For making me tell my kids You were good."

VI: That You May Believe

And still the fireworks went on. The world kept celebrating. But inside that porch, the Fourth of July had turned into a battlefield.

He stayed on the porch until the sun broke through the treetops. His hands never stopped shaking. But he never dropped the photo.

He never blamed the nurse. But he never stopped blaming God.

Something broke in him that night—not like glass, but like the last leg of a chair giving out.

He folded, quietly.

Functioned.

But only on the outside.

My parents moved like people who'd lost gravity. Like even the daylight had become heavy. Not just for a day. Not just for a week. From that moment on, everything felt heavier.

And then—

The funeral.

Kevin and I were little. Too little to understand what was happening.

I wore a clip-on tie. It scratched my neck, and I kept tugging at it.

I remember people crying. A lot of grown-ups.

I remember the box at the front. It was small. Too small. And it was the wrong color. I don't know why I thought that, but I did.

I pulled on my dad's sleeve.

"Can we wake Nicki up now?" I asked. "I wanna go home."

Kevin nodded beside me. "Yeah. She's probably just sleeping."

Dad didn't say anything. Didn't even blink. He just looked at us—really looked—as if we'd blurred out of focus, then suddenly snapped back into view. And something... changed. Like a door that wouldn't close finally clicked shut.

He bent down, kissed Nicki's forehead. Then stood, reached for our hands. We didn't understand, but we knew we were going with him. And together, we walked out of the church.

And even now, when I think of Nicki, I don't remember the funeral. I remember that weightlessness, that stillness, that ache in the space where a child's laughter should have been.

A pause.

"We call it her Independence Day."

Some brows knit, confused at first.

Then understanding began to settle.

"Independence—from the pain she was in. From a body that never let her speak, never let her run. From the seizures. The feeding tubes. The long nights..."

I looked down at my desk, gathering the words. "She was trapped. And then... she wasn't."

No one moved.

"She didn't get fireworks," I added softly. "But heaven did."

Someone sniffled. Bree shifted. The room went reverent—no one even moved.

Diego cleared his throat. "So… that's what you meant by miracle?"

I looked up. "That's part of it."

But something happened that night, too. Something just for us.

Later that night, Kevin and I were asleep when I felt it—a breeze, soft and sudden. Windows were closed.

I slipped into Mom and Dad's room.

"*Dad,*" I whispered, *"there's a wind in my room."*

He looked up. Cleared his eyes, "What?"

"*It's Nicki,*" I said. "*She said bye.*"

He sat up slowly, heavy with the weight of the day, then followed me back to my room. We stood silently beside the bed. The air had gone still again—until, just as he tucked the blanket, he felt it too. A chill. A whisper.

Neither of us spoke.

Mom never felt it. Kevin slept through it.

But Dad would later tell me: he believed it—not a dream, not a child's fancy. A moment. A message.

That breeze—quiet, gentle—was everything.

A girl saying goodbye.

For a moment, no one spoke. The room felt like it had shrunk.

Bree's pen slipped across her notebook—just a flick, a barely-there twitch. She didn't look up. Just stared at the page like it had betrayed her.

Wright opened his mouth—then paused. Even he could feel it.

"You said," Bree finally muttered, "that your dad cursed God for not being a father."

I nodded. Slowly.

She looked up then. Not angry. Just... exposed. "Yeah. That tracks."

The room held its breath. No one moved. A few students glanced toward Professor Wright—waiting. Expecting.

He shifted forward slightly, re-crossing his arms. Not defensive. Commanding. Like a man reclaiming the field.

"You're calling that a miracle?" Wright asked, trying to keep his voice even. "That a man suffers and keeps going—that's divine now?"

His tone was calm. But clipped.

I kept my eyes on him—not out of defiance, but clarity.

"No," I said. "The miracle isn't that he didn't quit."

A pause.

VI: That You May Believe

"The miracle is that the pain didn't poison him. That grief didn't hollow him out. That somehow, he chose to love again."

Wright tilted his head, the faintest narrowing of the eyes. "And yet... she's still gone."

"She is," I said. "But she's free. And he didn't become what broke him."

For a moment, Wright didn't respond. The air between us was dense.

Then, from across the room, Reid spoke up: "Her Independence Day."

I turned—surprised. But Reid didn't look at me. He was staring down at his desk, like the words had come from somewhere deeper than his voice.

Even Bree had stopped writing.

Wright exhaled—barely audible—but it wasn't a sigh of dismissal. More like pressure building under a surface he wasn't sure he could hold.

"Pain either breaks something," he said, "or bends it."

"Or bends it into something stronger," I said. "Tempered. Refined. Like metal in fire."

I wasn't trying to win. Just to offer something true.

"Maybe that's why I'm telling you all this. Not to argue. Not to prove a point. Not even for a grade."

I looked slowly across the room—at the ones who had laughed earlier. They weren't laughing at all now.

"Because sometimes the fire doesn't destroy you. It tempers you. And sometimes... the miracle is what comes out of the fire."

I looked back at Wright. He was still holding my gaze.

"You talk like certainty is strength," I said. "But sometimes, what takes more strength is staying open. Letting the story keep going."

A flicker in his expression. Barely there. But it was something. I could've left it there. But something pushed me. Quietly, gently: "If you're so sure this doesn't matter... then why does it matter to you so much?"

Something flickered. In his jaw, maybe. Or in the space behind his eyes. But he didn't answer.

A crack. Not in his face—but in the silence that followed.

A hesitation that wasn't academic. A pause that wasn't planned.

Then Wright blinked. Straightened. Said nothing.

But the weight in the room had shifted.

For the first time all semester, the conversation didn't belong to him.

It belonged to the room.

Ethan tapped the end of his pen against the desk, staring out the window like he was seeing something farther than the horizon.

Aisha looked down, eyes wet but not weeping.

Even Diego had stopped trying to look amused.

Then Lena spoke.

"Can I ask something?" she said, hesitating for the first time all semester.

I nodded.

"If she'd lived… if she'd gotten better somehow—" she stopped, chewing the words—"would it have still been a miracle?"

I thought about it.

"Yes," I said. "But it would've been a different one."

She looked puzzled.

"The kind we recognize," I said. "The kind we cheer for. Healing. Escape. Happy endings. A blind man seeing. A crippled man walking."

"And this one?" she asked.

"This one asked more of us."

I didn't say it bitterly. I wasn't angry anymore. Just honest.

Bree exhaled hard through her nose. "So you're saying the pain was the point?"

"No," I said. "I'm saying the love survived the pain."

She looked away.

"And that matters?" she asked.

"Yes," I said. "It matters because it's rare. Because not everyone makes it through the fire still soft."

Silence again. But it was different now. No longer stunned—*searching*.

Liam's hand moved slightly—half-raised, half-aborted. Then his voice cut through from the back.

"My mom lost a baby," he said. "Long before I was born."

He didn't look up.

"She stopped going to church. Said she couldn't talk to a God that let babies die."

Another beat.

"But she still packed my lunch every day. Still kissed me on the head before school. Still hummed when she did the dishes."

He paused.

"I don't know if that's a miracle. But it never felt like nothing."

No one responded. Because what do you say to that?

I let his words settle into the silence. Then I stepped in—not to one-up, not to pivot. Just to carry it forward.

"I'm not trying to convert anyone," I said. "I'm not here to make you agree."

I looked across the room again. A few heads tilted. Some arms slowly uncrossed.

"I'm telling you this… because I've seen too much not to."

Another breath.

"I've seen what happens when grief turns people bitter. I've seen what it costs to keep going when everything in you wants to stop. I've seen someone lose a child and not lose himself."

And then I looked at the whole class.

"All these stories… I'm telling them so you'll see what I see. So you'll look again. So you'll stop waiting for burning bushes and realize that maybe, just maybe, the fire's already here—but it hasn't consumed you."

A few students leaned forward unconsciously. Like something was drawing them in they didn't want to admit.

Wright said nothing. But he wasn't blinking much anymore.

I straightened—not to stand taller, but to steady myself. And then I said it.

"That's why I'm telling you this."

A pause.

"That you may believe. So you'll stop waiting for burning bushes and realize maybe… the fire's already here. But it hasn't burned you up."

No one breathed.

Then someone—maybe Reid—let out the softest *"Yeah"* under his breath.

Not in agreement. Not in understanding. Just recognition.

I almost missed it. But that single word—barely breathed—landed like a stone in water.

The room didn't erupt. There were no grand revelations. Just stillness. Deep, focused stillness. Like everyone had moved a half-inch closer to something without knowing exactly what.

Professor Wright didn't respond.

But for once, he wasn't waiting to.

And that, in its own way, was a miracle.

A breath.

A beat.

Then I said it—softly, but certain:

"That you may believe."

VII: The Crossing We Carry

"You said something earlier," Wright began, adjusting his glasses with precision. His voice was measured—but not neutral. "That pain might lead to something stronger. That grief can shape rather than destroy."

He paused—eyes scanning the room like a general taking stock of his troops. "It's a compelling sentiment," he continued, "but let's be honest— Nietzsche said the same thing nearly 150 years ago. *That which does not kill us makes us stronger.* And for centuries, theologians have debated whether suffering is a refining fire or simply chaos dressed up in metaphor."

His tone sharpened slightly.

"Kierkegaard believed faith had to be absurd," Wright began, lifting his voice just enough to reassert control. "That the leap to believe in something beyond reason wasn't a weakness—it was the point. *The absurd,* he called it. To believe in a paradox. A God-man. A resurrection. A miracle."

He stepped away from the lectern now, pacing lightly. The room's attention was his again—for now.

"Then there's Viktor Frankl—existential psychologist and Holocaust survivor. He didn't look for miracles. He looked for meaning. He said suffering ceases to be suffering the moment it finds meaning. That the human spirit doesn't just endure pain—it organizes itself around it, creates narrative out of horror. It survives *because* it can tell a story."

A few students were scribbling again. Bree, especially.

"And Aquinas—centuries earlier—saw suffering as part of divine providence. A test. A purifying fire. Not chaos, but choreography. Every trial allowed by God for the shaping of the soul. It's all... very noble. Very structured."

He returned to the whiteboard, marker uncapped, and wrote **PROVIDENCE** in neat block letters. Then circled it. Twice.

"But let's be honest," he continued, still not looking at me, "when we cherry-pick moments of human endurance and call them divine, we're not always engaging theology. We're often doing something else entirely—eisegesis, as we call it. Reading meaning *into* experience, not extracting it *from* revelation. We want it to matter, so we make it matter."

The marker squeaked against the board as he underlined **MEANING** beneath **PROVIDENCE**.

"And that's where we tread dangerous ground. When every coincidence becomes providence. When every trauma, instead of being grieved and processed, is dressed up in divine language. We stop engaging critically, and we start moralizing."

Pens scratched against paper. Bree's, most of all.

"Aquinas romanticized suffering," she said suddenly, leaning forward, tapping her pen. "That's the problem with providence—it assumes pain serves a higher function, which makes it easier to justify systems that allow people to suffer. If we frame suffering as 'soul-shaping,' then we risk excusing the institutions that perpetuate it."

Wright raised an eyebrow, intrigued.

"Frankl had it right," she continued. "People don't need miracles— they need agency. The moment suffering finds meaning isn't some divine intervention—it's psychological restructuring. We adapt because we have to. That's survival, not revelation."

Wright turned back to the board, marker hovering. "And that's exactly the point. Pain doesn't prove divinity—it proves human resilience. Theology wants to assign purpose to suffering, but suffering doesn't ask for meaning. It just exists."

Bree nodded slightly—but something about her posture shifted.

Not in surrender. But in avoidance.

Like she'd taken the argument to its limit but wasn't ready to push past it.

That's when I felt it.

That slow knot tightening at the base of my ribs.

He wasn't just pushing back—he was reducing suffering to abstraction. To theory. To tidy categories of people who'd never once had to sit on the edge of a hospital bed and hold someone together with words they weren't sure they believed.

It wasn't personal to him. It was academic.

But to me, it was my father. It was the wrench. The war. The little girl who died on the Fourth of July.

And now it was being turned into a case study for intellectual distance.

He paused again, arms crossed loosely.

"I'm not saying pain isn't powerful," he concluded. "I'm saying that power isn't necessarily divine. That's the difference between theology... and testimony."

That's when Chloe broke in. "But there's no justice in that," she said, voice tight. "What kind of God lets you suffer just to teach you something?"

For a split second, something in Wright's eyes faltered—like the question hit a bruise he hadn't expected to expose. But then it was gone, replaced with that clinical calm.

He didn't flinch. Didn't soften. He just looked at her with the same unreadable steadiness.

Her tone wasn't combative. It was cracked open—like she was speaking from a place that hadn't healed yet.

For a second, no one said anything.

Wright's expression didn't shift. His silence didn't offer comfort, just observation. The kind that made you wonder if he even heard the pain underneath the question.

That's when she spoke again. Quieter this time.

"So... are you saying it doesn't matter what it meant to him? Or to us?"

Wright's reply was smooth. Too smooth. "I'm saying that when we assign cosmic significance to personal pain, we risk interpreting trauma through the lens of confirmation bias. It becomes about what we need to see, rather than what's actually there."

Reid leaned forward, arms on his desk. "But if it changes you—if it keeps you from giving up—isn't that real enough?"

Wright didn't flinch. "Real, yes. Divine? That's a separate question."

That's when I stepped in. Not with a question. With a statement.

"What if suffering isn't proof against miracles," I said, "but the way they unfold?"

The words landed like a gravitational pull. The room went still. Not tense—just listening.

Wright didn't interrupt. Not yet.

I glanced around. "We say miracles are evidence of God. But we expect them to look like rescue—instant, dramatic, impossible. But what if sometimes... the miracle *isn't* what saves you, but what keeps you standing after everything falls?"

Gabe muttered under his breath, "Still sounds like a way to make sense of stuff that doesn't make sense."

I turned to him. "I'm not trying to make sense of it. I'm trying to show you what it became. What it did."

Wright pressed his fingers together in front of him, elbows resting lightly on the podium. "That sounds dangerously close to eisegesis. You're reading meaning into the experience, not extracting meaning from it."

Bree clicked her pen twice, then stopped.

She wasn't looking at Wright anymore. Wasn't looking at anyone.

"*You ever pray?*" she asked suddenly.

Not loudly. Not challenging. Just... quiet.

The words barely reached the air, but I caught them.

I turned toward her, unsure if she was talking to me or to herself.

"Not now," she clarified, her smirk flickering—but not staying. "I mean when you were younger. Before you... you know. Started believing this was real."

I answered.

She nodded slowly, eyes still on the desk in front of her. "*Yeah. Me too.*"

Then, before anyone else could pick up on the shift, she leaned back in her chair, flicked her pen open again, and exhaled.

"Doesn't mean it worked."

Just like that, she pulled herself back into the debate.

A few seconds passed—too short to call silence, too long to ignore.

I glanced toward Wright.

He was watching me—watching us.

I straightened slightly. Not in defiance. In patience.

"No," I said, quietly. But it didn't land like concession. It landed like a closing argument.

"I'm not inserting meaning." I looked directly at him now. "I'm remembering."

A few students looked up again. Wright's pen had stilled.

"You can quote Kierkegaard and Frankl and Aquinas all day," I said. "But none of them were there."

I let that hang.

"He worked himself into the ground. Built a business from nothing. Slept fifteen minutes a night because he still felt like he was on watch. Not metaphorically—literally. He didn't believe the war was over. He couldn't. Because the second he let his guard down, it all came rushing back."

No one said a word.

"And for years, it was quiet. No flashbacks. No explosions in his head. Just motion. Just survival."

I looked around the room. "Until the day we crossed that bridge."

Wright blinked—just once—but it was enough.

Now it was my turn to hold the silence. Not to control the room. But to invite it into something real.

VII: The Crossing We Carry

"Not metaphor," I said. "A real bridge. Steel cables. Wooden planks. Just me, my brother, my mom—who never let go of his hand—and my dad... walking across."

The classroom stilled again. This wasn't theory anymore. It wasn't abstraction. It was the moment the floor gave out.

"He stopped. Mid-step. Stared off like he was listening for something only he could hear."

I looked down—just for a second. Then back up. "That was the day the war came home."

I didn't want to tell this story. But some truths don't wait for permission.

The room was silent. No movement, no pen-clicking, no nervous glances. Just the quiet weight of something settling.

I exhaled, pressing my thumb absently against the edge of the desk. It was smooth—too smooth. The desks there had been different. Rough wood, splintered edges. I remembered the weight of a rifle against my shoulder, the damp heat pressing in. The smell of metal, sweat, earth.

"Tây Ninh Province. 1967."

The heat was the same. The weight was the same.

But the air? The air was different.

It carried something heavier than humidity—something that pressed into the lungs, thick and unrelenting.

By then, everything blurred. Days. Dirt. Death. Orders. None of it made sense anymore.

They were told they were part of a strategic sweep—a push into Tây Ninh Province. A place near the Cambodian border, thick with jungle and quiet lies.

The papers would call it Operation Junction City later—one of the biggest air-ground assaults of the war. Twenty-five thousand men moving like shadows through brush and broken nerves, trying to smoke out ghosts of their own.

But no one said that then. Not to the grunts. To my dad and his platoon, it was just another day where nobody told you why you were dying—only that you needed to keep moving.

The mission was simple on paper:
Advance. Secure the river. Cross the bridge. Keep pushing.

But nothing in Vietnam was ever simple.
Especially not the bridges.

Earlier that morning, someone in camp had rigged a radio—tinny, barely holding signal, but still working.

A song came blaring through the static—loud, raw, defiant. A voice growling about escape, about needing to get out of this place before it killed them. The guys nodded along. Some sang under their breath.

No one laughed. No one rolled their eyes. Because for too many of them, it really *was* the last thing they'd ever do.

Then the radio crackled. Shifted. The next song came on— something gentler. Softer. *A Kind of Hush,* by Herman's Hermits. A melody about silence, about something sacred passing between people without words.

My dad said later it made the jungle feel quieter somehow.

Not safer. Just… suspended.

Like the whole world had pulled tight on a single thread. And no one knew what would snap first—your nerves or the silence.

He was still humming it, almost without realizing, when they reached the bridge.

Wooden slats. Worn cable. River below so dark you couldn't see the bottom—and didn't want to.

It looked abandoned. Too abandoned. That made it worse.

Simmons grunted beside him. "Junction City, my ass," he muttered. "Feels like we're marching straight into hell with a flashlight and a broken map."

Henderson—still too green to be scared—was up front. He grinned as he adjusted his helmet. "I'll take point. Ain't no gooks out here this late. They sleep, same as us."

He didn't wait for permission. Just stepped forward. One plank. Then two. Then ten.

The jungle held its breath.

A shift in the air—too still, too expectant. The river beneath barely rippled, its surface black as polished stone. Somewhere in the trees, a bird called once—sharp, clipped—then silence.

Simmons inhaled sharply, like he was about to say something.

Then hell opened.

CRACK—CRACK—BRRRRRRT.

Gunfire erupted like a thunderclap from the far tree line.

Automatic. Close. Mean.

The jungle exploded.

Bullets tore through the air—snapping wood, slicing leaves, punching flesh.

Henderson didn't scream. Didn't even fall forward. He just dropped. Like the strings holding him up were cut all at once. His face hit the planks sideways—jaw slack, eyes wide. Already gone.

"AMBUSH!"

Simmons shouted it, but no one needed the warning. The world was already on fire.

Gunfire cracked from the far treeline—high, fast, endless. AKs. RPKs. Maybe a few M1 carbines stolen from ARVN units. The jungle screamed.

The guy behind Dad caught a burst across the ribs—bones shattered, red mist sprayed wide. Another went over the side of the bridge screaming, his calf half gone, blood pumping in sick rhythm as he hit the river below.

Someone was yelling. Maybe a medic. Maybe nobody. The bridge was chaos. Dad hit the ground flat. Rolled. Swung the Pig forward.

And then he unleashed hell. The M60 roared to life like a dragon unchained—belt-fed fury, tracer rounds streaking through the green like lines of fire drawn by the hand of God.

"RIGHT FLANK—COVER IT!"

He wasn't a sergeant. Didn't wear stripes. But when he shouted, they listened. Because *he sounded like someone who expected to live.*

"FOUR O'CLOCK! TREE LINE—LAY IT DOWN!"

Grenades thumped. Claymores popped. Screams. Smoke. Dirt raining from above.

He crawled forward two feet—two inches closer to death—shifted position and fired in short bursts. Shell casings burned his arms. Smoke stung his eyes. His finger squeezed and released, controlled, disciplined. The barrel still glowed red. The jungle screamed back.

They were outgunned. Outflanked. But not out yet.

One round clipped his shoulder—burned a stripe through his sleeve, didn't break skin but tore cloth and pride. Another hit the wood just past his thigh—splinters dug into his calf like shrapnel.

"FALL BACK TO THE TREE LINE—ONE AT A TIME!"

"I GOT THE BRIDGE!"

He didn't stop.

One of the new kids froze—face blank, eyes locked on Henderson's body. Dad barked, "MOVE, GODDAMMIT—GO!"

The kid snapped out of it and ran. Lived. Barely.

An RPG hissed from the other side. Missed. Hit a tree. Boom. Half the canopy dropped.

Still the Pig kept screaming.

One belt. Then another. Three hours of blood and smoke and ghosts.

When the last echo died, the air was so thick with gunpowder and sweat it felt like breathing metal.

Half the bridge was gone—splintered wood soaked in blood.

Three men didn't move. One was missing an arm. One was missing most of his face. Another had bled out before the firefight was halfway done—but they hadn't noticed. Too much death to count in real time.

The rest were half-men now. Bandaged. Limping. Shaking. Some cried. Quietly. Ashamed.

They pulled back. Regrouped behind a burnt-out tree line. Dragged what was left. Wrapped bodies in ponchos, not body bags—they hadn't brought enough.

Eventually, the radio crackled. Dustoff inbound.

The chopper came, its blades beating the air like war drums.

Dad didn't speak. Just sat on the ground, the pig across his lap, smoke still rising off the barrel like breath. Blood stained his boots. None of it was his.

Simmons limped over, arm in a sling, field dressing clinging to mud and what might've been someone else's blood. He pulled a cigarette from behind his ear, but no lighter.

VII: The Crossing We Carry

So he pressed the tip to the hot barrel.

Fssssss—light.

The smoke curled upward, thin and gray against the jungle's thick air. The river below was still, indifferent. Somewhere in the distance, a bird called once, then went silent.

Nobody spoke.

The jungle didn't care who lived.

Simmons took a drag, exhaled slow, watched the smoke disappear like breath into history.

Then, finally—

"You ever wonder," he said, voice gravel and fatigue, "why you're still breathing?"

Dad didn't answer. Because it wasn't wonder. It was math.

He was alive because everyone else had died first.

Because the Pig had kept singing.

Because sometimes the miracle isn't survival.

It's knowing you did everything you could... and the nightmares still come.

And all he wanted was *not* to feel a goddamn thing.

Years passed.

The war didn't follow him home all at once. It waited.

Quiet.

Like a fuse no one had lit—until one ordinary day, something struck the match.

He stepped onto another bridge. This one didn't shake with gunfire. It swayed gently in the breeze. A small swinging bridge on the edge of town.

Steel cables. Wooden planks. Trees hanging over the river like they were tired too.

It was supposed to be a quiet walk. Just him, my mom, my brother, and me.

We were kids. Thirteen, fifteen. We thought it would be fun—crossing the river, listening to it ripple below us, pretending the planks would crack beneath our boots.

But something changed mid-crossing. He slowed. His eyes locked on something that wasn't there. Not here, anyway.

It was July 7th, 1984. Gilman, Wisconsin.

We were headed to a softball tournament—just another Saturday, on paper. But the weight of the month already hung heavy.

Nicki had died ten years earlier. July Fourth.

Her birthday was coming—July 21st—and none of us said it out loud, but we all felt it.

Grief never really leaves. It just changes shape.

Dad had been quiet all morning. Not tense. Not angry. Just... heavy.

VII: The Crossing We Carry

We parked near the cheese factory—still running, still humming. The smell of warm whey and curds hung in the air like something familiar and faintly sour. The low churn of machinery blended with distant summer sounds: the clink of a metal bat, the pop of a glove, a burst of laughter from the fields beyond.

It felt normal. Too normal.

The steady drone of compressors filled the air, layered with the distant thump of a hammer from someone's backyard project, a dog barking somewhere down the block, a screen door slapping shut.

We walked toward the fields, gravel crunching underfoot, dust rising in soft clouds behind our steps.

Took the shortcut over the swinging bridge by the river.

Just a span of wood and wire—planks worn smooth, steel mesh fencing on either side. Enough to hold you up. Not enough to make you feel safe.

The bridge swayed gently with every step, the wood creaking, the cables groaning faintly like they remembered a weight heavier than ours.

Below, the river moved slow and dark, glassy in the heat— mirroring the trees that leaned in from both banks.

Tall oaks. Willows bent low. Their limbs drooping like arms too weary to lift anymore.

In the stillness, you could hear it all: birdsong, the whistle of wind through leaves, kids laughing faintly from the ball fields beyond.

Mom held my dad's hand like she always did. Like maybe she knew something was coming.

Halfway across, the loudspeakers kicked on. First some static. Then music.

A soft, uncanny melody—one that didn't belong on a bridge. It drifted out across the river like a memory trying to find its voice.

A Kind of Hush.

Dad stopped. Dead still.

One hand still in Mom's. The other halfway raised—like it remembered something his mind hadn't meant to.

His eyes locked on the far side of the water, but he wasn't looking at it. He was somewhere else.

Another bridge. Another silence. Same song.

He didn't blink.

He didn't breathe.

Then: "Right flank—cover it."

Low. Flat. Automatic.

Then louder: "FOUR O'CLOCK—MOVE! MOVE!"

He let go of Mom's hand. Dropped into a crouch.

Arms curling like the Pig was still in his grip. **"AMBUSH! GET DOWN!"**

VII: The Crossing We Carry

I froze. My brother stepped back. Mom reached for him, whispering, "John… it's okay. You're safe."

But he wasn't. Not in Wisconsin. Not in 1983.

He was back on a jungle bridge. Back where blood soaked planks and friends didn't come home. And we—his family—were just shadows flickering through the smoke of something he couldn't escape.

That day wasn't just a flashback. It was a fracture.

The VA would later call it combat amnesia. Said the brain buries what the heart can't handle—until something digs it up again.

But it wasn't a trigger. It was a landmine.

A song.

A date.

A daughter.

A bridge.

And just like that… the war wasn't memory anymore.

It was now.

But we were still on that bridge. My dad standing, confused. My mom holding his hand like she always did. And me—just a kid, finally seeing the war that never left him.

The silence that followed wasn't empty.

It was thick—alive with something that hadn't been in the room before. No one looked at their phones. No one scribbled notes. Even Professor Wright sat still, arms crossed—but looser now, like the tension wasn't quite armor anymore.

He didn't speak. But the look in his eyes wasn't debate—it was memory.

Lena didn't speak, but I caught her watching Wright—not with judgment, but curiosity. Like she was filing something away. Like she'd noticed the tremor in his silence.

I let the quiet stretch for a beat longer, then drew a breath.

"That bridge," I said, voice steady. "It wasn't just a flashback. It was a fault line. And everything we thought was buried came rising to the surface."

Diego exhaled through his nose, running a hand over his face. He glanced toward Reid, then back at me—but his usual smirk was nowhere to be found.

For the first time, he looked like someone thinking, not just arguing.

A few students shifted, not in boredom—but in discomfort. In thought.

"He didn't remember what happened to him for years. Not in detail. Not until that moment. That was the beginning—not the end."

Another pause. Then: "It almost destroyed him. But maybe it had to break him… so he could begin to heal."

Reid finally spoke. "History forgets the messy stuff," he said. "But maybe that's where the real truth hides."

Wright didn't speak. He watched me like he wanted to—but didn't have a handhold anymore.

"That moment didn't come with a flash of light," I said. "It came with screams. With tears. With a man crouching on a bridge, barking orders at ghosts." A few students looked up again. "But that's when the miracle started. Not with peace… but with pain."

I looked down for a moment—not out of shame, but gravity.

Then back up.

"We wait for miracles to save us. But sometimes, the miracle is the thing that stops us long enough to realize we need saving."

Someone exhaled softly—maybe Chloe.

I turned back toward Wright.

"You asked if survival is divine." I shook my head. "No. But transformation might be."

No one moved. No one laughed.

And for the first time, it didn't feel like anyone was trying to win. It felt like someone had just told the truth.

Wright leaned back slightly. Not in retreat—more like someone realizing the ground had shifted beneath him.

"You're saying that kind of trauma," he said slowly, "is divine intervention?"

His tone wasn't mocking this time. Just careful. Measured. Like he was feeling for the edge of something too big to define.

"No," I said. "I'm saying sometimes, pain is the doorway. And walking through it is the miracle."

He didn't answer. But he didn't look away.

From the far side of the room, Reid cleared his throat. "Maybe that's the point," he said. "Maybe we don't always see the miracle when it's happening. But looking back…"

He glanced toward me. "…we realize it was the only thing that could've gotten us through."

Bree chimed in softly. "That bridge… it wasn't just memory. It was a moment of transformation, right?" She looked at Wright. "I don't think that makes it less real. I think it makes it more."

Chloe sat forward, elbows on the desk. "You keep asking for evidence," she said, "but maybe evidence isn't always a number or a lab report." She looked toward me, then back at Wright. "Maybe sometimes, it's survival with meaning."

Wright didn't argue. Didn't agree, either. But something in his face—not softened, but… cracked. Just a little.

And in the quiet that followed, no one seemed ready to move on.

That's when Gabe spoke up.

He didn't look at Wright. He looked at the desk in front of him, like he wasn't sure if he was talking to us or himself.

VII: The Crossing We Carry

"My brother came back from Afghanistan different." He paused. Swallowed. "Not angry. Not loud. Just… hollow. My mom said it was like his soul had a limp." He finally glanced at me. "I never thought of that as a miracle. But maybe… maybe him still being here *is* one."

A few people turned toward him. No one said a word.

Kai leaned forward next, elbows on the table, fingers laced tight.

"I was in a car wreck two years ago. Lost a friend. I walked away with just a broken arm."

He exhaled sharply through his nose. "People kept saying it was luck. But I remember the paramedic telling me, 'I don't know how you survived this.'" He looked up, voice quieter now. "I still don't know why I did. But I stopped calling it luck."

Wright didn't speak. His hands were folded now—not crossed. Not defensive.

And then, from the far right row—Ethan, who hadn't said a word all semester.

His voice was calm. Almost too calm.

"My dad used to say pain was proof you're still breathing." He looked straight at Wright. "But that always felt hollow. Like surviving was the only point." He turned slightly, eyes on me now. "But what you're saying? It's different. You're saying pain isn't the point. It's the starting line."

That landed. Even Wright shifted.

Then—Liam cleared his throat.

His voice still had that gravel to it—like it had been dragged through something deep.

"I said before," he began, "that God doesn't stop the pain. He stands in it with us."

He looked toward me. "That story... what happened on that bridge... That's exactly what I meant."

He let the silence hang for a second.

"Your dad didn't get spared. He got *seen*. He got *held*—by your mom, by your family. Maybe even by God, in a way he didn't recognize yet."

Then he turned, looked straight at Wright. "We keep asking why God didn't stop it. But maybe the better question is—what did He do with it?"

He looked at me—like he wasn't ready to agree but wasn't ready to fight anymore either.

That was enough.

I turned to face the room. "We keep waiting for parting seas and thunderclaps," I said. "But sometimes, the miracle is just... that we keep going. That we don't give up. That we let the fire change us without turning us to ash."

That's what he did. One bridge. One step. One breath at a time.

Diego sat forward slightly, elbows on his desk. For the first time, his voice lacked its usual edge.

"So you actually think that was a miracle?"

Not mocking. Not challenging. Just asking.

VII: The Crossing We Carry

He wasn't teasing. He wasn't testing. He was just… trying.

This time, even the professor didn't look like he had a counterpoint.

He didn't need one.

Because something had already shifted—and not just in him.

It was the room.

VIII: All the Same Fire

The room was still. Not silent. Still. The kind of stillness that doesn't ask for quiet—it demands it.

No one moved. No pens. No screens. Just stillness.

They just sat in it. The aftermath.

What had started as a classroom debate had become something else—something heavier. Something none of them were quite ready for, but no one wanted to leave behind.

Professor Wright stayed seated. His arms crossed—not in defiance, but in a way that seemed... protective. Not of himself. Of the structure he was trying to hold together.

VIII: All the Same Fire

Then Lena spoke. Quiet. Thoughtful.

"I've never been sure what I believe. But that story... the bridge, your dad... that didn't feel like a 'point.' It felt like... something sacred."

She looked down after she said it, like she wasn't sure she should've spoken at all.

Diego followed, rubbing the back of his neck.

"You know, I was thinking about that. What you said earlier—about miracles not always being rescue, but reckoning."

He looked at me.

"It reminded me of a concept we cover in trauma therapy— narrative reframing. You take a traumatic memory and you give it structure. Not to control it, but to contain it. So it stops owning you."

He hesitated.

"That... that's what that bridge story was. That wasn't sentiment. That was survival."

For a moment, no one corrected him. Because maybe it wasn't just survival. Maybe it was sacred, too.

Bree leaned forward, elbows on her desk.

"But how do you know the difference?" she asked. "Between something meaningful and something we just assign meaning to because we're desperate to believe there's a point?"

Her voice wasn't sharp. Not like before. Just honest. Tired, maybe.

"That's the danger, isn't it?" she added. "Saying everything happens for a reason when maybe... it just happens."

Professor Wright saw his opening.

"Well," he said, unfolding his arms, "that's precisely the kind of epistemological fault line this course is designed to explore. What constitutes belief? What separates narrative from revelation?"

He stood, walking slowly to the whiteboard, rubbing out the phrase I'd written earlier.

"Religious epistemology is the study of how we come to know what we say we believe. Aquinas called it a 'rational ascent.' Kierkegaard argued that true belief required absurdity—that it had to leap over logic to mean anything."

He looked out at the class, measured.

"But if belief is only valid through personal story... how do we guard against delusion? Against fabrication? If every trauma becomes divine because someone survived it—do we not risk flattening theology into sentiment?"

The question was pointed. Designed to wrest control back.

But no one jumped to agree.

Reid finally sat up straighter.

"I get what you're saying, Professor. But maybe the point isn't about flattening theology. Maybe it's about expanding it. Maybe survival is part of faith history, not a detour from it."

He looked at me briefly, then back at Wright.

"I mean, Jesus didn't avoid suffering. He leaned into it. And we call that the foundation of Christianity. Not because it's clean—but because it's honest."

Professor Wright didn't answer right away. Instead, he turned to the board—where the word **MEANING** still lingered.

He stared at it for a moment.

Then, without a word, he lifted the marker and drew a slow, deliberate circle around it.

Then looked at Diego.

"So, from a psychological perspective, meaning-making... is healing?"

"Sometimes," Diego said. "But not always. Meaning-making can go wrong. Survivors sometimes create meaning that blames themselves. Or God. Or others. That's why therapy isn't about answers—it's about process."

He paused. "But when it works... it's transformation."

Wright nodded, once.

"Which brings us," he said, "to the theological question: if suffering is part of the process, is it necessary? Or merely... instrumental?"

That's when Gabe raised a hand—reluctantly. Like he didn't want to speak, but needed to.

"Honestly?" he said. "I used to think this stuff was just structure. Equations. Data. Like, miracles were just statistical anomalies we called divine because we didn't understand them."

He shrugged.

"But after hearing that story about your dad… I don't know. Maybe design and chaos aren't the only choices. Maybe meaning isn't something you prove. Maybe it's something you endure into."

Even Bree didn't argue.

Liam, quiet since his earlier statement, finally leaned forward again.

"I said before," he began, voice low and gravel-edged, "that God doesn't always stop the pain. He stands in it with us."

He looked directly at me.

"What happened on that bridge… that's exactly what I meant."

He turned to Wright.

"We keep asking why God didn't stop it. But maybe the better question is—what did He do with it?"

Wright's jaw flexed. He didn't argue.

That's when I spoke again.

"My dad came home from war in one piece. But he didn't stay that way. The bridge cracked him open. But it didn't destroy him."

I looked at the room.

"Not immediately. But slowly… he started to unravel. The nightmares came first. Then the tremors. The silence. The guilt."

I let the weight settle.

"And that's when it got worse. Because that's when my mom got sick."

A few students leaned in, eyes shifting.

"She was diagnosed not long after that bridge moment. The doctors said two years. Said the cancer was aggressive. And it felt like another grenade had gone off—just in slow motion."

I exhaled. Not from nerves. From gravity.

"But he didn't leave. He didn't run. He didn't self-destruct."

A pause.

"He broke. Quietly. Slowly. But he broke. Hollowed out by what came next."

"He Couldn't sleep. Couldn't sit still. The flashbacks kept getting worse—until the difference between memory and reality just... vanished."

I glanced across the room.

"That's when he checked into the VA. Not because he wanted help. Because he didn't know what else to do."

The reverence in the air wasn't for triumph. It was for the absence of it.

"He spent months there. Disconnected from time, from family, from everything. We'd visit, and some days he didn't even remember we'd come. Other days, he was convinced he was still on patrol."

Diego, quiet until now, finally spoke.

"That sounds like dissociative PTSD. When the brain stops processing the trauma as memory and starts living in it like it's present-tense."

I nodded.

"That's what they said. The doctors called it a protective response. I'm not sure what it protected. But it sure didn't feel like living."

Aisha shifted in her seat. Bree had stopped writing. Wright didn't try to cut in this time.

"There was one guy there—Keith Marshall. A vet from South Dakota. Native guy. My dad didn't talk to many people back then, but Keith got through. They'd drink, late into the night. Swap stories. Or sit in silence. It wasn't healing. It was survival."

I looked down, let the memory settle before continuing.

"They both had their demons. And for a while, they made room for each other's."

I straightened slightly, locking eyes with Wright.

"It didn't make him better. Not yet. But it kept him alive."

The silence that followed wasn't awkward. It was honest.

Even Professor Wright stayed quiet. Arms folded. Eyes narrowed— not in judgment this time, but thought.

No one reached for their notebooks. No one checked the time.

Because something in the room had shifted. Not just perspective. Posture Even breath. And sitting in that stillness, I remembered another silence—one far colder.

One that smelled like antiseptic and rubber gloves. One that buzzed under fluorescent lights and made you forget what season it was.

VIII: All the Same Fire

It came after the bridge. After the screaming. After the moment everything cracked open and refused to close again.

That's where we found ourselves—at the VA.

My brother and I living in a camper near the hospital. My mom sleeping in a chair beside his bed, night after night, praying he'd recognize her when he woke up.

Because for weeks, he didn't. Not always.

There were days he'd wake up in a sweat, shouting coordinates. Barking orders. Calling for medevac like we were still bleeding out.

And the worst days?

He didn't yell at all.

I paused, letting the weight of that time settle—of what it took from all of us. Especially her.

She carried him through it. Carried us. And no one seemed to notice.

Bree's voice came quiet, but deliberate. "Did anyone protect your mother?"

The question didn't land like accusation. It landed like revelation. I blinked.

"No," I said. "She protected everyone else."

Bree didn't press further. She didn't need to. The silence that followed said enough.

They said Tomah was the place to go.

The doctors told my mom it was one of the best VA centers in the state. That if anyone could help my dad, it would be them. That he'd be safe there. That he'd be understood.

But in 1984, PTSD was still new—at least the name was.

They didn't even call it that when my dad came home. They called it combat stress, battle fatigue, or just being difficult. It wasn't until 1980 that the term post-traumatic stress disorder officially made it into the medical books—acknowledging, finally, that the damage wasn't weakness. It was impact.

Real. Physical. Chemical. Visible on scans, even if no one could see it in his eyes yet.

But even with the new label, the care was still finding its footing. The doctors meant well. The nurses tried. But nobody really knew what to do with men who had survived fire and come home filled with ghosts.

My dad didn't want to go. He said he was fine. Said he didn't need a shrink to tell him what was already broken. But Mom had seen enough. The blank stares. The sudden rages. The crouching in the hallway with his hands over his ears because something on TV had sounded like a mortar.

He hadn't been sleeping. Not really. Maybe an hour a night—if that. He'd built a business by then. Worked long hours. Put on a face for customers. Laughed when he had to.

But he was unraveling.

The VA was a last resort.

VIII: All the Same Fire

When they admitted him, he didn't speak.

Didn't complain.

Didn't cry.

The walls were clean but colorless. The hallways wide but airless. A sterile quiet blanketed everything—but it wasn't peace. It was sedation. A lullaby for broken men who forgot what sleep felt like.

Some of the patients shuffled through the corridors like ghosts— numb, vacant-eyed, never meeting anyone's gaze. The other vets called them "Zoomers." Said they did the "Thorazine shuffle." Tiny, rapid steps that went nowhere. Just pacing out the rest of the war in slow motion.

One guy, they called "Torch." No one knew his real name. He'd tried to set himself on fire. More than once. Kept a lighter hidden somehow. Said if he had to die, he wanted to feel it. All of it.

There was a rec room—a pool table with one leg shorter than the others, some mismatched dumbbells, a bench press with cracked vinyl, and a stack of half-finished puzzles with missing pieces. Outside, a small nine-hole golf course stretched across the edge of the property. Nothing special— just a few fairways, some battered flags, and weathered clubs that looked older than most of the staff. But it was there. A strange offering of calm next to corridors lined with ghosts.

They *tried* to make it relaxing.

But it felt more like a prison wearing a smile.

He was quiet that first week. Just stared past the staff, past the other vets, past his own reflection in the polished metal of the elevator. His boots squeaked on the floor. His hands twitched when someone got too close. He kept reaching for a weapon that wasn't there.

The flashbacks didn't come all at once. They crept in, like jungle fog. Slow. Heavy. And then, without warning—they exploded.

One morning, during rounds, a nurse leaned in to take his vitals. His body recoiled. His eyes widened. And in an instant—he was back there.

Vietnam.

The room twisted. The lights flickered like flares. The hum of the heart monitor turned into rotor blades. The nurse's pale blue scrubs became jungle green.

He grabbed her wrist—tight, rough—not to hurt, but to survive.

"Stay low—MOVE! MOVE! They're in the trees!"

He shoved the tray over. The metal clanged against the wall. Voices shouted. Two orderlies rushed in.

But he didn't see them.

He saw gooks on the ridge, Simmons bleeding out beside him, the smell of blood and cordite thick in the air. He dropped to the ground, arms moving like the Pig was still strapped to his chest.

"Suppressing fire!" he barked.

His body shook. His breathing ragged.

Then—hands on his shoulders.

"John," someone said.

VIII: All the Same Fire

"GET OFF ME—FIRE! FIRE! DON'T JUST STAND THERE—THEY'RE COMING—"

"John—it's okay. It's not real. You're safe. You're in the hospital."

He looked up—eyes wild, unfocused.

And just like that, the jungle vanished.

Fluorescent lights. Linoleum tile. A nurse in tears. The tray overturned beside him. Blood from a busted IV tube smeared across his arm like shrapnel.

He went quiet. Shaking.

"I didn't mean to..." he whispered. "I didn't mean..."

That night, they sedated him. He didn't speak the next morning. Or the one after that.

Even Mom's voice—soft, persistent—couldn't reach him.

Until Keith found him.

He wasn't a therapist. Wasn't a doctor. Just another patient in the psych wing. A Lakota Sioux from Eagle Butte, South Dakota, with eyes like old scars. His chart said 81st Airborne—first tour as a medic. Second tour, rifleman.

He'd gone back by choice.

That alone told Dad something.

They didn't talk war. Real vets don't—not at first. They measure each other by silence. By how deep the stillness goes before it cracks.

Keith didn't push. Just showed up. Sat beside Dad outside the rec room, day after day—quiet, steady. Then one afternoon, he pulled out a cigarette. Offered it without a word.

Dad hadn't smoked in years. He'd buried the cravings under dumbbells and routine, built himself like a fortress. But that cigarette—it wasn't a vice. It was an invitation. A surrender that didn't feel like losing.

He took it.

Keith struck a match.

They smoked.

Then Keith said, "You ever work with medics?"

Dad nodded.

"I was one," he said. "Sixty-six. Eagle Butte boy. Got sent to the jungle to hold people together. First tour, I patched holes. Second tour, I made 'em."

He paused—jaw tight, eyes gone somewhere else.

"Too many holes in my brothers. Holes that didn't need to be there. Holes that didn't bleed right, didn't close right, didn't get buried right."

He shook his head.

"So I stopped trying to fix 'em. Figured if the bastards were gonna make holes, I'd give 'em a few of their own. Give 'em a reason to remember us."

Another breath.

"I stopped asking who was right. I just kept score."

He didn't say it for shock. He said it because it was true.

"You can only try to stop the bleeding so many times before you start wondering what the point is. So I went back—figured if I was gonna lose myself, I'd do it holding a rifle instead of gauze."

They smoked in silence for a while.

Then Keith added, "I used to think my hell was deeper. That I'd earned it more. That what I saw gave me some kind of license to suffer worse."

He flicked his ash.

"But it's all the same fire, man. Doesn't matter how you got burned."

Dad didn't say anything. But his shoulders dropped—just a little.

And that night... he didn't scream.

Not once.

Keith didn't stop with cigarettes and silence.

He knew what he was doing.

He watched my dad the way only another combat vet could. Not for weakness—but for fracture. The tremors behind the stillness. The rage coiled just beneath the quiet.

And after a few days, he changed tactics.

"Hey," Keith said one morning in the courtyard. "You still in there?"

Dad didn't look up.

Keith took a long drag from his cigarette, then ground it out under his boot.

"You think being quiet makes you strong?" he asked. "Think it means you're in control?"

No response.

Keith leaned in, voice low but cutting. "It just means the ghosts are winning."

That got a flicker.

"Yeah," Keith nodded. "I said it. Because I've been there. Shut down. Sealed off. Telling myself I could carry it all alone."

He gestured with a jerk of his thumb. "You think I ended up in here because I was handling it well?"

Still nothing from Dad.

Keith stood. Walked a few paces, then turned back.

"You know what the trick is?" he asked. "To get another vet to talk?"

Dad didn't move.

Keith stepped in closer. "You push. You poke the wound—not because you want to hurt them—but because if they don't bleed, they rot. You think silence saves you? It buries you."

Still no eye contact.

So Keith said the one thing that cracked it: "You think your hell's hotter than everyone else's?"

Dad flinched. Subtle—but there.

Keith nodded like he'd been waiting for it.

"Don't flatter yourself," he said, calm but hard. "It's all the same damn fire."

And then, without warning, he sat again. Pulled out another cigarette.

This time, Dad took it without hesitation.

From then on, it wasn't just smoke between them.

It was strategy. Keith began showing him how to read the signs— how to hear what wasn't being said. How to lean in, press just enough, and then sit back in the silence long enough for the truth to come out.

"You don't need to fix them," Keith told him once. "You just need to let them know they're not alone. That's the part no one gets. The silence ain't the killer. The isolation is."

It wasn't therapy, exactly.

But it was healing.

Dr. Palmer, the VA psychologist, picked up where Keith left off. He was older—thin-framed, wiry, sharp. A WWII pilot who traded his wings for a clipboard and a quiet chair. He didn't preach. He didn't condescend. He just nodded when Dad talked and gave him room when he didn't.

Between Keith and Dr. Palmer, something began to thaw.

Not fast. Not loud.

But real.

And that's when the shift happened.

Dad didn't just survive the hospital. He started learning how to help others survive too.

Healing didn't come all at once. It came in flickers. A nod instead of silence. A full night's sleep. A story shared instead of swallowed.

And in those small flickers—he started becoming someone who could sit with other people's fire, not just his own.

Someone who didn't just survive—but helped others believe survival was possible.

The house didn't feel smaller when he came home. It felt quieter. As if sound itself was waiting to see how he would move through the space.

Mom never said much about those early days after he returned. But she didn't have to. I remember the way she moved around him—never tiptoeing, never afraid—but always with this gentle awareness, like she knew he was still carrying something breakable inside.

Some nights, he'd sit in the living room after dinner, hands folded, eyes fixed on a spot that wasn't there. The TV would be on, but he wouldn't be watching.

One night, I asked him what he was thinking. I was too young to understand the weight of what I'd interrupted. He just looked at me, then over to Mom in the kitchen. And after a long moment, he said, "I'm just grateful for the quiet."

"Dad," I asked, "why don't you ever pray?"

VIII: All the Same Fire

He didn't answer right away. Just kept staring at the wall, like he was trying to decide if the truth would hurt me. Then, slowly, his eyes found mine. They weren't angry. Just... tired.

"Some things," he said at last, "don't feel like they have answers." That was all.

But Mom caught my eye, nodded once, and smiled—not at him, but at me. That was the first time I realized silence could be its own kind of conversation. A kind of mercy.

The room had gone still, and for a moment, I wasn't in a classroom—I was exposed. That story wasn't part of the syllabus. It wasn't curated for effect. It was just truth. And saying it out loud felt like stepping off something high, hoping the silence would catch me.

Maybe that's what vulnerability really is—naming your ghosts in front of strangers.

I thought of Dad then. How long it took him to speak. How often he chose quiet instead. And I wondered if maybe this was my version of that porch—only I hadn't turned around.

I stayed. I spoke.

And now I waited to see what silence would do next.

The classroom felt different now—like the temperature had shifted a few degrees, though no one had moved.

"You talk about ghosts," Reid said suddenly, not as a challenge, but a reflection. "But what if it's not about what haunts us... but what won't leave?"

I looked at him. "Exactly."

There was this one night—I must've been thirteen. Dad was sitting on the back porch, staring out into the dark, a beer untouched beside him. I opened the screen door to say something—I don't even remember what now. A question. A joke. Something small. But I saw his shoulders tense, just slightly, and I froze. I let the door close again.

I never did ask.

And years later, that moment still lingers—not because of what was said, but because of what wasn't. That's the thing about ghosts. They don't scream. They wait. Quiet. Patient.

"Ghosts aren't just things we fear," I said, turning back to the class. "Sometimes they're memories that refuse to go. Regrets that keep knocking. Love we didn't get to say. They follow us—not to scare us, but to remind us."

Bree wasn't smirking this time. Her pen was still. Diego leaned forward, elbows on his knees, brows furrowed.

"My dad carried his ghosts in silence," I said. "But grace isn't the absence of ghosts. It's what lets you live with them—without letting them define you."

Professor Wright's eyes narrowed slightly—focused, not dismissive.

"And sometimes," I added, "grace looks like a man who didn't pass his pain forward. Who bore it. Bent under it. But never broke anyone else with it."

The room didn't exhale. It just held the moment—like maybe they were seeing their own ghosts a little clearer now.

VIII: All the Same Fire

The room in front of me had gone quiet again.

Not out of awkwardness—but reverence.

As if the story hadn't ended. As if it was still echoing through the walls, rewriting something just beneath the surface of us all.

I looked around the room. No one was on their phones. No one was whispering. Even Wright had stopped scanning his notes. He just sat there, arms crossed—not defensive anymore. Just listening.

"I want to go back to something Keith said," I said, voice steady. "Something that stuck with me. Maybe more than anything else."

A few heads lifted.

"He said, 'It's all the same fire.' Doesn't matter where you got burned. Doesn't matter what kind of uniform you wore, or what war it was, or even if it was war at all. Trauma levels us."

Liam nodded from the far side of the room.

"And the miracle," I continued, "isn't that the fire stops. It's that someone steps into it with you—and doesn't run."

Wright shifted slightly but didn't interrupt.

"That's what Keith did for my dad. And what Dr. Palmer did too. They didn't fix him. They didn't offer cheap answers. They just showed up— and refused to let him carry it alone."

Diego, who'd been quiet so far, leaned forward.

"As a psych major," he said, "that's one of the hardest things to explain to people outside the field. Real healing doesn't start with solutions. It starts with presence. With safety."

He looked over at me. "You said earlier that sometimes the miracle is the thing that stops you long enough to realize you need saving. That's clinically true. Neurologically true. Our systems are wired to protect us—but sometimes, they shut down completely. The miracle is when someone gets in far enough to turn the switch back on."

Bree tilted her head. "So... is that psychology? Or faith?"

"Both," Diego said. "And neither. It's connection."

Wright uncrossed his arms.

He didn't smile. But he didn't push back either. And for the first time in weeks, it didn't feel like a debate anymore. It felt like something had shifted.

Not just in him.

In all of us.

I didn't quote a verse. Didn't have to. But one kept ringing in the back of my mind: *"The Word became flesh and dwelt among us..."*—John 1:14

That's what Keith did. What Dr. Palmer did. What my dad learned to do.

They didn't offer escape. They offered presence.

And maybe that's what belief actually begins with.

Not certainty. Not proof. But someone stepping into your fire—and staying

IX: Thieves in the Temple

The board still read **MEANING**, underlined, but no one was looking at it anymore.

Kai tapped his pen absently, then looked over at Gabe. "You know what stuck with me?" he said, not loud, just into the stillness. "It wasn't the breakdown. It was the build-back. The part where your dad starts helping other vets... even after everything."

Gabe nodded slowly. "Yeah. I was thinking about that, too. From a systems standpoint, trauma is like... a stress fracture. Pressure builds until something breaks. But recovery—that's a redesign. He didn't just patch himself. He started... engineering trust."

Professor Wright raised an eyebrow, clearly intrigued.

IX: Thieves in the Temple

Diego leaned forward, fingers interlocked. "That's a real concept in trauma therapy. We call it post-traumatic growth. It doesn't mean you're better because of what happened—it just means you adapted. You found new purpose. New meaning. But that takes work. And usually, people don't get there alone."

Ethan spoke next. Calm. Measured.

"It's weird," he said. "I used to think trauma was just something to survive. You endure it, then move on. But now... it's starting to feel like survival is the beginning. Like it tells you what still matters."

Wright, arms folded, let that breathe for a second before stepping in.

"Let me offer another lens," he said, picking up the marker again. "In the study of miracles, particularly in religious traditions, we often divide them into healing, nature, and provision categories. Miracles that restore. That defy. That sustain."

He drew three circles on the board. "What we've heard so far—combat flashbacks, recovery, endurance—these may fall under a fourth category: narrative miracles. Not events that alter the physical world, but that rewrite the internal world."

He turned back. "But here's the question—are those truly divine acts? Or are we just finding order in chaos because we need to?"

That landed heavily. But it didn't shut the room down.

It opened it.

And I could feel the shift again—subtle, like pressure changing before a storm.

I've told this part before, but it never stops feeling like a warning wrapped in grace.

I leaned forward.

"My dad came back from the VA different. Not healed. Not whole. But something had shifted."

They waited.

"When he got home, the business was already gone. The people he'd trusted—guys he'd hired, mentored—they'd robbed him blind while he was in the hospital."

Gabe looked over, eyes narrowed. "What'd they take?"

"Lumber. Cash. Customers. Even tools. They gutted the place from the inside out. Sold what wasn't theirs. Lied to my mom's face."

Kai winced, like he understood this one in a language the rest of us didn't.

"That's what kills a business," he muttered. "Not competition. Not economy. Internal theft. Once trust's gone—game over."

I nodded. "By the time Dad came back, there wasn't much left. And here's the thing… he didn't rage. He didn't throw punches. Didn't scream."

Ethan leaned in slightly.

"What did he do?"

I glanced down. Then back up.

"He looked at my mom. And he got to work."

IX: Thieves in the Temple

Dad came home from the VA to the sound of silence—not peace, but absence.

The yard was too quiet. Not like the usual morning calm, but something hollow. Like the land itself knew what had been lost.

This wasn't just a place of business. This was home.

My dad had built it board by board, mostly from scraps the factory tossed away—crating wood they were going to burn. Night after night, after long shifts and little sleep, he'd come home and pry nails from those boards, pull staples with bare hands until his fingers bled, then stack each piece meticulously along the side of the garage.

2x4s. 2x6s. 1x8s. Each size had its place.

He taught my brother and me how to do it too—five cents a board if we got the nails out clean.

It was our first job. Our first lesson in sweat equity.

Some of the nails were easy. But others—what we called screw nails—were ring-shank nails, spiraled like a thread and often coated in glue. They held fast. If you tried to muscle them out with a crowbar, the heads would snap right off.

I learned something one day, almost by accident: if you tapped the nail gently with the hammer first—just a little—it would break the seal. The glue would loosen, and the nail would slip free like it had never been stuck at all.

Dad saw me do it and stopped me. "What are you doing?" he asked. I showed him. He didn't just nod—he shouted for everyone to come see. Made me do it again. And again.

It wasn't just a trick. It saved hours. It saved hands. It turned work into craft.

After that, the piles grew—tall stacks of reclaimed lumber sorted like treasure. We bundled the boards, lined them up by size, and even sold the nails we'd pulled—bent, but still usable.

The board ends, too short scarred, or twisted for reuse, went into the burn barrel. Afterward, we sifted through the ashes for salvageable nails. Sometimes with a magnet. Sometimes by hand.

Nothing was wasted. We took every scrap and made it into treasure for someone.

Word got around. Farmers started showing up, asking to buy lumber. Then carpenters. Then came the orders for custom cuts and deliveries.

He hired help. Bought a flatbed truck. The factory even began buying the cleaned wood back. The side hustle grew into a full-blown lumber yard—all anchored to our home. It stood on the land where we lived, stacked beside the barn and the house he'd built himself.

That house wasn't stick-built. He stacked 2x6s like a pioneer—row upon row, locking them in with nails and grit, building not just walls, but shelter in the truest sense of the word. The barn too. Every inch of it told a story of refusal—of a man who wouldn't let hardship write his final line.

And we drove those nails ourselves—20-penny spikes, thick and long enough to hold generations. It took a helluva swing to get them in clean. But we learned. Learned to grip the handle near the end. Learned the weight, the arc, the sound a good strike made.

IX: Thieves in the Temple

One swing—that was the rule. Miss, and you'd hear the groan. Bend the nail, and you'd catch a glance.

We challenged each other. Who could set more in a row? Who could sink a nail flush with a single hit? Who could finish a wall without splitting the wood?

It wasn't just construction. It was discipline. It was bond. Every board we laid, every nail we drove, carried a rhythm—like music, like memory, like legacy.

And beneath all that wood, buried in the swing of every hammer, was something more: the belief that if you built it right, if you put your sweat into every inch, it just might last longer than you.

And then he left—to get help. To finally face the ghosts he couldn't outrun. He went to the VA so he could come back whole.

But while he was gone… the ones he'd trusted gutted everything he'd built.

They didn't break in. They didn't wear masks. They smiled while they stole.

Lumber disappeared—trucks full of it. Given to friends. Used to build their own homes, their own barns. The hand tools vanished too. The circular saw he'd used for years. The planer. The jointer. The workbench drawers left half-open, stripped bare.

And the worst part?

The cleaned lumber—the stuff the factory still wanted—was sold out the back door, cash pocketed. For months. Unchecked.

When Dad walked into the garage for the first time since returning, he didn't say anything.

He just stared.

The stacks were too low. The tools out of place. The rhythm was gone—the order he'd spent years imposing on chaos had unraveled into something unrecognizable.

He stepped outside. Walked the perimeter like he used to, scanning for rot or loose boards. But this time, the damage wasn't from weather or wear.

It was betrayal.

There was no screaming. No slamming of fists or doors.

He just stood there in the middle of what used to be his livelihood, hands at his sides, shoulders not slumped—but weighted.

Mom found him standing by the barn, eyes fixed on the place where the stacks of lumber used to tower.

She didn't ask what was wrong. She didn't need to.

Instead, she stood beside him. Quiet. Steady. Like always.

"I'm sorry," she whispered.

He shook his head once, slow.

"No," he said. "They didn't take anything I can't rebuild. Not really."

But they had.

They took trust. They took time. They took the years he couldn't get back.

IX: Thieves in the Temple

The temple had been looted—the tools, the timber—but not the heart that built it. The altar still stood.

And still... he didn't explode.

Something had shifted since the VA.

The fire was still there—but it didn't consume him. Not this time.

Because now... he had her to hold.

And she needed holding.

He turned to Mom.

She'd been the one holding everything together while he was away. She was the one who never left his side when he didn't even know where he was.

But now... she was sick.

The diagnosis had just come: uterine cancer.

The doctors never said Agent Orange caused it. But they never said it didn't.

And part of me always wondered—how could they not be connected? The exposure. The fallout. The way it clung to our story long after the war ended.

Dad didn't ask questions. Not out loud.

He just shifted gears.

He'd lost a business. He wasn't going to lose her.

So he got to work—again.

This time, not in the lumber yard, but beside her, helping open a toning parlor. Something gentle. Something healing. Resistance equipment for circulation and strength. A place where she could find a little power in a body that was slowly turning against her.

He painted the walls. Built the frames. Drove her to every appointment and back again.

He didn't talk about miracles. But he started becoming one—just by staying.

And that's where the shift really showed. Not in the money. Not in the muscle. In the way he stayed soft.

The fire hadn't left. But it no longer owned him.

The room wasn't quiet because it was empty. It was quiet because something had just filled it. Not like a switch had been flipped—but like something sacred had slowly settled, thick in the air, like dust after a collapse.

The hum of the HVAC faded to the edge of awareness. No pens clicked. No backpacks rustled. It wasn't that they didn't *want* to speak. It was that words hadn't caught up yet.

The story had landed like a body dropped into still water—quiet at first, but the ripples were still moving through the room.

Kai spoke first.

His voice was lower than usual. Slower.

IX: Thieves in the Temple

"I keep thinking about that business," he said. "All that time your dad spent building it. Sorting every board by length. Knowing what he needed and making it work."

He paused, tapped his pencil once.

"I'm studying business. And I've spent a lot of time reading case studies about theft, mismanagement, recovery. But this?" He shook his head. "This wasn't just a business loss. It was betrayal. And he didn't sue. Didn't spiral. He just... shifted."

Then he looked across the room, eyes scanning the quiet as if measuring it against something he couldn't quite name.

"I don't know if that's a miracle. But I know it's rare."

Gabe shifted in his seat, like he wasn't sure if he should speak—but then he did.

"Can I just say," he began, glancing at me, "the way your dad built that house? The barn? The entire property—stacking 2x6s like logs, turning castoff wood into something strong enough to live in... that's not just resourceful. That's design. That's structure. That's not luck."

He leaned forward now, elbows on his knees.

"I know it's not the main point of the story, but from an engineering perspective? That kind of vision—taking lumber that was meant to be scrapped, sorting it by type and size, aligning the weight distribution, building a home from the bones of something that was supposed to be burned?"

He shook his head slowly.

"He could teach a class in that kind of structural logic. Honestly. Most people wouldn't see potential in that mess of broken crates. But he did. He built something that could withstand storms, seasons—hell, even betrayal. And he didn't use blueprints. He used instinct. That's rare."

Then Gabe sat back, voice quieter now.

"And it's kind of poetic, isn't it? The same materials other people threw away—he made a home out of them."

He let it hang for a moment longer.

"Sounds like a metaphor."

A few students nodded—not because it was clever, but because it was true.

Even Wright's eyes flicked toward the board, where the word **MEANING** still hovered like a dare.

There were nods around the room. Then Aisha spoke, her voice gentle and grounded.

"You know," she said, "I'm not in engineering. I'm studying psychology. But I see parallels here: resilience isn't just surviving—it's reconstructing the broken parts so they hold something even stronger."

She paused, then continued:

"Your dad used abandoned wood. He used it to reclaim safety and peace. In my field, we talk about post-traumatic growth—how trauma can destroy, yes, but also how rebuilding with intention can create new purpose. He didn't just mend a house—he modeled hope."

IX: Thieves in the Temple

There was a quiet pause. Even Professor Wright didn't interrupt. I looked at him—really looked. He still had his arms folded, but his posture had changed. Less like a wall. More like someone bracing for something they weren't sure how to hold.

He opened his mouth—then closed it.

So I spoke instead.

"I know it sounds like all this was just... more pain. More weight. Another chapter in a story that never lets up."

I looked around the room, slow.

"But that's the miracle."

Someone—maybe Lena—tilted their head.

"Not the pain," I clarified. "But what he did with it."

I tapped the desk once, gently.

"He came back from the war broken. Came back from the VA gutted. Came home to betrayal, to a sick wife, to a business that was nothing but ashes."

A beat.

"And he chose laughter."

I let that settle.

"He didn't disappear into a bottle. Didn't numb it. Didn't destroy what was left. He built something else. Not out of certainty. Not even out of belief. But presence."

I looked back at Professor Wright.

"You asked earlier—what do miracles point to? Maybe it's this: That after everything burns, someone still shows up with a hammer and starts building again."

The room didn't move.

No one needed to.

Because somehow, that moment—like so many in this conversation—had become sacred.

And the fire wasn't the end.

It was what revealed what had been forged—resolve, softness, presence.

The fire didn't finish him. It tempered him.

X: Unless a Seed Fails

The board still read **MEANING**, underlined twice. No one had erased it. And for some reason, that felt right.

Professor Wright stood just to the left of the board—arms crossed, one foot angled toward us, the other toward the marker tray like he couldn't decide whether to teach or retreat. His posture wasn't aggressive, but it wasn't relaxed either. It was careful. Calculated. Like something was forming in front of him that he didn't yet trust.

"We keep circling the word miracle," he said finally, breaking the silence. "But we haven't agreed on what that actually means."

He turned and uncapped a marker. In broad, clean strokes, he wrote:

MIRACLE = ?

Then turned back to us.

"We've heard war stories. Healing stories. Even that one about the tree prank." He gave a half-smile at that—dry, not dismissive. "But the question is, are we calling these miracles because they defy explanation… or because they comfort us?"

Chairs shifted slightly. Arms crossed. Eyes narrowed.

Then he raised the tension.

"If your father's transformation is a miracle," he continued, looking directly at me now, "then what do we call the man who doesn't come back? The one who stays lost in flashbacks? Who drinks himself to death, or disappears from his family?"

He let it hang for a second.

"Did he just… miss the miracle?"

There it was. The turn.

Wright wasn't trying to mock me. I knew that. This wasn't the smug smirk of a skeptic—this was the scalpel of a philosopher, cutting through sentiment to see if anything underneath could hold. He was pressing. The way good professors do. The way they're trained to.

And still—it stung.

Reid raised his hand. Not defiantly, but with something like urgency.

"I think that's the wrong question," he said. "You're asking us to define miracles like lab results. But what if they're not universal? What if they're personal? Like—someone finding peace who didn't have it before. Isn't that miraculous, even if it's just for them?"

Wright nodded once, then turned to the board and wrote in smaller letters:

PERSONAL = MIRACLE?

He tapped the cap of the marker against his chin. "It's meaningful," he said. "But is it divine? Is it God intervening? Or just resilience?"

Liam hadn't said much. But when Wright mentioned the word "resilience," he nodded, like it was something he'd carried longer than he let on.

Bree leaned forward, elbows on the desk, her hair tucked behind one ear.

"Why does it have to be either/or?" she asked. "Why can't it be both? I mean… Scripture says God works through people. Through pain. Through process."

She paused. The usual edge in her voice had softened. "Maybe the miracle isn't always magic. Maybe it's endurance."

That surprised me. Bree didn't give ground easily.

Then Gabe jumped in—his words measured, as though testing the waters before committing fully.

"If we start calling everything a miracle," he said, "doesn't it cheapen the word? I mean, getting through a hard time… that's part of life. But is that divine intervention? Or just not quitting?"

He looked at me then. Direct.

"Your dad went through hell. But was it a miracle? Or just a man refusing to fall apart?"

Before I could respond, Aisha spoke—quiet but certain. No hand raised. Just presence.

"It's both," she said.

The room turned toward her.

She adjusted her glasses and set her pen down carefully beside her notebook.

"You asked if survival is a miracle. I think it can be. Because I've seen the other side of it."

She looked around the room, then directly at Wright.

"I usually say I chose nursing because of my grandmother. She had a stroke when I was eleven. I remember sitting in that hospital, watching the nurses—not just treat her, but *see* her. Talk to her. Hold her hand. Even when she couldn't talk back."

Her voice wavered slightly, but it didn't falter.

"She didn't get better. She died six months later. And I do think something miraculous happened. Because she wasn't alone. And that mattered."

She paused, fingers tightening on her notebook.

"But that's not the full story."

A few students leaned in.

"My cousin died two years ago. Young. Fast. No warning. That's when everything changed. That's when I stopped just believing in care—and started believing in presence. In showing up when nothing makes sense."

She looked down, then back up—eyes clear now.

"Sometimes the body keeps score... and sometimes the soul does too. And I want to be there when no one else knows how."

I didn't respond. I didn't have to.

That line stayed with me.

She looked right at Wright.

"You asked if being seen counts as a miracle. I think it does. Especially when it would be easier to look away."

Wright didn't respond. He just... stood there. Taking it in.

I exhaled and found my voice again.

"My dad didn't believe in miracles. Not for a long time. Not after Nicki died. Not after the war. Not even after the VA."

The room quieted.

"But something shifted. He didn't become someone else. He didn't have a vision or a conversion moment. He just stopped flinching. Stopped waiting for the next disaster. And he started showing up again—even in the middle of everything falling apart."

I let the sentence breathe.

"He laughed again. He told jokes. He helped my mom through chemo. Not with some perfect, scripted plan. Just... by being there."

Liam nodded from across the room, his voice rough as ever when he finally spoke. "That sounds like resurrection."

Professor Wright stepped forward again—not to challenge, but to clarify.

"I hear what you're saying. And it's powerful. But let's stretch this a little further. In John's Gospel, miracles aren't events—they're signs. They point beyond themselves. They reveal something about who Jesus is."

He took a step closer, softer now.

"So the question is… do these moments—your dad's story—do they point to something greater? Or do they just help us survive?"

I let that settle. Then answered.

"They do both," I said. "They help us survive. But they also remind us we're not doing it alone."

I took a breath.

"There's this moment in the Gospel of John—Jesus tells His disciples that their grief won't last forever. That yeah, it's real. It's heavy. But it's not the end of the story."

A few heads lifted.

"He compares it to childbirth. Says that when a woman gives birth, she's in pain—but when the baby's born, that pain doesn't vanish. It just gets… outweighed. Because what comes after is worth it."

I looked at Wright.

"So Jesus doesn't promise a life without suffering. He promises that something new can come *through* it."

Wright didn't push back. Not this time. He just nodded, slow and quiet, like maybe the conversation had turned into something he wasn't expecting—but no longer wanted to fight.

And for a moment, the room felt... still. Not finished. But settled. Like something that had been circling had finally landed.

But miracles don't land clean. They don't come with trumpets or hallelujahs. Sometimes they come limping. Bruised. Stripped of everything except the decision to keep going.

I looked down, then back at them.

"He didn't find peace at the VA," I said. "Not exactly. What came next... that's where it started to shift."

I could feel the room leaning in again.

"He came home in 1985, expecting to rebuild. But the business was almost gone. My mom was getting sick. And everything he'd worked for— everything he thought he could protect—had already started to collapse."

A beat.

"But something was different. He didn't rage. He didn't shut down. It was like... the fire was still there, but it didn't own him anymore."

I glanced at Wright—who didn't interrupt.

"He turned toward what mattered. And stayed."

And somehow—right in the middle of all that collapse—something else began to take root.

My dad started laughing again.

Not loud. Not often. But deep.

It wasn't performative. It wasn't polite. It was rooted in something older than joy—something like breath finally returning to a body that had forgotten how to breathe.

It started with small things. A dry joke. A crooked grin. And then one day, it grew into a prank so elaborate, it might've made a lesser man question reality.

And then came the tree.

It was the spring of 1986.

The air was wet with thaw and sawdust, and the yard smelled like second chances. Not new ones—just salvageable ones.

Dad stepped out the front door carrying a spade and a flat shovel— one for breaking, one for lifting. He paused at the edge of the lawn, eyed a bare patch near the driveway, then stabbed the blade into the earth. One foot on the metal. One breath. Then he began to dig.

The radio crackled in the background, half-buried under the scrape of steel on cement, the creak of old lumber. A driving beat pushed through the static—loud, defiant, just barely melodic.

Something about wild boys and fire.

Dingus lifted her head from the porch. She was a mutt—a little black-and-white dog with big ears and zero shame. Ears twitching. Waiting.

And then—she let loose.

She threw her head back and howled like she was a backup singer—off-key, unbothered, utterly committed. Long, stretched, caught between playfulness and something else. Something like recognition.

We used to joke she could hear something in that song we couldn't—some signal under the noise. Like she was singing back to a memory.

Dad wiped his forehead with the back of his hand, glancing toward the porch. "She's got good taste," he muttered.

Jeff—one of Dad's closest friends—scoffed from where he sat on the porch step. "Or terrible taste."

Dad didn't answer. Just kept digging.

And then, without a word, he reached for the Miracle-Gro—big scoops, generous, reverent.

Jeff raised an eyebrow. "Didn't know you were buying into that crap."

Dad didn't look up. Just shrugged. "Figured I'd try something new."

He didn't just want shade. He wanted proof—something that could grow where so much had died. So he fed the roots like they were prayers.

The thing about Miracle-Gro back then—it still had a reputation. Snake oil. Gimmick. Guys like them didn't touch it. They believed in shovels, sun, and time. But that morning, Dad upended the box like he was feeding something hungry.

The sapling went in: a small maple, barely three feet tall. Thin trunk. Nervous leaves. It didn't look like much.

But he watered it like it was a child.

The next morning, Jeff pulled up and nearly dropped his coffee.

The tree had grown.

Not a little. A lot.

It stood over six feet now, fuller, stronger. The kind of growth that shouldn't happen overnight—not even with a thunderstorm and divine intervention. The leaves looked thicker. The trunk, firmer. Even the shadows it cast were different.

"Jesus, John," Jeff said, stepping out of the truck. "What the hell kind of Miracle-Gro is that?"

Dad didn't smile. Didn't even glance up. He was pulling weeds like he'd been up for hours.

"Stuff's unreal," he said.

Jeff stared. Walked around the tree like it might hiss or blink. He knelt, touched the dirt, flicked a loose root with his finger like it might recoil.

The bag of Miracle-Gro was still there. The hose coiled beside it. A small gardening trowel sat like a witness.

Jeff looked from the tree to Dad. Back to the tree.

That night, after Jeff left, Dad dug up the tree. Quietly. No flashlight. Just muscle memory and half-moonlight. He carried the sapling behind the barn and set it beside two others he'd picked up days before— one a little larger, one just slightly smaller.

The next morning, Jeff came back.

And the tree had grown again.

Seven feet now. Thicker. More leaves. It looked like it had lived there for **years**.

Jeff stood by the truck, one hand on the door like it might steady him. "You've got to be kidding me."

He walked forward in slow, reverent steps—like the tree might be radioactive. Circled it. Muttered to himself. Touched the bark, the base, the branches. Tapped the trunk with the back of his hand like knocking on a door.

"This isn't normal," he said. "This isn't even horticulture. This is witchcraft."

Dad didn't say a word. He was drinking coffee out of a chipped mug that read *#1 DAD*, a Father's Day gift from a time before grief dulled the humor.

Jeff eyed the Miracle-Gro box again. "This stuff illegal?"

Dad just sipped. Shrugged. "Maybe you should get some."

Jeff circled one more time, then finally looked at Dad head-on.

Jeff said, "You didn't do this. No way. This thing's been here longer than three days. I'd bet money."

Dad didn't respond. Just sipped again, like it was the only thing keeping him from laughing.

Then he set the mug down, stretched his arms, and finally— finally—grinned.

"Why don't you go grab the others behind the barn?"

Jeff caught it. "What?"

"The other two," Dad said, setting the mug down. "Time to finish the job."

Jeff stood there a beat. Processing.

Then turned and walked.

And that's when he saw it.

Three trees. Same species. Three heights.

Like a visual timeline of deception. Small, medium, large.

Same dirt still clinging to their roots. Same tags from the nursery. Identical maples—just staggered.

Jeff stared.

"You've got to be kidding me," he said again, but this time the words came with a grin.

When he came back around the barn, Dad was already laughing.

Not a chuckle. Not a smirk.

A full, guttural, shoulder-shaking laugh—the kind that only comes when something heavy inside finally *lets go*. His eyes were squeezed shut. His shoulders trembled. He leaned forward and braced himself on his knees like the joy might knock him over.

Jeff doubled over too, dropped the shovel, and wheezed between laughs. "You bastard," he said. "I was about to buy stock in that stuff!"

Dad couldn't stop. He just kept laughing. The kind of laugh that doesn't rise—it releases. Not from humor. From relief.

They stood like that for a long while. In the sun. In the dirt.

Two grown men laughing beside a tree that shouldn't have grown.

That afternoon, they planted the real tree. No tricks. No bait. Just two men, one hole, and the kind of soil that could finally hold something again.

Someone snorted in the back of the classroom.

One of those sharp, involuntary bursts that slips out before your brain has a chance to stop it.

It cracked the moment wide open.

A few students tried to hold it in—but that only made it worse.

Laughter broke out again—looser, real.

Even I was laughing—head down, hand to my mouth, the kind of laugh that comes from somewhere deep, somewhere tired.

Because sometimes, after all the grief and grit, you just need permission to laugh. To remember that joy isn't betrayal—it's proof you survived.

Even Wright let out something like a breath—not quite a laugh, but not denial either.

And that joy?

It didn't stop with his friends.

It started one spring afternoon—long before any of us had the emotional vocabulary to process it, let alone explain it.

Dad painted two words across a massive boulder in the backyard:

SEX STONE

No context. No warning. Just blocky, uneven letters in cheap white paint—slapped across a boulder the size of a small cow. He didn't even clean the dirt off first.

We stared at it.

"Dad?" Kevin asked.

"Yeah?" Dad said, wiping the brush on a rag.

"What's… what's the Sex Stone?"

Dad didn't pause. Didn't grin. He just shrugged.

"Felt right," he said.

And that was that.

He never explained it. Never referenced it again. Just went about his day like he hadn't just consecrated the yard with the most baffling phrase imaginable. He didn't invite curiosity. Didn't give us a knowing wink. It wasn't funny. It was just… *there*. Like a warning. Or a prophecy. Or both.

And every so often—without fanfare—he'd refresh it.

No ceremony. No comments. Just him, a can of paint, a brush, and a quiet hour near sundown. Touching up the letters with the slow care of someone tending a gravestone.

After a while, it became myth.

Friends would come over and spot it from the porch. You could see it from the kitchen window if the sun hit it right.

"Is that thing really called the Sex Stone?" someone would whisper.

"Ask him," we'd say.

No one ever did.

It was like an inside joke he hadn't let anyone else in on yet. A joke with no punchline. Just the setup. Endless, unexplained, and permanent.

Years passed. The joke stayed. It grew into the soil like ivy. Every time I thought maybe he'd grown out of it—maybe it had weathered off, maybe he'd let it fade—there he'd be, brush in hand, blocking out the E again.

We never questioned it anymore.

Until the day my future in-laws came over.

Mick and JoAnne

It was the first time our parents were meeting.

JoAnne was the kind of woman who said "Oh dear" when someone swore on TV. She brought banana bread to strangers. She ironed her church clothes the night before and underlined her Bible with a ruler so the verses stayed straight. She was soft-voiced, gracious, impossibly kind—and *very* devout.

Mick, her husband, was quieter in some ways but quicker to laugh. Big handshake. Bigger grin. The kind of man who could fix a busted screen door with one hand and quote Ecclesiastes with the other.

X: Unless a Seed Fails

This meeting was important. I'd prepped my parents like I was coordinating a peace treaty.

And this was the first time she was coming to our house.

I briefed my parents in advance. Told Dad this mattered. Told Mom that JoAnne was pious. That she was gentle. That she might cry if someone so much as used "hell" as an exclamation.

They nodded. Promised to behave. Mom even baked her special green bean casserole with the crunchy onions on top. Dad cleaned the porch and shaved. It was the most prep he'd done for anything short of war.

For the first hour, everything went perfectly.

They arrived on time, holding a Bundt cake like it was sacred. We gave them the tour—living room, kitchen, barn, the spot where the swing used to be before the storm took it. Dad was charming in that old-man Midwestern way. Mom was gracious. Everyone was smiling. Nothing had caught fire. Hope was alive.

Then it happened.

JoAnne stepped onto the back porch to admire the view. It was golden hour. The sun was just dipping, casting long shadows across the yard.

And that's when she saw it.

The boulder, bathed in amber light. The words, glowing like they'd been neon-lit from heaven: **SEX STONE**

She squinted. Tilted her head like she thought maybe it said SEED STONE. Maybe SET STONE.

Then her brows furrowed. Her head cocked just slightly to the right—the universal sign of polite confusion—and she took a slow step forward.

But no.

She turned, coffee mug still in hand, and said: "John?" Voice polite, lips tight. "What exactly... is a sex stone?"

You could feel the molecules in the air stop moving.

Mom froze with a fork halfway to the casserole.

I stared at the back of Dad's head, silently praying he would say something—anything—moderate.

He turned.

Met JoAnne's gaze.

A beat passed.

Then another.

He set down his coffee.

Took a breath like he was about to launch into something philosophical—maybe geological, maybe biblical.

And then, with the calm of a man reading off a grocery list, he said:

"It's a fuckin' rock."

Silence.

Not stunned silence. Not confused silence.

Biblical silence.

The kind of silence that falls when someone touches the Ark… and nothing happens. At first.

And then Mick lost it.

A full, guttural, wide-chested laugh—deep and helpless. The kind of laugh that rises from the gut and breaks through like it's splitting ribs. He set his coffee down, grabbed his side, and just bellowed.

"That's the best damn thing I've ever heard," he said, wheezing through it.

JoAnne gasped.

I choked.

JoAnne's eyes widened. Her lips parted. Her hand tightened on the mug like it might save her.

Mom made a noise—somewhere between a gasp and a snort.

Then it happened.

She started laughing.

Not giggling. Not tittering behind a napkin. Laughing. Bent over, hand on her ribs, shoulders shaking like someone had just slapped holiness into her.

Even JoAnne couldn't hold out. Her laugh came like a betrayal— quick, sharp, surprised. Like she'd been ambushed by joy and just gave in.

A crack in the shell. A bark of disbelief. Then full-throated, surprised laughter—like joy had ambushed her, dragged her into the deep end, and dared her not to enjoy it.

And Dad? Dad cracked into the widest grin I'd seen on his face in years. He laughed hard, from the gut. No guilt. No sadness. No filter.

It was the kind of laugh that comes from somewhere earned. From the part of a man that's still healing, but has stopped pretending it doesn't hurt.

For a moment, all the years fell off him.

The war. The trauma. The lost daughter. The VA visits. The night terrors. The hollow weight of all those months when he couldn't make his body smile.

Gone.

Just a man, a rock, and a living room full of people who had no idea how badly they needed to laugh.

That wasn't immaturity. That wasn't defiance. That wasn't denial.

That was resurrection.

He wasn't just surviving anymore. He was being unburied.

Not because the grief had vanished. Not because he forgot the names he couldn't save. But because he'd stopped carrying them alone.

That day, the Sex Stone finally made sense.

It was never about the joke. It was about the joy.

It was a fuckin' rock.

And for the first time in a long time, it held something holy.

Someone near the back was still chuckling. Not mockingly. Just that kind of quiet, shoulder-shaking laughter that sticks around after a story lands a little too perfectly. A few others were wiping their eyes—not from sadness, but from laughing too hard. Even Bree, who never smiled easily, had her head down, a smirk tugging at the edge of her mouth.

It was like—for a moment—they'd forgotten the trauma. Forgotten the flashbacks, the betrayal, the grief. Because something else had taken hold.

Joy.

Earned, unfiltered, unapologetic joy.

I looked around the room. Took it in.

Even Wright let out something like a breath—not quite a laugh, but not denial either.

And that joy? It didn't stop with his friends. It drifted. Settled. Stayed. It was the kind of joy that hangs in the air like steam—fragile, warm, fleeting if you rush it.

I waited. Let it breathe.

Then I asked the question I hadn't planned on.

"Let me ask you something," I said, quieter now. "If you knew someone who had been through war... through loss... through a lifetime of pain and regret—and you didn't know any of that—and then you met him, and all he gave you was laughter... would you believe it?"

A few eyes flicked toward me. I let the pause settle.

"Because that's what he did. That was my dad. He carried enough pain to bury a man. And somehow, he still gave joy away like it cost him nothing."

Someone near the front—maybe Ethan—murmured, "That's rare."

I nodded. "Yeah. It is."

Wright hadn't said a word yet. But when I glanced at him, I saw something different in his posture—not resistance, not theory. Just a kind of quiet... respect.

And the laughter? It didn't stop.

Not because the moment wasn't sacred. But because maybe it was.

"Is that what you'd call a miracle?" Diego asked finally. "Joy?"

Took a breath. Measured it.

I turned to him. "Not just joy. The kind that's impossible. Implausible. The kind that shouldn't survive what it came through. That's the miracle."

Bree tapped her pen against her notebook, the rhythm sharp. "But you said he was angry at God. Still was. So... how does someone carry that much weight and still choose to laugh?"

I hesitated. Not for effect. For accuracy.

"Because sometimes laughter isn't an escape," I said. "It's proof. That something survived the wreckage. That a part of him—of us—could still lift."

Aisha tilted her head slightly. "So you're saying joy is... defiance?"

"Maybe," I said. "Or maybe it's what comes when defiance gives up, and all that's left is what's real. Maybe the deeper the sorrow, the sharper the humor. Because it has to be."

Wright leaned on the edge of his desk, arms still crossed. "So now we're saying grief manufactures joy?"

"No," I replied. "Not manufactures. Distills. You ever meet someone who's suffered long enough that they laugh at the things other people cry over?"

A few heads nodded.

"It's not because they don't feel. It's because they've already felt the worst. Laughter becomes the breath between sobs. It becomes proof that they're still here."

Bree's voice cut in again, lower this time. "So he didn't forgive God. But he still... gave?"

I nodded.

"He never wrapped it up in a neat bow. He didn't sit me down with sermons or promises. But he gave himself. Quietly. Consistently. Even when it cost him."

Someone in the back whispered, "That sounds like belief."

I let the silence hang.

"I think," I said, "it was something older than belief. More stubborn. Like muscle memory. Like his soul had been shaped in a way that kept moving forward, even when his heart still limped."

Wright shifted again—not out of discomfort, but curiosity.

"You keep coming back to that," he said. "Forward motion. Survival as sacred. But we haven't answered the question—if your dad didn't believe, what do you call all this?"

I didn't look away.

Didn't flinch. Didn't explain. Just spoke what I knew.

"I call it a seed," I said. "Something planted before he knew it, watered by suffering, hardened by fire. A seed that waited."

He tilted his head. "And what do seeds need?"

"Time," I said. "Time. And just enough light."

The room held still. A few students wrote nothing at all. Others scribbled without looking up.

"You know the Gospel of John starts that way," Bree muttered. "The light shines in the darkness, and the darkness has not overcome it."

She didn't say it sarcastically. More like she was testing the words in her mouth, checking if they still fit.

Wright crossed his arms again. "You've been giving us stories, not arguments."

"Exactly," I said. "Because people don't believe in arguments. They believe in witnesses."

Liam spoke from the side, quiet but certain. "Sometimes people don't need to be convinced. They just need to be seen."

Heads nodded again.

"I think," I added, "that joy isn't what happens when things are fixed. It's what breaks through even when nothing is. It's not the victory—it's the proof that something inside us wouldn't die."

Aisha leaned forward. "So what do you do with that kind of joy?"

I looked at her. "You honor it. You don't bottle it up or slap theology on it. You let it live. Because maybe that's what makes it holy."

Even Wright didn't argue that.

There was a pause. A long one. No one eager to fill it. The kind of silence that feels earned.

Then Reid said, "Sounds like your dad never stopped burning. He just stopped letting it consume him."

I smiled, just barely. "Yeah. That's about right."

No one moved for a long time.

And somewhere, maybe not aloud, I hoped they were starting to see it.

Not the fire. Not the trauma. But the joy that somehow survived it. Still burning. Still stubborn. Still there.

I looked down at my desk, just for a moment, then back at them. "That's what he meant when he said, 'It's necessary to go through the fire to be tempered and refined.'"

"Some things only grow after they've been buried. Not hidden—buried. Pressed down, broken open, and left alone for a while. That's how seeds work. They don't bloom because they're protected. They bloom because they surrender to the dark first. Unless a seed fails."

I looked around the room again, slower this time. "My dad didn't bloom in spite of the fire. He bloomed because of it. Because something in him had to fall first. Had to die. That's where the roots came from.

The fire didn't consume him. It cultivated him.

Because he didn't fail. He grew.

XI: As If by Fire

"Tempered," Wright repeated, almost to himself. "That implies purpose. That the heat isn't just punishment, it's process."

He let the idea breathe.

"You're saying suffering doesn't just test belief—it creates it?"

I nodded. "Not always. But in my dad's case? Yeah. The pain wasn't proof of God. But the fact that he could still love—still give when emptied out—that felt like evidence of something holy."

Diego leaned back. "But what if that's just... personality? Some people are generous. Some people survive. Doesn't make it divine."

"Sure," I said. "But generosity without a source burns out. My dad never claimed a reservoir. Never claimed faith. And yet it poured out of him, even when he was empty."

Reid added, "Sounds like a paradox. He rejected God but lived like a believer."

"He never rejected," I said. "He wrestled. There's a difference."

Bree looked up, expression unreadable. "And maybe the wrestling is where it becomes real."

Wright raised an eyebrow. His expression was curious now—not combative. "So you're saying faith might begin as friction?"

"Or fracture," I said. "Sometimes it starts with something that breaks. But it doesn't end there."

Liam rubbed the back of his neck. "My dad said once that faith is what keeps you from sinking when the floor gives out. I thought that was just metaphor. Now I'm not so sure."

Aisha spoke gently. "Faith without language... faith without clarity. That's still faith?"

"Sometimes clarity comes later," I said. "Sometimes it never does. But the way my dad lived, the weight he carried, the kindness he still managed—there was something sacred in that. Not preachy. Just persistent."

Wright tilted his head. "And you... when did that click for you?"

Wright shifted in his seat, and for a moment, the weight of the room didn't feel heavy—it felt suspended. Like something just beneath the surface was about to break through. Wright shifted in his seat. "Let's not lose the thread," he said, voice lighter now. "You've painted a vivid picture of endurance, but let me ask this—what separates that kind of endurance from any other form of resilience? What makes it faith and not just survival instinct?"

His voice was still measured, but something about it had shifted. Less challenge. More curiosity. Like he was testing not just me, but himself.

I let the question hang. Let the class hold it for a second.

"Because resilience bends," I said. "Faith rebuilds. Resilience keeps you afloat. Faith sets the course."

Diego shook his head slightly. "That sounds like semantics."

Bree leaned forward. "But you said your dad didn't believe."

"He didn't call it that," I said. "He never said the words. But he lived in a way that suggested something was shaping him—something bigger than grief."

Aisha raised her hand, then dropped it. "So what do you call that kind of faith? The unspoken kind?"

"Maybe it's proto-faith," I said. "Maybe it's what happens before belief has language. Like a shadow cast before the light."

Wright nodded slightly—still guarded, but listening.

"And what if he'd never found language?" Wright asked. "Would you still call it holy?"

"Yes," I said. "Because I don't think belief is what you say when things are easy. It's what remains when everything else has been scraped away. He gave joy when he had none to spare. He showed up when his body told him not to. He loved without asking anything back."

Reid chimed in, "Sounds like a kind of liturgy. Not churchy—but consistent. Devoted."

"I think that's what it was," I said. "A kind of holy repetition. Not for show. Just to survive."

Diego clicked his pen. "You're saying someone can live out faith without admitting it?"

I nodded. "I'm saying maybe the admission comes later. Maybe the actions come first."

Bree looked up from her notes. "Like the body believing before the mind catches up."

"Exactly," I said.

Liam crossed his arms. "And how does that become your story?"

I hesitated.

"That's where the fire comes in," I said. "Where the tempering happens. Because I didn't believe just because I wanted to. I believed because I was broken. And I remembered the way he bent, but didn't break."

A hush settled again. Not silence. Just collective listening.

"You said before," Wright added carefully, "that he gave without ever demanding recognition. That he carried weight in ways no one saw."

"He did."

"Then maybe belief," Wright said, "isn't about answers at all. Maybe it's about endurance."

I nodded slowly.

"That's the only kind I've ever seen hold up."

That was when Lena, softer now, said, "So when did you believe?"

I looked up. Not surprised. Just… steady.

"It was 2003," I said. "I was divorced. Twice. Raising two sons from two different marriages—by myself. I was working nonstop just to keep the lights on. Trying to keep them fed. Trying to keep them from seeing how close I was to breaking."

Wright didn't respond right away. He studied me like the room had gone translucent.

"So was that the moment? The bottom?" he finally asked.

"No," I said. "That was the fracture. But belief didn't come just because I needed it to. It came because I saw someone else survive it with something intact."

Bree closed her notebook, softly. "Is that how you define faith? By what stays when everything else leaves?"

"I define it by what's left standing. When all your plans fail. When the world doesn't bend the way you hoped. When you've got nothing but silence—and somehow you keep going."

Reid nodded once, then leaned forward, elbows on the desk. "So your dad became that proof. Not through words, but through presence."

"Exactly," I said. "It wasn't what he said. It was what he carried."

Diego looked unconvinced. "But doesn't that just make him strong? Stoic? I still don't see where God fits in."

I turned toward him. "What if strength is the evidence? What if joy in the midst of ruin isn't a coping mechanism—it's a byproduct of something deeper?"

Wright interjected, "That's poetic, but it leaves the skeptic with nothing to hold. If you say faith is invisible and only recognized after suffering, how do you distinguish it from luck or willpower?"

"I don't," I said. "Not until later. Sometimes not until it's passed on."

Aisha said softly, "Like inheritance."

"Yes," I said. "Like a story that didn't start with me. Like something I didn't earn, but was given. Not in a sermon, but in the way he lived."

Wright raised a brow. "So he was your parable."

I nodded. "Every miracle starts as a mystery. But some people live in a way that lets you see the shape of it, even if you can't name it yet."

Someone—I think it was Lena—murmured, "That kind of legacy sticks, doesn't it?"

I gave a small smile. "There's an old family Bible in my house. One of those big family ones, the kind with the gold trim and our name engraved on the front. My parents gave it to me years ago—our name engraved on the cover. I don't read it much. Don't even remember the last time I opened it."

A pause.

"But I haven't thrown it out either."

No one commented, but I caught Wright's glance. Curious. Measuring. Like he knew that detail might come back around.

Wright leaned back, studying me. "But you've still not said how that qualifies as a miracle."

I let the silence sit a moment.

"Maybe the miracle wasn't what happened to him," I said. "Maybe it was what didn't."

Diego blinked. "Meaning?"

"He didn't become bitter. He didn't break the people around him just because he'd been broken. He kept showing up, even when no one asked him to. That kind of quiet defiance against despair? That's rare. That's sacred."

Bree added, "Sounds like a sign that doesn't announce itself."

"Exactly," I said. "It's like those first signs in the Gospel—small things. Water into wine. Nothing flashy. Just enough to show something had shifted beneath the surface."

Wright looked down at his notes, then back up. "So you're saying miracles don't always interrupt the natural order?"

"No," I said. "Sometimes they move within it. Like grace hiding in plain sight. Like joy that shouldn't exist—but does."

Wright gave a small nod—less agreement than acknowledgment. Like he'd seen something he couldn't quite name.

The room settled into a silence that wasn't empty. It was full—of thought, of weight, of things not yet said.

XI: As If by Fire

And me? I kept thinking about what came next.

Because belief doesn't just live in theories. It lives in the days that test them.

The room was still. Not silent—just listening. Like even the air had paused to take it in.

I kept thinking about inheritance—about how belief isn't always taught. Sometimes, it's transferred through presence. Through resilience. Through acts that don't look like theology, but become it.

And sometimes, it takes time to recognize the miracle. To see what was passed down in the quiet, in the giving, in the staying.

I hadn't planned to tell this part. Not out loud. Not here. But sometimes the sacred things rise to the surface when you're not looking. And once the memory surfaced, it didn't ask for permission—it just waited to be told.

And like all sacred things, it arrived quietly—with a chipped mug, a silence, and a name I hadn't spoken in years.

That's when I remembered the envelope.

The diner off Highway 29.

The drive to the diner felt longer than it was. Just over an hour, but heavy. Not with traffic. With shame.

I'd called again. Not because I wanted to—but because I had no other choice. Two boys. Nearly 70 hours a week at work. Scraping together groceries, daycare, rent. Still falling short. Again.

Every time I dialed that number, it felt like swallowing glass. Another reminder I hadn't come as far as I thought. That independence was still a distant shore.

The radio was low—Rodney Atkins' "Watching You" drifted through the speakers. I almost turned it off when the chorus hit, the kid singing about being just like his dad.

But I didn't. I let it play. Let it press on the bruise.

Because in that moment, I wasn't the dad in the song. I was the one pulling over to ask for help again. The one trying not to drown in what I couldn't provide.

The tires hummed against worn asphalt, the kind that rattled through the steering wheel like a metronome of regret. The lines on the road blurred into a kind of silence. I passed silos leaning like tired men, bare trees that looked like they were praying or bracing for impact.

The farmland rolled past, slow and steady, while my thoughts moved faster—rehearsing explanations, crafting softened versions of the truth, even though I knew he wouldn't ask for any.

The air was too crisp. The sun was too bright for how I felt. Every mile felt like another inch of pride being peeled away.

About a mile off Highway 29, I turned down a quiet stretch into Abbotsford and pulled into the lot of Abby Café. The place looked like it hadn't changed in decades—cracked vinyl booths, faded blinds, the kind of spot where the coffee tastes like it's been burning since sunrise.

Neither of us ever mentioned the drive. That's how we handled things back then. Say less. Show up.

He was already there when I arrived. Worn flannel. Calloused hands wrapped around a chipped mug. He didn't smile, but he stood when I walked in.

"Hey," he said. Sat back down like we'd just talked yesterday, even though it had been months.

He already knew why I was there. Probably knew it before I even called. That wasn't the first time I'd needed help. Probably wouldn't be the last. But he didn't let me feel it. He didn't make me wear that shame.

The waitress came over, called us both "hon," poured the scorched-smelling coffee into chipped mugs, and vanished with the jingle of her keychain, like the whole moment was too fragile for witnesses.

I talked first. Not about the money. Not yet. I talked about the boys. About the car. About work slowing down. I gave him the full sob story like I'd rehearsed it—and maybe I had. I said I didn't know how I was going to make it this month.

He didn't interrupt. Didn't flinch. Just nodded now and then, his eyes steady and unsparing—not harsh, just unwilling to look away. Like he was watching the rubble settle, waiting to see what could still stand.

Then he set his mug down. Looked right at me.

"It's necessary to go through the fire," he said, "to be tempered and refined."

He said it like it had been waiting inside him. Like it didn't come from him, but through him.

I stared at him. That line didn't fix anything. But it shifted the ground beneath me. Quietly. Clearly. It didn't offer a ladder—but it offered light. And sometimes that's enough.

And then—without fanfare—he reached into his coat, pulled out a small, creased envelope, and slid it across the table like it might shatter if he let go too fast.

"I know it's not much," he said. "But it'll get you through."

I didn't touch it. Just stared at it sitting on the fake wood laminate between us—its surface worn smooth by years of elbows, spills, and small talk. It looked like me, in a way: scuffed, dulled by time, but still holding.

The envelope was thin. But it landed like a stone. Like it held both my shame and my redemption—pressed into the same breath. One part mercy. One part reminder. All weight.

The flap was sealed with a sliver of tape, barely holding. Like grace holding its breath—uncertain if it would be received, or even if it should be. His hand lingered for a breath longer than it needed to—as if passing it off took more than muscle. As if part of him was letting go of more than paper.

My name was written in his all-caps handwriting—sharp, deliberate. Like he needed to make sure it was unmistakable. That this offering, this gesture, this grace—it was mine.

I felt the waitress watching from across the counter, pretending to clean a coffee pot that had already been wiped dry. She didn't say a word. But I saw her eyes flick down, then away. Like she knew the shape of that kind of moment. Like maybe she'd lived it too.

Part of me wanted to push it back. Another part had already done the math—medical payments, utilities, house payment, gas. The number wasn't even that big. But what it meant? That was tectonic.

That's when I realized something: my dad was living on disability. PTSD, full rating. Mom was sick again. Diabetes, cancer. He was the one keeping her meds sorted, checking her sugar, adjusting pillows when she couldn't get comfortable. Every day he took care of her quietly—no ceremony, no complaint.

And I sat there, suddenly aware of the miracle in front of me.

Not the money.

But the man.

Still, he'd driven that hour across worn roads to meet me here. And he gave what he had.

He never once said, "You should've planned better." Never once asked how I'd gotten myself into this mess. He just gave. Quietly. Like it was the most natural thing in the world.

I looked at him again. He looked tired. Worn. But not hollow. Not bitter. Just… present. Solid.

It didn't feel like help. It felt like mercy. Like a life preserver tossed by a man who was treading water too.

If there was a miracle in my life, it wasn't that the envelope had cash. It was that it came from a man who had every right to keep it—and didn't.

He gave it freely.

And in that moment, I saw something I hadn't before.

The fire hadn't burned him away.

It had made space for something new to grow.

I remember the drive home. Long, quiet. The kind of quiet that makes you hear your own heartbeat.

I kept turning his words over in my head: 'Tempered and refined.'

How could someone like him—someone who'd buried a daughter, lost years to trauma, watched his wife's body fail in slow motion—still believe the fire meant something other than destruction?

What did he see in that heat that I couldn't?

And maybe that was it. Maybe it wasn't about what he saw. Maybe it was what he refused to unsee. What he chose to hold onto when the easier option was to let go.

I pulled into the driveway and sat there a long time. My boys were inside—young, loud, oblivious to everything I'd just carried home with me.

But before I stepped through that door, I did something I hadn't done in years.

I got out of the car. Walked around back. Kneeled in the dark. And prayed.

Not eloquently. Not confidently. Just... honestly.

I didn't ask for money. I didn't even ask for strength.

I just said: "Show me what he sees."

XI: As If by Fire

When I finally came inside, the house was dim. Toys in the hallway. Crayons scattered on the kitchen table. One of the boys had fallen asleep on the couch with a blanket over his face. I stepped over a pair of sneakers and made my way to the bedroom where I kept my Bible—mostly unread, mostly untouched. I hadn't opened it in months.

I didn't even know why I reached for it. Muscle memory, maybe. Desperation.

I flipped it open without thinking. No bookmarks. No plan. Just the weight of habit and hope.

My eyes landed on 1 Peter 1:7. I sank to my knees.

"...these have come so that the proven genuineness of your faith— of greater worth than gold, which perishes even though refined by fire— may result in praise, glory and honor when Jesus Christ is revealed."

I didn't read the rest.

I couldn't.

That was the moment it took root.

Not because I understood everything. Not because the pain stopped. But because, somehow, I believed.

Not in answers. But in presence.

In the same God who had walked with my dad through fire, and now... maybe, just maybe, was reaching for me.

"It wasn't the parting of the sea," I said quietly. "But it was a miracle all the same."

No one responded. Not right away. They were still caught in it—still feeling the weight of something unsaid.

Bree was watching me, expression unreadable. Not skeptical. Not moved to tears. Just... still. Like she wasn't ready to speak because she hadn't figured out what the moment had done to her yet.

Diego leaned back again, arms crossed, but he didn't jump in with a rebuttal. Not this time.

Wright finally said, "So it wasn't about being saved from the fire. It was about finding something sacred inside it."

I nodded. "That's where it happened for me. Not in a church. Not in a healing. "Just in the quiet. In the decision to believe maybe this wasn't all survival. Maybe it was... being refined."

Reid asked, "Would it have meant less if you hadn't opened that Bible? If the words hadn't lined up like that?"

"No," I said. "That just confirmed it. The real miracle had already happened. I was willing to ask. Willing to see."

Aisha wrote something down. Then looked up. "So faith isn't just belief. It's availability."

"Yes," I said. "And sometimes that starts with being broken enough to listen."

Wright tapped his pen once, thoughtful. Then he said, "You know, I've spent my whole career arguing that miracles require interruption— divine disruption of the natural world. But this?" He gestured vaguely, as if pointing to the weight of the story that still hung between us. "This feels like something else. A miracle that whispers instead of shouts."

"It does," I said. "Because maybe some of the loudest miracles don't make a sound."

He considered that. "Or maybe we've defined miracles too narrowly. Maybe the criteria aren't thunder and lightning, but grace and timing."

Diego crossed his arms. "Or maybe it's just coincidence. A man gives his son money. A verse in a Bible happens to match a metaphor. That doesn't make it divine."

Wright let out a soft breath, almost like he'd been pulled back from something. Like he'd been halfway to admitting it, almost—until Diego's voice snapped the line taut. He nodded slowly. "Coincidence," he repeated, but this time like he didn't want the word in his mouth.

He shifted his posture slightly, more reserved now. Academic footing returning. "Sometimes we see a pattern, and we want it to mean something. That's human nature. Narrative impulse. We crave shape and intention."

He tapped his pen once against his notebook, eyes now lowered. "And that's where we have to be careful. To distinguish what moves us emotionally from what holds up under scrutiny."

Wright looked up again, slower this time, as if weighing the cost of every word. "But I will admit this… the alignment here—it's hard to ignore."

Diego said nothing. Just watched.

"I'm not calling it divine," Wright added quickly, as if reminding himself. "But it… unsettles. And maybe that's the closest I can get for now."

He turned his pen in his fingers.

"Maybe," he said slowly. "Or maybe that's where discipline comes in. To not cheapen the word, but also not dismiss what we can't fully define. I'm not saying I believe what you believe." He looked at me then—level, honest. "But I can't deny the impact of the moment. Or the alignment. Or how rare it is for something to feel... orchestrated without being explained."

I didn't speak. I let him sit in it.

He continued, quieter now. "Coincidence is a defensible term. But sometimes, it feels like calling a symphony background noise just because you don't know who's conducting."

A hush spread through the room again. This time, not from uncertainty—but from recognition. Not agreement, but the sacred tension just before belief becomes being.

Ethan cleared his throat. "Still feels like a miracle to me. Not flashy, but real."

Gabe, who hadn't spoken in a while, added, "Feels like the kind of thing you only notice if you're looking. Like... the moment's small, but what it does to you isn't."

A girl near the window—Lena, maybe—murmured, "But maybe that's the point. Maybe miracles aren't about visibility. They're about impact."

Diego frowned. "Or it's just a powerful moment. Powerful doesn't equal divine."

XI: As If by Fire

Bree stared at her notebook. "You ever think maybe some people only survive because they believe it meant something? Whether it did or not?"

Reid said, "Belief doesn't have to be true to be transformative. But what if it is true?"

The energy in the room shifted again—divided now. Not hostile, but layered. Not a room waiting to be convinced, but one beginning to question its own questions.

I watched it unfold—how something that began as just my story had become a mirror. A reflection of what people were willing to see.

Reid said, "Like a seed falling, breaking open, creating space for something new."

Bree added, "Or maybe the miracle isn't what happens. It's what changes because it did."

I smiled, just slightly. "Exactly."

Sometimes the miracle isn't in the fire itself. It's in what survives it.

I still don't have language for all of it. But every time life bends close to the flame again, I remember that diner. That envelope. That line about being tempered.

And I keep going—not because I've escaped the fire, but because, like him, I've learned to walk through it.

Not untouched.

Just… tempered.

XII: Hear My Voice

The conversation had changed. Not in volume, but in gravity. It had drifted—quietly, deliberately—from spectacle to substance. From parted seas to steady endurance. From lightning bolts to the slow kindling of belief.

Bree wasn't trying to corner definitions anymore. Diego, usually restless, had gone still.

Even Wright—so quick to challenge the sacred—had softened, as if his questions had begun to listen for their own answers.

They'd stopped asking, "Are miracles real?" Now they were asking, "If they are... what kind of people do they make us?"

Aisha had called transformation a slow-burning miracle. Reid said it felt like something blooming from ash. Even Lena—thoughtful, reserved Lena—had leaned forward, arms crossed, but eyes wide open.

That's when Wright spoke. Not as a skeptic. As a man who had finally admitted there was something under the surface—something he couldn't quite name.

"You said something earlier," he said slowly, "about your father. That he carried something sacred. That he didn't become what tried to break him."

I nodded. "He gave joy away," I said. "Even when he had none left for himself."

Wright tapped his pen once, then stopped. "So what changed? Did it ever crack?"

I didn't answer at first. Not because I didn't know. Because I wanted the silence to do what it always did: make room for something truer.

"He broke," I said. "But not in ways people recognize. No shatter. Just silence."

Diego asked, "Then how?"

I exhaled. "He started talking."

"Like… to someone?" Reid asked.

I nodded. "To God. Like they'd been speaking for years, and he was just tired of pretending they hadn't."

Ethan's voice was quiet. "But why then?"

"Because pain doesn't just disappear. It compacts. It thickens. Until one day, it reaches a pressure point—and something gives. For him... it gave in the form of prayer."

Wright raised a brow. "You're saying faith is the breaking point?"

"No," I said. "It was the voice waiting in the quiet after."

Bree leaned back. "Still sounds like projection. Like he built a voice out of need."

"Maybe," I said. "But that voice didn't soothe him. It shook him. It told him things he didn't want to hear. That's not comfort. That's call."

Aisha leaned in. "Isn't that kind of the point, though? Faith doesn't always rescue. Sometimes it confronts."

Wright nodded, slowly. "You've talked about survival. And transformation. But let's be specific: if a man starts talking to God in the middle of the night—where's the line between miracle and breakdown?"

Diego added, "Yeah. And what if that voice is just desperation wearing a mask?"

I let the question breathe before answering. "When something echoes in you—so deep it doesn't feel like it came from you—so steady it doesn't leave you alone—that's not delusion. That's direction."

Lena tilted her head. "So the test of a miracle... is where it takes you?"

"Exactly," I said. "The voice didn't pull him out of pain. It pulled him deeper into presence. Into the people who still needed him. Into himself."

Reid's voice was soft. "So it's not about clarity. It's about movement."

I smiled. "Yeah. Muscle memory of the soul."

Even Wright allowed a breath of something like a laugh.

"There's a verse," I said. "*My sheep hear my voice. I know them, and they follow me.*'

But it doesn't say how long they wander before they recognize it. Or how long the voice keeps speaking before they admit they've heard it all along."

Wright didn't speak. But he didn't look away either.

The quiet in the room felt different now—less like hesitation, more like expectation.

I took a breath.

"He didn't announce it," I said. "Didn't cry for help. That's not how it works with men like him. You just... start seeing less of them. Hearing less. Until one day, the silence isn't just quiet. It's dangerous."

I hesitated. Not because I didn't want to share it—but because some moments lose their sacredness once spoken.

"There was a night even quieter than this one," I said. "A silence that wasn't waiting for a question. It was waiting for voices."

It was 2007.

Forty years had passed since Vietnam, but the war had never left him.

The headlines spoke of Iraq and Afghanistan—new conflicts, yet the same echoes. The evening news debated military surges and casualties, while the internet hummed with distractions—celebrity scandals, the first iPhone, the rise of social media.

He often laughed, bringing joy to those around him.

But beneath the laughter, remnants remained. Not in visible wounds or medals, but in the quiet moments between.

Nightfall was the enemy—bringing sleep, and with it, the nightmares. Relentless. Unyielding. The same horrors replayed, refusing to fade.

Sleepless nights grew heavier, exits felt closer, and his hands trembled more often. The war had never truly ended—it followed him into the dark.

Mom had taken ill again. Not the kind of illness that charges in and knocks you down—but the kind that seeps in slow and takes pieces. One breath at a time.

That night, the darkness felt heavier. Like the air itself had thickened, pressing in from all sides. The moon hung behind a veil of clouds, its light cold—casting warped shadows like bruises. Every creak of the house sounded sharper, more pointed—like the walls themselves were holding their breath.

She'd fallen asleep early. He sat beside her in the dim light, watching the slow rise and fall of her chest. His hand moved through her hair, slow and practiced, like it had a thousand times before—but this time, it lingered. Longer than usual. Like it knew.

Then it slipped away.

He stood in the hallway, still. Listening.

The silence wasn't gentle. It wrapped around him like wire—tight, unrelenting. The heater clicked inside the walls, the sound too sharp, too sudden. The old clock ticked in the next room, each beat echoing like distant gunfire.

Outside, the trees stood motionless against the windless sky, skeletal limbs reaching up like they were pleading with something that wasn't listening.

He moved to the closet. Slow. Measured.

Took out the .357 Magnum.

It was cold in his hand. Solid steel, weighty with history. The blued finish had dulled—worn smooth at the grip by years of being held, cleaned, put away… and taken out again. A tool. A memory. A verdict.

He opened the cylinder—soft click.

Checked the chambers. Not out of caution. Out of ritual.

The box of cartridges waited in the top drawer. His hand didn't tremble. He might have been loading a stapler, screwing in a lightbulb. Just a task. Just one more thing to finish.

He slid six rounds into place. One by one. Each tiny metallic chime barely audible, but definitive.

Then he spun the cylinder, slow. The sound whispered around the empty room and landed with a soft lock.

Loaded.

Final.

Undeniable.

He sat in the recliner. The leather groaned beneath him, the sound low and familiar—like an old friend who knew how this night might end. Like it recognized him. Like it understood.

The gun rested on his lap. Heavy. Still. A weight that didn't ask for explanation.

No tears.

No shaking.

No note.

There was nothing left to say. Nothing left untried. Just the hollow quiet of a man who'd outlasted too much.

He looked around the room one last time—not with sentiment, but with finality. The stack of bills on the counter. The coat still draped over the kitchen chair. The dent in the wall from a long-ago fight no one remembered anymore. Ordinary things. Quiet witnesses.

He lifted the gun.

Barrel to temple.

Metal met skin—cold, inevitable.

His thumb pulled the hammer back. A quiet, exact sound. Not dramatic. Just decisive. The sound of a door closing. Of a breath held too long.

The room didn't protest.

Even the shadows stopped moving.

Time narrowed.

The stillness thickened—so absolute it felt sacred, or maybe sacrificial.

Then—

The phone rang.

3:30 a.m.

It cut through the dark like a blade.

He blinked. Once.

Then looked toward the kitchen wall where the receiver sat, its cord coiled like a sleeping serpent.

Who the hell is calling now?

He let it ring again. And again.

Then something—instinct, maybe—moved his hand.

He picked it up.

"John?"

A man's voice.

Calm. Warm.

Unhurried.

"This is Jeff. From Tomah. VA chaplain's office. We've met... maybe once? Don't know why I'm calling. Just... felt like I should."

Dad didn't speak. He couldn't. His throat had closed tight.

Jeff didn't fill the silence. He just waited.

"I, uh…" Dad cleared his throat. "It's late."

"I know," Jeff said. "That's kind of the point."

There was a pause. Not awkward. Just… wide.

"You were in Vietnam, right?" Jeff asked.

"…Yeah."

"Jungle unit?"

"…Yeah."

"67?"

Another pause.

Then: "Yes."

Jeff exhaled slowly. "You remember the smell of diesel and death? How it clung to your boots like it was trying to come home with you?"

Dad froze.

That detail. Too sharp. Too close.

He almost asked who the hell this was. Almost hung up.

But Jeff kept talking—gently. Carefully. Like someone trying to coax a wounded animal out from under a porch.

"You still see it sometimes, don't you?" Jeff said. "The fire. The faces. The pieces of boys you had to pretend weren't boys anymore."

Dad didn't answer. But the tears started.

Quiet. Steady.

Jeff's voice stayed even, unhurried. "I still smell it too. Forty years, and it hasn't washed out."

Dad clenched the receiver tighter. "You were there?"

A beat.

"I was there."

He clenched the receiver tighter. Every word Jeff spoke felt less like sound and more like a tuning fork—vibrating with something ancient. Familiar.

The words hung in the air, settling into the silence like they belonged there. Like they had always belonged there.

Another pause.

"I knew a guy," Jeff continued. "Took shrapnel to the ribs. Refused morphine. Said he didn't want to forget how it felt to be alive."

Dad swallowed hard. "That makes no sense."

"No," Jeff said gently. "But it sounded like truth at the time."

Dad blinked. His voice came quieter this time, almost cautious. "Were you... a medic?"

Jeff didn't answer right away. When he did, it wasn't with a title.

"A healer," he said.

Just that. No rank. No role. Just a word—ancient, unshaken—that hung in the air.

A quiet breath passed between them.

"John," Jeff said after a beat, "I know tonight feels like the end of something. But what if it's not?"

Dad's lip curled. Not in anger—resistance. "You don't know what it's been like."

"I do know what it's been like," Jeff said. "Your hell's no hotter than anyone else's."

Jeff continued, steady. "You think this pain makes you weak. But what if it's the opposite? What if carrying it this long—without answers, without help—is proof of strength, not failure?"

"The fire didn't consume you," Jeff said. "It cultivated you."

Dad exhaled slowly. "I remember one patrol," he said. "Eleven days left. Mind was somewhere else... past, future, not sure. I wasn't in my body. Then my foot caught a root. Yanked me straight to the ground."

He let the memory settle between them.

Jeff's voice came quiet. "You sure you caught the root?"

Dad frowned. "What?"

"Maybe the root caught you."

The silence held for a beat. And then Jeff added, gentler now, like a psalm whispered over a wound: "There's a time for that, too. A time to be thrown down. A time to be yanked back. A time and a purpose, under heaven."

Dad's voice cracked. "That was a time to kill."

Jeff didn't flinch. "And this?" he said. "This might be your time to break down. And maybe... to build again."

He paused, his voice steady but soft. "A time to heal."

"You're not done yet."

Dad's breath caught—like he'd just been told something true he hadn't heard in years.

A long silence.

Then Jeff said, softer, "Funny how the things we can't say out loud... are the ones that stay the longest."

Dad nodded, unseen. Voice gravel. "I... I can't..."

"I never said you had to," Jeff replied.

Another beat.

They talked for the next three hours. Like they were long lost friends catching up after a lifetime apart.

About Mom. About the ache of long caregiving. About the nights when sleep felt dangerous. About guns that waited too patiently and voices that didn't come soon enough.

At one point, Jeff said softly, "You thinking about doing something you can't take back?"

Dad's voice cracked. "...Yeah."

Jeff was quiet for a long beat.

Then: "Then I'm glad I called."

Outside, the night began to lift.

And as the sun breached the edge of the trees, golden light spilled across the floor—across the gun, still resting on the carpet.

Unfired.

Undisturbed.

Dad sat with the phone still in one hand, the other hanging limp, knuckles white, empty. The silence pressed in, heavy, as if it had its own weight. His breath was uneven, shallow. He studied the sunlight inching across the floor—the way it spread, slow and deliberate, touching everything without hesitation.

For weeks, the light had been an indifferent thing. Just another cycle in days that blurred together. But now—now it reached him, steady and warm. It was in no hurry, as if it understood something he didn't. As if it knew he needed time.

He swallowed hard. The gun had not moved. His body had not moved. But something—something had.

And for the first time in weeks, the light felt like more than weather. Light—warm, golden—felt like permission.

If this was coincidence, he thought, then it's the best-timed miracle I've ever seen.

Later that morning, he called the Tomah VA.

"Hi," he said. "Is Jeff working today? From the chaplain's office?"

XII: Hear My Voice

There was a pause.

"We don't have a Jeff here," the voice said.

The words hung there—hollow, dissonant—like a wrong note struck in an empty room.

He stared at the phone. Had he misheard? Or had the world itself just tilted a few degrees off-center?

Skepticism flickered first. This had to be a mistake. He *knew* Jeff had been there—had listened, had prayed, had called at just the right moment.

He called back twice more. Asked for full names. Records. Callback numbers.

And that was when something inside him shifted. Not snapped. Not burst. But turned. Like a compass needle—not forced, but drawn—finding true north.

And for the first time in years, he didn't feel like a ghost.

For days, my father replayed that conversation in his mind, unable to shake the feeling that something beyond chance had reached out to him. And so, the following Sunday, he found himself stepping into a church—not out of comfort, but obedience.

He sat in the back, arms folded. The same way he sat through briefings in Vietnam—tight-jawed, bracing for orders.

The pastor was speaking on obedience.

Not glory. Not blessing. Just obedience.

"Faith," he said, "is not a feeling—it's a movement. A response. A step."

The words hung like smoke—slow, sinking.

"It's easy to believe when the road is smooth, when the answers come quickly. But faith is forged in struggle. When the night is longest. When the silence is deafening. When you don't feel strong enough to take another step—faith is stepping anyway."

The pastor's voice deepened.

"History is written by those who step forward in faith. One man. One woman. One soul willing to stand when others sit. To believe when doubt surrounds them. To fight when the battle seems lost."

A pause.

"God doesn't reserve His favor for the strongest, the fastest, or the most righteous. He gives it to those who move in faith. Those who trust when they cannot see. Those who rise when they have every reason to fall."

Dad sat in the back pew, arms folded, unmoving.

But something inside him shifted.

And in the pause between words—between one breath and the next—The voice came. Not with a whisper. With a command.

"Stand up."

He didn't move.

"Stand. Now."

His fingers gripped the edge of the pew, white-knuckled.

"Walk to the front."

He blinked, heart pounding. Sweat rising at the back of his neck.

"Now."

Mom leaned in slightly. "What, honey?" she whispered, but he didn't answer. His eyes were locked ahead.

His body obeyed before his mind caught up.

He stood.

People turned. The pastor hesitated mid-sentence.

Dad stepped into the aisle like a man walking through floodwaters. Heavy. Reluctant. Pulled by something he didn't choose—but couldn't ignore.

Halfway down the aisle, the voice spoke again.

"Kneel."

He dropped to his knees. Right there. No altar call. No invitation. Just raw obedience.

The floor was cold. Hard. Real.

A gasp rippled through the room. The pastor stammered, unsure whether to continue or stop.

The voice pressed harder.

"Say it."

He didn't understand.

"Say it out loud."

He closed his eyes. Heat rising in his throat.

"What?" he whispered. "Say what?"

He felt breath catch, muscles lock.

"Say it."

His lips parted.

"Few," he said—soft, unsure.

"Again. Louder."

"Few."

"Again."

"Few."

"Say it like you believe it."

He inhaled, chest burning.

Then shouted: "FEW!"

The word shot from his chest like a flare. Not a number. A truth. Few who hear. Few who move. Few with faith. But those few... they carry favor.

A silence fell across the room so thick it felt holy. Sacred. Like the air itself was holding its breath.

The pastor stepped back, stunned. A woman near the front pew gasped.

And still the voice came.

XII: Hear My Voice

"Again."

"FEW!"

He felt it leave his body like a declaration. Like something ancient clawing its way to light.

Then—Nothing.

The voice went still.

The moment passed.

He stood, legs trembling, and walked back to Mom.

Sat beside her.

She looked at him—not afraid, not confused. Just steady. Soft.

"You okay?" she asked.

He nodded. Still catching his breath. Still shaking.

"The few with faith have favor," he said. "Few. Faith. Favor."

She took his hand.

He squeezed hers back.

"It's done," he whispered.

The voice was gone.

But the word remained.

The pastor stopped by the house after the service. He didn't call ahead. Just showed up. Said he'd been thinking about what happened.

He used the word 'unsettled'—not in confrontation, but like a man holding a thought too big to carry.

They sat at the kitchen table. My mom had just made a fresh pot of coffee, but the pastor barely touched his. He kept glancing toward dad like he was trying to read a page written in a language he didn't quite believe existed.

"I don't mean to disrespect what you experienced," the pastor said finally. "But... that moment. In the service. It wasn't something I could explain."

Dad didn't flinch. Just waited.

The pastor folded his hands. "You said God told you to go. Told you to kneel. Told you to speak." He hesitated. "John, God doesn't speak to us like that. Not audibly. Not directly. That's not how He works."

Dad tilted his head. "You think it wasn't God because you didn't hear Him?"

The pastor blinked.

"Maybe you didn't hear Him," Dad said, "because you already decided it couldn't be Him."

There was no anger in his voice. Just something... steady. Settled.

He paused, letting the silence settle between them like dust in a beam of light.

"It's the Psalms, isn't it?" Dad said quietly. "The way they speak like God's still talking. Raw. Honest. Like the soul doesn't have to be polite to be heard."

The pastor shifted in his seat, just slightly.

Dad leaned in, fingers laced together. "I know what you think. You've said it more than once—that the Psalms are dangerous."

The pastor didn't deny it. Just cleared his throat.

"I said some people think that," he replied. "That they're too emotional. Too much about human feeling—not enough about divine truth."

"That's what you're afraid of, isn't it?" Dad said. "Emotion. Because if it's emotional, then it's not theological. If it stirs something before it explains something—then it can't be trusted."

Dad tapped the edge of the table, thoughtful. Then said, steady as the tide, "Psalm 85 says God speaks peace to His people. So if He's talking, maybe it's time to start listening."

He let the weight settle.

"And John 10 says His sheep hear His voice. He knows them. And they follow. So maybe it's not about whether He's speaking, but whether we recognize it when He does."

Dad tapped his fingers on the table again. Not impatient—just setting the thought in place. "If these two passages say the same thing—that God is talking to us—why can't He talk to me? Or you?"

The pastor hesitated, then exhaled. "They were written at different times. By different people. I'm not sure you can equate them."

Dad nodded, barely missing a beat. "Exactly." He leaned forward, not in challenge, but in certainty. "Two different voices. Saying the same thing. At different times. Different people, same message. It's only complicated if you ignore the pattern."

He sat back again, letting the weight settle. "So either it's coincidence—or truth carried through different hands."

The pastor didn't speak this time. Maybe because there was nothing left to argue.

Then Dad said, calm as sunrise, "Psalm 27 says the Lord is my light and my salvation. So what else is there to fear? If He's the strength of my life, then nothing else gets to claim that power."

He let the words land.

"And John 8 says Jesus is the light of the world. If we walk with Him, we don't stay in darkness."

The pastor opened his mouth, but Dad kept going.

"Psalm 62 says to pour out your heart to Him. That He's a refuge. And John 14 says, don't let your heart be troubled—believe in God, believe also in Me."

A pause.

"Psalm 119 says God's promise preserves your life, even in suffering. And John 6 says the words Jesus spoke are spirit and life.

Same message. Different mouths."

He sat back, arms resting on the edge of the table.

"No degree. No seminary. Just a man who's lived long enough to know when truth shows up more than once, it's probably worth listening to."

The pastor was quiet now. The kind of quiet that isn't offended—just convicted.

He looked down, not in retreat, but in realization—as if wondering what truths he'd memorized but never lived.

"You still think those words don't carry weight?" Dad asked. "Because they're honest? Because they cry out from pain instead of speaking from pulpits?"

The pastor looked down. "I was taught that Psalms are... complicated. That they reflect the messiness of man. I've even heard some say they're the devil's poetry—too dark to be trusted."

Dad didn't laugh. He didn't even blink.

Instead, he said, "That sounds like something the devil would want you to believe. That our grief, our cries, our praise, our repentance—are too messy for God to use."

He leaned forward again.

"Psalms weren't written to scare us away from God. They were written to remind us we can run to Him."

The pastor exhaled slowly. Like someone letting go of a defense he hadn't realized he'd been holding.

"My moment in the church?" Dad said. "That wasn't about noise. Or theater. It was obedience. The sermon was about that, remember? Not glory. Not blessings. Just faith that walks."

The pastor nodded once. Still quiet.

"God spoke," Dad said. "He told me to move. Told me to kneel. To speak. And when I didn't understand, He told me again. 'Say it.' 'Say it louder.'"

He looked the pastor in the eye.

"And I did."

Another pause. Then, softly:

"He told me, 'Few.'"

The pastor raised an eyebrow. "Few?"

Dad nodded. "Few. Faith. Favor. The few with faith have favor."

The pastor sat back slowly. Processing.

And then Dad added one more.

"You want something scriptural? Here's one: John chapter five. 'He who hears My word and believes in the One who sent Me… has passed from death to life.'"

He let that sit.

"I was in that chair with a gun in my hand, about to cross one way. And God met me in that moment and gave me another way."

Silence wrapped the room.

No one spoke. Even the clock on the wall seemed to hush.

Finally, the pastor cleared his throat. "I don't know what to do with all this."

XII: Hear My Voice

"You don't have to," Dad said. "Just don't dismiss it because it didn't fit your plan."

Then he stood, refilled the pastor's coffee without asking, and added, "Sometimes God talks loud enough for one man to hear it clear—and quiet enough that the rest of the room stays skeptical."

The pastor didn't argue.

Because when someone has *really* heard God... you don't have to believe them.

"When He says, 'Hear My Voice...'"

Dad paused—like the words had rewritten something in him.

"Listen."

The pastor didn't argue. Because some words don't need agreement to carry truth.

And *few* ever forget when they hear the voice for themselves.

XIII: 5:24

It started with a cough. Not loud. Not disruptive. Just enough to interrupt the rhythm of Wright's pacing as he scribbled another quote across the whiteboard: *"The silence of God is the loudest sound in suffering."*

He capped the marker, turned slowly, and let the silence settle like it was part of the lecture.

"Who said that?" he asked, one eyebrow lifted.

No hands went up.

"Anyone?"

A beat. A shuffle of pages. No one looked directly at him.

Finally, from the second row, Bree offered, "Elie Wiesel?"

Wright nodded. "Correct. He wrote it in *Night*—his memoir as a Holocaust survivor. He endured Auschwitz and Buchenwald, witnessing immense suffering, including his father's death."

He let the words settle.

"A man who watched his father starve, freeze, and fade in a camp infirmary—yet still, he wrote about God. Or more specifically... God's silence."

He stepped forward, voice softening. "And that silence? He called it the truest experience of faith he'd ever known."

The class quieted.

I watched Lena's hand tighten around her pen, watched Diego lean back, his usual smug grin curiously absent. Reid stared ahead, unblinking. Bree had that same guarded look she always wore when things veered too close to something real.

Wright looked at me now. Deliberate.

"Thoughts?" he asked.

I didn't blink. "Silence doesn't mean absence."

Wright cocked his head. "Doesn't it?"

"It can mean waiting. Or listening. Or grief. Or restraint."

He leaned against the desk, arms crossed. "So you're saying God's silence is... what? Compassion?"

"Maybe. Or maybe it's the only honest response when words aren't enough."

He smirked. "That's poetic. But is it theology?"

Bree cut in. "Sounds like an excuse."

A few heads turned. She shrugged. "I mean, come on—how convenient. When God speaks, it's love. When He's silent, it's wisdom. If He acts, it's a miracle. If He doesn't, it's mystery. It's like no matter what happens, God gets credit. Or a pass."

Reid leaned forward slightly. "But what if that's not about letting God off the hook? What if it's about people needing a frame for chaos?"

Wright nodded. "A framework for pain. Exactly. Humans have always turned to gods for that. Greek. Norse. Hebrew. It's not new—it's instinct."

Diego added, "So is denial."

Wright looked at him. "Go on."

Diego shrugged, but his voice held weight. "It's easier to say 'God's got a plan' than admit life is meaningless and people just die."

"Faith as anesthesia," Wright said, tapping his marker against his palm. "So what happens when the anesthesia wears off?"

Bree answered before I could. "That's when you either wake up—or double down."

Lena finally spoke. Her voice was quieter than usual, but steady. "What if the silence isn't absence? What if it's the space where we decide who we are?"

That one landed.

Even Wright paused.

And for a moment, the room wasn't a classroom—it was a confessional.

Reid, still watching the board, murmured, "My uncle prayed every night when he was in hospice. Every single night. Until the last one. Then he didn't say a word."

"Why not?" Bree asked.

Reid swallowed. "He said, 'God already heard me. If He's going to do something, He will. If not, He's got His reasons.'" He looked up. "Then he died."

Wright was quiet. Just for a breath.

Then he wrote one word on the board in all caps:

INTERVENTION.

"What do we expect," he asked, turning to us, "when we talk about God intervening? Lightning bolts? Burning bushes? Or just... not dying?"

Aisha raised a hand slowly. "What if the intervention is internal? What if it's the strength to face death differently?"

Wright nodded. "You're describing transformation. Not interruption. Which raises the question: Are we calling emotional growth divine because we're scared to admit it might just be... psychological adaptation?"

Bree spoke again, sharper now. "Or maybe it's just us dressing up survival in robes and calling it holy."

I met her eyes. "Is survival not holy?"

She looked away.

Wright tapped the board again. "We've explored the nature of miracles. Now let's interrogate the silence. If a miracle is God acting, then silence is God... not acting. And that's where most faith dies. Not in fire. But in the absence of it."

The word absence hung there.

I looked around the room.

"You all keep asking what silence means," I said. "But you're asking like silence is always passive. What if it's surgical? Precise. Intentional."

"Like what?" Diego asked. "Like a parent letting their kid fall so they learn a lesson?"

"No," I said. "Like a doctor making one clean cut so they don't have to make ten messy ones."

Aisha nodded. "Or like someone choosing not to speak because the words would only wound more."

Wright smiled faintly. Whether it was respect or sarcasm, no one could quite tell. "That's very generous."

Bree didn't look at me when she spoke. "Or maybe silence just means there's nothing left to say."

Then Lena said it.

The sentence that hit like a stone dropped in a still pond.

"Then what does it mean when God doesn't show up?"

The room didn't shift. It stopped breathing,

Lena's voice hadn't wavered. But something inside the question had. It wasn't anger. It wasn't doubt. It was grief, wrapped in skin, trying not to shake.

No one answered right away.

Even Wright—the master of quick rebuttals—seemed slower to respond.

The air in the room felt different now. Thicker. Like the walls had drawn closer, waiting.

I took a breath. Not for courage. Just to slow the flood behind my ribs.

"Sometimes," I said, "it doesn't look like God shows up."

A pause.

"Not because He didn't. But because we expected Him to come with lightning—and He came in silence instead."

Bree folded her arms tighter, but she didn't look away.

Lena stared down at her desk, pen motionless.

And Wright... he watched me like he knew I was about to leave the discussion.

And walk into something else.

I didn't plan on telling them.

But some stories aren't chosen. They arrive.

And that's when it changed. I stopped being a student in that room. And started remembering.

It was the last night of June 2014. A Monday. The air in the Midwest hung like wet wool—thick, unmoving, heavy with a kind of sadness that didn't announce itself but soaked through everything. Even the trees outside seemed tired, their limbs too lazy to rustle.

Inside the house, the air conditioner hummed a steady rhythm upstairs—a mechanical lullaby, background music to a life trying to stay ordinary.

My mother moved slower that night. Not fragile. Just... careful. Like her bones knew something she hadn't yet accepted. Her face still held its usual softness, the kind that made people feel safe without knowing why. She smiled through it. Of course she did. She always smiled through it.

Because that's who she was.

Dad had gone to bed early. For once, sleep had found him easily. No night terrors. No racing mind. No ghosts. Just rest. That was new. That was a gift.

She didn't wake him.

She never would have.

She knew the creak of every board in the floor and how to step around them. She moved like memory—familiar and gentle. She didn't want anything dramatic. Just a marshmallow. One of the big ones. Her guilty pleasure.

She didn't bother with lights.

She didn't reach for a glass. Didn't turn on the TV. Just stood there in the kitchen, barefoot on the cold linoleum, one hand resting on the counter, the other still cradling the peppermint like it held more than flavor.

Maybe memory.

Maybe mercy.

Outside, the yard light cast a pale amber glow through the window, catching the edges of the room in a soft hush. Beyond that—darkness. Real darkness. The kind you only find in the country, where stars do all the talking and silence means something.

The hum of the refrigerator filled the room like a low, steady breath. The clock ticked once. Then again.

And then—without warning, without sound—she was laid down. Not collapsed. Not fallen.

Laid.

As if some invisible hands had eased her to the floor with reverence, like a sacred offering returning to stillness.

Her body met the ground like it had been invited. Like the earth itself had opened its arms and whispered, *Rest now.*

And the peace she had prayed for, night after night, finally found her. Not in a rush. Not in a blaze. But in quiet.

In completion.

Not sleep.

Surrender.

Not silence.

Stillness.

And just like that, she was gone.

Not with thunder. Not with trembling. Just breath, exchanged for something eternal.

No final cry. No rush of air. Just a moment that passed unnoticed—until it didn't.

No one saw it happen. No one heard.

But somehow, heaven did.

And maybe that was the miracle—That she didn't have to ask. Didn't have to wait.

She just... let go.

And God caught her.

Dad woke to a different kind of silence.

The kind that feels thick in your lungs. Like the air has weight. Like something has shifted and you're the last to know.

It was exactly 5:24 a.m.

He saw the numbers glowing on the alarm clock first, then sat up with a strange sense of knowing.

He reached out for her like he always did.

Nothing.

He didn't rush. He just reached. Like a man trying to hold something the world had already let go.

That wasn't new. She sometimes couldn't sleep. Would read, or sit in the living room. But something inside him stirred—primal and unexplainable.

He sat up. Called her name softly.

No answer.

He stood, slow, the kind of slow that tries not to panic.

The stairs creaked under his weight. The hallway was still dark. Her name fell again from his lips, just above a whisper.

Still nothing.

And then he saw her.

The moonlight caught her just enough—curled on the kitchen floor like she was resting. Her face turned toward the pantry. Her hand still wrapped loosely around that marshmallow.

Untouched.

Uncrushed.

He froze.

His breath caught in his throat.

For one impossible second, he believed she might stir. That she'd blink and smile and scold him for worrying. That she'd say, "I just needed something sweet," and everything would go back to how it was.

But it didn't.

Because something had changed.

Not violently.

But completely.

He dropped to his knees, his whole body folding like paper. Not from shock—but from grief so vast it stole his bones.

The fire hadn't consumed him. It had carved him out—left space only grief could fill.

And then the sobs came.

Not tears. Not weeping.

Sobs that ripped through the quiet like thunder, that bent him forward until his forehead touched the floor.

He held her hand—the one not holding the marshmallow—and called her name like it was the only word he'd ever known.

"I love you."

"I'm sorry."

"You don't have to hurt anymore."

"It's okay now."

Again and again, as if words could stitch her back into time.

The hum of the air conditioner carried on, unaware, unchanged. But now it sounded like absence.

He looked again—and it undid him.

There was something about her face that he couldn't explain.

A glow—not a light from outside, but something internal. A calm radiance, the absence of pain. It was like every moment of her suffering had left all at once. Her brow was smooth. Her cheeks were soft. Her whole body rested like she was being held.

And that glow—it undid him.

He sat with her for what seemed like an eternity.

No clock mattered.

The light changed. The shadows shifted. The hum of morning crept into the world. But he stayed there—kneeling beside her, hand in hand, as if the kitchen floor had become holy ground.

And then—he prayed.

Not with eloquence. Not with scripture rehearsed. Just a whisper cracked wide open:

"Father, I thank you that you have heard me. I knew that you always hear me..."

The words from John 11, the same ones Jesus spoke before calling Lazarus from the grave.

But Dad didn't speak them to resurrect.

He said them because he believed she had been heard. That someone had listened as she slipped from this world into the next.

He didn't recite to call anything back. He prayed because he believed she had been heard. That in her peace, in her passing, she was heard and carried home.

And only then—finally—did he pick up the phone.

It was just after 7:00 a.m.

"The phone rang. I answered on the first buzz. It was Dad.

His voice cracked before the words came.

"I've got some bad news," he said slowly. "I... I want to prepare you."

There was a pause—just long enough to steal breath.

I knew.

I could hear it in the way he exhaled. Like something had broken open inside him and he didn't know how to hold it anymore.

"I found her this morning," he said. "In the kitchen."

His voice wavered like a man trying to hold back a flood.

"She looked peaceful. She was holding a marshmallow... like she was just about to take a bite."

He swallowed hard on the line.

"I think she was already gone when I came down. But she wasn't afraid. She looked..." His breath caught again. "...held."

My knees buckled. I sat down without meaning to.

"I'm sorry," he whispered. "I didn't want you to hear it this way. I just... I need you. I need you to call your brother, too."

Another pause.

Then: "Jordan's still sleeping upstairs. He doesn't know."

My son. Fifteen years old. Asleep in the same house where his grandmother had just died.

That changed everything.

He wasn't just asking me to come grieve. He was asking me to help protect the innocence still wrapped in sleep under that roof.

"I don't want him to wake up to this," Dad added. "We should tell Jordan together... your son shouldn't have to hear it alone."

He lived almost an hour and a half away.

I didn't pack a bag. I didn't even think about shoes. I grabbed my keys with a hand that didn't feel like mine. My heart was too heavy for my chest.

The drive was a blur.

Trees. Signs. Mile markers I couldn't read. The wheel clenched tight between my palms, like I was trying to hold the world together through sheer grip.

While I drove, the ambulance came.

Dad had told them not to use sirens. Not out of denial, but reverence. He didn't want the noise to scare my son. Or to puncture the stillness. Or maybe because something about the moment had already declared itself sacred.

By the time I arrived, the ambulance had gone.

The gravel crunched under my tires. The house stood still.

Inside, it was quieter than I'd ever known it. Not empty. Just... hushed. Like it knew something holy had happened.

Dad stood in the kitchen, hollow-eyed. His shoulders hung in a way that felt foreign—like they were carrying centuries. He didn't speak. Neither did I.

We just looked at each other. And in that silence, everything spoke.

I went upstairs.

My son stirred when I opened the door. His little face scrunched with confusion.

"Dad? Why are you here?"

I sat beside him and took his hand.

"Something happened last night."

His eyes welled up instantly. Like he already knew.

And he cried. The kind of crying that breaks a parent.

So I held him. And I cried too.

We stayed that way, three generations caught in a single breath of loss.

Later, the coroner came. He told us it had been a massive heart attack. Sudden. Painless. There were no bruises. No signs of a fall. Just... stillness. Peace.

Dad told him about the marshmallow—how it had still been in her hand when he found her. Uncrushed. Unmoved.

The coroner looked confused. "It doesn't make sense," he said. "If she collapsed, you'd expect her to crush it. Or drop it. But it's perfect."

That marshmallow became everything. Proof. Hope. A whisper from God.

She didn't fall. She was laid down.

We didn't talk about it much, but we all felt it. That marshmallow was more than strange—it was sacred.

At the funeral, we made marshmallow bouquets. People didn't get it. They didn't need to. It wasn't for them. It was for her. For us. For what we'd seen. She had lived in pain for years.

But when Dad found her—she wasn't in pain. Her face was calm. Her brow unknotted. Her skin soft. Her expression—restful.

He told me later, "God tucked her in. That's the only way I can explain it."

That day didn't break him. It started something. Something quieter. But more real than anything before.

He started praying again. He opened his Bible. He called people he hadn't talked to in years. Forgave people he swore he couldn't. Because grace had walked into his kitchen.

And he would never forget what it looked like.

I didn't realize I'd gone silent until I looked up. The room was watching—every eye, every breath, every still hand.

No one said a word.

Not Wright.

Not Lena.

Not even Bree.

For a moment, the classroom wasn't a classroom. It was a sanctuary—not because of ritual, but because something holy had just taken up residence in the open air.

I glanced at the clock.

8:47 a.m.

It had only been three and a half hours since I'd woken up. But somehow, it felt like days.

Part of me was still in that kitchen. Still watching my father kneel. Still hearing the prayer that broke open a world.

"5:24," I said suddenly.

Wright's brow lifted slightly.

"That was the time," I explained. "When my dad woke up. 5:24 a.m. Exactly."

The numbers hung in the air.

"I didn't think much of it at the time," I added. "It just stuck with me. Etched into the memory like it was trying to mean something."

Lena's brows furrowed.

"Later," I said, "after the funeral, after the silence settled... I opened my Bible to John."

A pause.

"Chapter five. Verse twenty-four."

I didn't need to recite it. Didn't even want to. Because it wasn't about the words as much as what they meant.

"It talks about passing from death to life," I said. "Not after we die—but while we're still breathing. When we believe. When we hear. It says judgment isn't waiting at the end—it's already been handled. Life doesn't start when we're buried. It starts the moment we're heard."

I let it sit. No filler words. Just stillness.

"That wasn't the miracle of resurrection," I said quietly. "It was the miracle of being brought home. Long before ambulance sirens, my father's prayer, even before sunrise... she had already been received."

The room stayed quiet.

Then Bree's voice—sharper than usual. "How do you know it wasn't just coincidence? We all remember things that way when we want to."

I nodded. "That's fair."

Another voice—James, from the second row. "Or maybe it's not just about remembering. Maybe it's a sign. Like, you didn't pick that time. It picked you."

I didn't need them to believe. But they did. Or at least—they paused long enough to wonder.

A ripple moved across the class.

Lena, finally: "Or maybe it's both."

Wright shifted, sitting upright again. "All right," he said, his voice a shade more academic now. He cleared his throat, like someone trying to remind the room that class was still technically in session.

"Let's remember—we're exploring these ideas theologically, not just emotionally. Our goal is to understand the structures and implications of belief systems, not only personal experience."

But even as he spoke, his voice didn't quite hold its usual firmness.

I think he felt it too.

Some part of him wanted to dissect it. Another part wanted to sit in it.

XIV: Five Loaves and Two Fish

The room didn't breathe. It didn't shift. Even the air conditioner seemed to hush, as if some unseen line had been crossed. No one moved. The silence wasn't awkward—it was reverent. The kind that follows something sacred. Not necessarily holy—just real. Raw. Unearned.

Wright cleared his throat once. Not to interrupt, not to resume authority—just to remind his own lungs they were still working. But even then, he didn't speak.

It was Kai who broke the stillness first. Not loud, not flippant—just a low murmur as he stared at the edge of his notebook. "I still don't know if I buy all of this," he said. "But I get why people do."

For Kai, that was a confession. A man who mocked faith in week two was now admitting, aloud, that it wasn't stupid. Maybe it never was.

Wright turned his head slowly toward him. There was no smirk. No point to prove. Just the barest tilt of his chin. A nod—not of agreement, but of recognition. Like two people on opposite sides of a chasm had just seen the same bird fly overhead.

Diego leaned forward, no longer the amused skeptic. His arms rested on his knees, fingers tangled like he didn't trust his own hands. "It's weird," he said, quieter than usual. "I walked in here thinking I had a handle on what faith was. Like... blind optimism. Crutch stuff. But now I'm wondering if it's not about avoiding pain... maybe it's about going straight through it."

His voice cracked slightly at the end. He coughed once, glanced sideways, and then let the silence fill the rest. No joke to follow. No pivot.

Reid, still in the same position he'd held for most of the semester, lifted his gaze from the floor to meet mine. No words. Just a nod. Subtle, but weighty. The kind you offer when you don't know how to say *I'm sorry* or *thank you* or *me too.*

Lena was quiet longer than the others. Her hands rested on her notebook, unmoving. When she looked up, her eyes were clear—not with certainty, but with something softer. "I'm not ready to believe," she said. "But I'm done dismissing people who do."

Her voice didn't shake. It was even, firm, but it wasn't a wall anymore. It was a door, left slightly ajar.

The honesty in her voice pulled the breath from the room again. That one landed deep. I felt it press against my ribs.

Aisha's hands were folded in her lap. Her face was still, but her eyes shimmered. She hadn't spoken since the story had been shared. But now she whispered, not to be heard—just to be real. "That sounds like grace," she said.

Bree—who usually met everything with armor—didn't look at anyone. She stared at her desk, jaw tense, eyes glassy. She didn't speak. But something in her posture changed. Less defense. More presence. Something had cracked—not in defeat, but in honesty.

Even Gabe, who had offered snide remarks and hedged opinions for weeks, simply sat back, arms crossed, but no longer closed. "Yeah," he muttered under his breath, just loud enough for those nearby. "Maybe there's more to this than I thought."

Wright leaned back against his desk slowly, arms folded—not as a power stance, but as if holding something heavy in his chest. He looked at no one in particular. And then, finally, he spoke.

"Let's shift to Kierkegaard," he said, though the edge in his voice had softened—like someone quoting doctrine while nursing a bruise. "Faith as a leap. Not despite doubt, but because of it."

There was a subtle tremor in the way he said it. Like he was quoting someone else and trying to convince himself the words still held purely academic weight.

The shift wasn't dramatic. But it was real.

The class no longer felt like an arena.

It felt like a group of people—barely out of adolescence—trying to understand how to live in a world where grief and miracles share space. Where faith isn't an answer, but a language for what we can't explain.

No one looked at the clock.

Because for the first time all semester, time wasn't the point.

I leaned forward slightly, just enough for my voice to land clearly. "Professor," I said, "do you remember the story of the five loaves and two fish?"

Wright's gaze flicked toward me—not dismissive, but curious.

"Of course," he said cautiously.

I nodded once. "Then you know... sometimes the smallest offerings—barely enough for one person—feed thousands. And there's even more left over."

He didn't respond. But something in the room shifted again.

I let that hang. Then I added, quietly: "I've seen that happen. Not literally. Not with fish. But with grace."

And that's when I spoke again—not to steer the discussion, but because I couldn't not.

"I think... that leap he talks about? My dad made it."

I saw a flicker in Bree's eyes. The tiniest recoil—like maybe she understood how hard it was to keep speaking after all that.

"Over time, he became something unexpected. A shepherd. Not in title at first, but in presence. He started showing up for people in need.

Praying for folks who didn't even know they wanted prayer. He led without trying to lead. He became... safe."

The word lingered: *safe*. Not a word we usually associate with veterans—men who spent their youth hardening just to survive. But that's what he became.

I looked down for a second, fingers brushing the edge of my desk. Then back up.

"When Danette and I got engaged, we had a small ceremony planned. Just us, close friends, and family. Nothing extravagant. But I knew I wanted one thing above all else."

I looked around the room.

"I wanted my dad to marry us."

The silence didn't shift this time. It leaned in.

"Because he wasn't just my father anymore. He was a man who had walked through fire, and still offered warmth. He no longer looked for miracles—he made room for them in his own living."

I let the words sit for a moment. A long one. And then I added:

"By then, people in the community had started calling him 'Pastor John.' Not formally, not through any denomination—but because that's who he was to them. He'd sit with people in silence. Pray with them in waiting rooms. Hug like he meant it. And somehow, he helped people find a stillness they didn't know they needed."

Reid nodded again. Slightly. Like something in that resonated.

"I didn't ask him to officiate just because he was my dad," I continued. "I asked him because his life was the sermon I trusted most."

Wright didn't speak. Neither did anyone else.

Because sometimes, the most convincing theology is a life that's been lived honestly.

And sometimes, that's all the sermon we need.

After Mom's passing, after the quiet rearranged his soul, Dad didn't turn bitter. He didn't retreat into himself or silence or rage. He did what very few men of his generation ever do.

He opened.

Not all at once. Not loudly. But steadily—praying again, then aloud, then with others.

It began small—conversations with neighbors. A coffee shop moment with a friend. A pause in the grocery store when someone looked tired. "Can I pray with you?" he'd ask. Not in a pushy way. But with a sincerity that disarmed people.

They always said yes.

It wasn't long before folks started seeking *him* out. For advice. For prayer. For presence.

He never tried to become anything. But the Spirit nudged, and he listened.

Within a year, he was volunteering more at church. Greeting. Hosting a men's group. Stepping in when the pastor had a health scare. And then—slowly, but inevitably—he was asked to speak. Just once at first. A fill-in. A backup.

He wept afterward. "I never thought I'd do that," he told me.

But he kept doing it.

Because every time he spoke, someone stayed behind. Someone waited. Someone said, "You said what I couldn't put into words."

His faith didn't sound like doctrine. It sounded like breath. Like survival. Like memory turning to meaning.

Eventually, they asked him to lead the small church. Not full-time. Not formal. Just as a shepherd in the season of his life when he thought all shepherding was behind him.

He didn't seek the title.

But he carried it well.

He wasn't a preacher of thunder. He was a man of whispers and conviction. The kind who didn't tell you how to live, but made you want to live better.

So when Danette and I got engaged, there was never any doubt.

"Will you marry us?" I asked him one afternoon, our feet in the grass, his Bible in his lap.

He looked at me slowly. Tears rose before words. He didn't speak right away.

"I'd be honored," he said eventually. His voice was soft, but steady. "But only if I can say something about your mother."

"Of course."

He looked out across the yard then. The light was golden—the kind of golden that feels like memory already. "I still talk to her," he said. "Sometimes I ask if she can see what we're doing. Other times I just say thank you."

He smiled gently, the kind of smile that carries both ache and peace. "She loved Danette, you know. Really loved her. She said, 'She's strong. She'll keep you grounded, just like I tried to do for your dad.'"

That stayed with me.

That was the moment I asked him to officiate. It wasn't just about the ceremony—it was about bearing witness. Not to our love. But to his transformation. The man who once shouldered silence and pain like armor was now a pastor, a mentor, a vessel. His faith had grown—not from lightning strikes, but from steady rain. And this, he said, was the harvest.

We chose a quiet place for the ceremony. A chapel near the Snowshoe Lodge—a small theater-turned-sanctuary on the crest of Timms Hill, the highest point in Wisconsin. The main lodge, quaint and wood-framed, was called the Hill of Beans.

There were a few cabins tucked into the trees, a frozen lake stretching out beyond the pines. It wasn't grand, but it was perfect. Sacred, not because of architecture—but because of who would be standing at the front.

December 29th, 2017.

A snowstorm had swallowed the hill. The roads were slick, the air sharp, and everything outside was hushed under a blanket of white. But inside the chapel, warmth clung to every beam. The space—once filled with children's plays and small-town performances—had been transformed. Candles flickered. Music hummed low. And at the front stood my father.

Not just as a man. But as a living testimony.

He wore a dark suit and a humble expression. No notes. No rehearsed lines. Just a heart reshaped by loss and mended with grace. When he looked at Danette and me, his eyes shone—not just with pride, but with something weightier. Reverence.

He spoke simply—every word carrying the weight of years.

"I've known love," he said, voice steady. "Real love. The kind that wakes you up and holds you steady when the world starts spinning. The kind that forgives more than it remembers. That listens more than it speaks. That stays."

He paused, eyes distant. "Your mother gave me that. Every single day. She saw the man I was... and chose to love the man I could become. She never stopped believing in that man. Even when I didn't."

The room was silent, save for the soft sound of snow brushing against the windows.

"I still talk to her," he said again. "Not because she's gone. But because love doesn't disappear when breath does. It just moves. Becomes something quieter. But no less present."

Then he looked at us, his gaze steady. "My prayer for you," he said, "isn't just happiness. It's depth. Forgiveness. The kind of laughter that only comes after tears. The kind of faith that steadies you—not because it has all the answers, but because it reminds you that you're not alone."

XIV: Five Loaves and Two Fish

He took Danette's hand, then mine. "May your love be rooted in the kind of grace that held me through the darkest nights. The kind your mother gave freely. The kind I try to live out now—not perfectly, but faithfully."

It was the most sacred moment I've ever witnessed. And it wasn't about us. It was about him. About who he had become. About how he had let love—not bitterness—shape the rest of his story.

And in doing so, he gave the rest of us permission to believe we could do the same.

After the ceremony, we made our way to the Hill of Beans lodge, the snow coming down thicker now, blanketing the world in white. Inside, warmth wrapped around everything—wood-paneled walls glowing with firelight, voices soft with joy. Danette and I walked in still buzzing from the vows, her hand nestled in mine, her eyes brighter than I'd ever seen.

Dad sat quietly at a table near the window, watching. Just watching. The way a man does when he's lived long enough to know how fast moments pass. The kind of watching that sees layers—love, loss, the echoes of both.

We hadn't planned a big reception. Just a meal with those closest to us. The photographer we hired moved around the room like a breeze, catching smiles and clinks of glasses, nods from old friends. At one point, she came over and asked for the rings—wanted to take a few close-ups.

That's when Danette froze. She looked down at her hand and realized my mom's wedding ring—the one she'd worn that day—was gone.

Gone.

Time folded. The world shrank to the space where that ring used to sit—where memory and meaning had just slipped away.

My breath caught. And then I moved.

I didn't say anything. I just moved. Out of the lodge. Into the snow. Part of me knew it was irrational—but the louder part was already tearing through drifts, scanning every footprint, every shadow. The panic didn't wait. It hit all at once.

That ring wasn't just jewelry. It was mom. It was memory. It was the way we tried to bring her into that day—into that moment. And now... it was gone. I could already hear the regret forming in my mind, the self-reproach: *We should've had it resized. We should've checked.*

I bent low, hands shaking, eyes scanning the ground like a man looking for oxygen.

Inside, they were pulling up the last photo. A picture near the fenceline, overlooking the frozen lake. She was still wearing the ring then.

Danette's nephew relayed the news: "It has to be between that spot and the lodge."

I heard footsteps behind me—multiple. No one had waited. No one asked questions. They'd all come outside. Dad included. He didn't say much. Just pulled his coat tighter and stepped into the snow.

I didn't stop moving.

I was whispering now—not prayers exactly, but pleas. "Please. Please. Please let us find it..."

Then Danette's voice cut through the silence. Gentle, but sharp.

"Here."

We all turned. She was crouched by a tire track, one glove brushing aside the snow.

"There's a circle…" she said, her voice barely above the wind.

She dug slowly, carefully.

And then—she lifted her hand.

The ring was there.

Nestled in the snow—perfect, untouched—as if someone had set it there on purpose.

A tire had come close—maybe even grazed it—but instead of burying it, it had pressed it into a perfect outline. A mark. A halo.

Danette cradled the ring in her palm like it was fragile, sacred. Tears welled in her eyes.

"How is this even possible?" she whispered.

I didn't trust myself to speak. My hands were still trembling. I exhaled shakily, suddenly aware of the cold stinging my face.

And then, behind us, Dad's voice. Soft. Steady. Full of something that felt older than time.

"She wanted you to find it."

We turned.

He stood still. Snow settling on his shoulders. Hands tucked into his coat. Looking at the ring—not like it was a thing—but like it was a message.

I remembered something he told me, months after Mom passed. How he still talked to her sometimes. How he'd whisper into the wind, not knowing if she could hear him—but always feeling like she could.

In that moment, I knew exactly what he meant.

The ring wasn't the miracle.

The finding was.

The circle in the snow, the timing, the photo, the tire track. The way it hadn't been crushed. The way we knew where to look.

It wasn't dramatic. No fire from heaven—just snow, silence, and grace.

Just one small act of grace.

Like five loaves. Like two fish.

Like love that outlasts breath.

I didn't say anything at first.

The wedding memory clung like the last drift of snow on a windshield—stubborn, lingering, half-melted in the sun. I stayed seated, one hand still on my notebook, though I hadn't written anything in a while.

No one filled the silence. They were learning now—that some moments don't need bridges. Some stories just carry themselves.

XIV: Five Loaves and Two Fish

I cleared my throat. Not to command attention. Just to remind myself I was still here.

"We were supposed to honeymoon in Superior," I said quietly. "Northern Wisconsin. Danette found a cabin up near the lake. Secluded. Peaceful. We wanted something small."

There were nods. Familiarity. Everyone knew the need to retreat after something big.

"But then, just a few days before the wedding, one of Danette's friends called. Said she had a condo in Maui. Beachside. Said we could use it—for free. Her gift to us."

Lena's eyes widened. Bree blinked. Diego muttered something that sounded like "Wow."

"We didn't ask," I added. "We hadn't even hinted. But out of nowhere, we were handed this gift."

Aisha whispered, "That sounds like grace."

I smiled. "It felt like it. A moment where life offers something you didn't even think to hope for."

Wright, still perched on the edge of his desk, tapped his pen lightly against his notepad. "So... coincidence?"

"I mean, sure," I said. "If you want it to be. But to me? It felt aligned. Like it fit into something bigger. Because when I told my dad about it, that's when I found out..."

I hesitated for a breath. Then:

"...he'd been to Hawaii before. Once. On his way to Vietnam. But he never left the airport. They shuffled him from one gate to another, then onto a military plane. No island. No ocean. Just concrete. And then, war."

That stilled the room again. Not in pity—just gravity.

"It had been on his bucket list ever since," I said. "To go back. Not to erase what had happened, but to rewrite how it ended."

Kai looked up. "So the trip was never just about you?"

"No," I said. "That's what I mean by alignment. That unexpected gift—it didn't just bless us. It opened the door for something we didn't even realize we were holding."

Bree leaned forward slightly. "And did he go?"

"Not yet," I said softly. "But that moment—that conversation— planted the seed."

Professor Wright looked at me with a mixture of academic curiosity and something softer. "So this trip... it comes back around later? Ties in again?"

"It mattered more than we knew," I said. "But that's for later."

Reid tilted his head, eyes narrowed thoughtfully. "It sounds like the beginning of provision. Like... John six."

A few students glanced at him, surprised he'd made the reference.

"I think about that moment a lot," I said. "The disciples didn't see the whole picture when they handed Jesus five loaves and two fish. They didn't see the crowd, the leftovers, the miracle. They just saw the offering."

"And what was your offering?" Lena asked.

I paused.

"Our plans," I said. "We let them go. And something better came."

Aisha nodded. "Maybe that's what faith is."

The room stilled again—not for lack of words, but because the right words had already been spoken.

Gabe, quiet for most of the discussion, let out a soft exhale. "That wasn't chance," he said, mostly to himself. "People don't just give away Hawaiian condos."

Wright didn't jump in. His expression had shifted—less professorial, more human. He watched the room, then finally looked back at me.

"And your dad?" he asked.

I met his gaze. "He told us that day he'd always dreamed of going back. That Hawaii wasn't just a place to him—it was unfinished. Unredeemed. And maybe this... maybe this was his way of writing a new ending."

I remember, sometime after that, Danette and I were sitting on the porch—nothing dramatic, just a quiet evening. She looked at me and said, "Your dad has to go someday."

Not sad. Not even scared. Just... honest.

She looked at me for a long time, then said it—quietly, but without hesitation. "Your dad has to go someday."

Not sad. Not scared. Just... honest.

And then—after a beat—"But I hope he knows what he's leaving behind."

That stayed with me. Because it wasn't about loss—it was about legacy. About what lives on after breath runs out.

Diego leaned back in his chair, arms crossed, not skeptical—just thinking. "You think all of this is God?"

"I think God can use anything," I said. "Even a honeymoon. Even a ring. Even a missed layover from decades ago."

The clock on the wall ticked forward.

But no one looked.

"Or maybe," I said quietly, "it's just one small offering... and somehow, that was more than enough."

""And somehow, He still multiplies it."

XV: One Gift

The clock on the wall ticked louder than usual. The fluorescent lights buzzed faintly overhead, casting their usual sterile glow, but there was something in the air now—something less clinical.

The room was still in the gravity of the previous conversation, and no one reached for their phones. No one looked like they wanted to.

Wright stood by the board, tapping his marker, as though measuring every word.

Aisha rarely spoke, but when she did, people listened. "What about provision?" she asked—steady, clear. "Like… when you get something you didn't even know you needed?"

Wright turned to her. "You mean generosity?"

She nodded slowly. "Maybe. But not just that. I mean... when it feels like more than chance. When you're in a tight place, and something breaks open in just the right way. Doesn't that count?"

Wright's expression didn't change much, but he scratched his chin like he was buying time.

"Coincidence is powerful," he said finally. "Our minds are meaning machines. We're always connecting dots—even when they're random. It's called apophenia. We give significance to patterns because it helps us feel like there's order."

"But what if there is order?" Reid leaned forward, eyes sharp. "What if the dots really do connect?"

Professor Wright tilted his head slightly. "That's what faith says. But in here, we ask if the connection can be demonstrated. Verifiably."

Kai scoffed quietly. "That's a fancy way of saying you don't believe unless it prints out on a chart."

"No," Wright replied calmly. "It's a way of saying belief isn't invalid—but it's not the same as evidence. Faith may speak to truth, but scholarship asks how we know it's true."

"But some things," Lena said quietly, "can be true before they're proven. Or even if they never are."

That stopped him—not fully, but enough.

Professor Wright leaned back against the edge of the desk, crossing one ankle over the other. "There's a danger in assigning divine intention to every fortuitous outcome," he said. "You risk turning coincidence into theology."

"But isn't that what the Gospel of John does?" Bree asked, her voice more curious than confrontational for once. "Like… that moment in chapter two, when Jesus turns water into wine? No one expected it. It wasn't a healing. It wasn't life or death. But it mattered. It was a gift."

Several students nodded. Aisha sat straighter, clearly energized by the connection. Even Diego, who usually rolled his eyes at biblical references, looked intrigued.

"It mattered to the wedding host," Wright acknowledged. "But again—was it miraculous because of divine power? Or because of what it symbolized to the people who experienced it?"

Diego jumped in. "Or maybe both. Maybe it was symbolic *and* supernatural. Why does it have to be either-or?"

"Because 'miracle' implies suspension of natural law," Wright replied. "Something that cannot be explained by empirical evidence. But if it's just a timely event—like a friend showing up when you're struggling— that's not a miracle. That's support."

"But what if the support comes from someone who didn't even know you needed help?" Lena asked. "Or didn't even know why they were helping—but did it anyway?"

Wright raised an eyebrow. "Are you suggesting people are just vessels for divine will?"

"No," she said. "I'm saying… sometimes people are moved to do something, and only later do we realize why it mattered. Isn't that what faith is for? To fill in the meaning after the fact?"

There was a murmur of agreement from around the room.

XV: One Gift

"I think about John six," Reid said. "The loaves and fish. A kid offers his lunch—and it becomes enough. Nobody planned it. Nobody *expected* it. But that small thing made a way for something big."

Professor Wright nodded, almost respectfully. "It's a compelling image. But we're still talking in metaphors."

"Maybe," I said quietly, "but metaphors are how we name what we can't fully explain. Maybe that's why the Gospel tells stories—because sometimes the truth isn't in the logic. It's in the resonance."

The room didn't laugh. No one scoffed. If anything, a hush settled deeper across the rows, as if the idea had drawn out something unspoken in everyone.

Gabe, who rarely offered anything more than a nod, shifted forward. "My grandma used to say that God whispers through people who don't even know they're listening. That maybe the miracle isn't just what happens—but who it happens *through*."

Professor Wright tilted his head, measuring the comment. "That may be comforting," he said slowly, "but we must be careful not to retrofit spiritual narratives onto emotional events."

"Explaining it doesn't make it less divine," Aisha said. or "Naming it doesn't erase its sacredness."

"And isn't that what theology is?" Bree added. "The language we build to name what we believe?"

Wright folded his arms and smiled, not smug—genuinely interested. "You're turning this room more into a seminary than a university."

"We're turning it into a place that allows both," Reid said. "Faith *and* thought."

That stopped Wright for a beat.

It was the most civil resistance he'd faced in any of our sessions—and maybe the most honest. No one was trying to win anymore. They were trying to understand. And for the first time, it felt like the professor didn't have a ready answer.

He took off his glasses and polished them on the edge of his shirt, a thoughtful pause. "The Gospel of John is poetic," he said. "Its miracles are wrapped in metaphor, each with layers of theological intent. If you interpret them literally, you risk bypassing the symbolic power. If you interpret them only symbolically, you risk missing the reverence."

"Maybe reverence *is* the point," I said. "Not proving, not disproving—just recognizing that something mattered enough to remember."

The clock above us ticked. Somewhere, a heater rattled against the wall, the room still cold despite the rising warmth in our words.

Lena whispered, "What if the gift *is* the reminder?"

Wright didn't dismiss her. He just nodded—slowly.

Kai broke the silence again, this time quieter, more measured. "What if the miracle isn't the thing that happens? What if it's the timing? Like... the exact moment it happens. When it means the most."

"That's coincidence," Wright replied, almost automatically. But then he added, more softly, "Or at least that's how we classify it academically."

"Yeah, but we classify a lot of things academically that lose something in the translation," Kai said. "Like grief. Or hope. Or when someone forgives you and you don't know why."

Wright lifted his eyebrows—surprised, maybe, by how much had changed in just a few weeks. The discussion wasn't combative anymore. It wasn't even defensive. It had become communal.

"You're saying miracles are about meaning, not mechanics?" he asked.

"I'm saying they're both," Aisha said. "Because the Gospel of John doesn't separate those things. It's never just a sign—it's always a story. A person. A need."

"And a response," I said. "A provision. Unexpected. Unexplained."

"Unexplainable?" Wright asked.

"No," I replied. "But unignorable."

Bree jotted something quickly, then looked up. "You know that story in John where Jesus feeds the 5,000?" she said. "That wasn't just about food. It was about scarcity and sufficiency. About trusting that what we bring—small as it is—can matter."

Diego leaned forward, nodding. "Five loaves and two fish. It wasn't enough. But somehow, it was."

Professor Wright looked around the room. The temperature had shifted again—this time not just emotionally, but intellectually. He wasn't defending the curriculum anymore. He was… participating.

"And what about when there's no food at all?" he asked. "No fish. No loaves. What does belief do then?"

"It waits," I said. "Or it asks. Or maybe it just keeps walking."

"But is that still belief?" he pressed.

"That's when it *becomes* belief," Lena answered. "Not the kind you read about. The kind you live through."

No one had moved for a while. Backpacks remained zipped. Pens lay flat on desks. The normal end-of-class rustle hadn't begun.

Reid leaned back in his chair, arms crossed—but this time the posture wasn't closed. It was grounded. "We keep asking if these things are real. But I think the better question is: What do they reveal?"

"About what?" Wright asked.

"About us," he said.

Wright didn't respond right away. He looked at Reid, then out toward the window, where the early afternoon sun threw long bars of light across the linoleum floor.

"It's not wrong to need stories," Wright said finally. "But maybe their power isn't in their fact—but in their function. What they accomplish emotionally. Socially. Psychologically."

"You know," he added, shifting slightly, "we spend so much time trying to define things—to draw clean lines between what's spiritual and what's ordinary. But maybe... maybe that's the wrong project."

The class stayed silent, sensing the weight of the moment. Even Wright seemed to catch himself—like he'd said something truer than he'd meant to.

"Maybe the miracle," I said, "isn't just in what happens. It's in what it changes. In who it reaches. In who it leaves different than before."

Aisha looked over. "And maybe it's in how it echoes. Through time. Through people."

"Through us," Diego added.

Wright gave a quiet laugh—not dismissive, but thoughtful. "You're making it hard for me to grade you objectively, you know."

"You started it," Kai muttered, half-smiling. "All we did was follow the syllabus."

Everyone laughed. It was light, but not shallow. It broke the tension without cheapening the moment.

Wright leaned back against the edge of the desk again, arms folded now. "So here's the challenge," he said. "If these aren't coincidences—if they're not just luck or timing—then what are they? Are we really prepared to call them... divine?"

Bree hesitated, then nodded. "Yes. Because if we're not, then what's the point of studying any of this? If it's just language games and sociological trends, then none of it matters. But if it *is* something more..."

"Then we have to reckon with it," I said.

Reid nodded slowly. "Because if it's real, then it asks something of us."

Wright turned back toward the board, then paused. He didn't write anything this time. Just stood there, thoughtful.

Finally, he said, "Maybe it doesn't matter what we call it. Miracle. Coincidence. Gift. Maybe what matters is whether or not we let it change us."

The room was still.

And just then, the clock ticked loudly again—a signal, not a command.

But no one moved.

Wright finally straightened, uncrossing his arms as he reached for his pen again. "Belief has always tried to justify itself with stories," he said. "And the more powerful the story, the more convincing the faith. But correlation doesn't equal causation. Just because something feels miraculous doesn't mean it is."

He let the sentence hang there, like punctuation on the room's mood.

But this time, no one nodded.

I leaned forward slightly, hands folded on the desk. "Then let me tell you about a gift we didn't ask for. One that came at the exact moment we thought we'd lost the chance. You can call it coincidence if you want. But by the end of it, even I couldn't."

Bree tilted her head, curious. Aisha leaned forward, elbows on her knees.

Kai muttered under his breath, "Here we go..."

XV: One Gift

I looked up, just once, meeting Wright's eyes. "This wasn't a story I planned to tell. But since we're talking about unexpected gifts…"

It started with a photograph—Danette and me, barefoot in the sand, grinning like we'd just discovered something holy.

The wind had caught her hair mid-laugh, and I was looking at her like the world had stopped turning for a minute just to let us breathe.

The ocean behind us stretched out like glass, and the sun—low and gold—kissed everything in a way that made even shadows feel warm.

Maui had done that to us.

It rearranged things inside. What was supposed to be a quiet honeymoon in a cabin up north, something rustic and familiar, turned into a kind of unspoken renewal. A friend of Danette's, out of nowhere, had offered us her condo. Beachfront. No cost. "A gift," she said. "Something good to start your marriage with."

We didn't ask. Didn't even hint. Just received it—and something deeper took root—a sense that maybe grace sometimes wears a Hawaiian breeze and smells like saltwater and plumeria.

The island stayed with us even after we landed back home. In the slow way we unpacked. The unfamiliar silence of our apartment, now filled with tiny reminders—sand still clinging to our sandals, shells Danette had collected, a bottle of pineapple wine we kept forgetting to open. There was a kind of hush around us, like the trip had softened the edges of the world for a while.

We were still living in that hush when Danette looked at me from across the kitchen table. It was late afternoon, one of those moody Wisconsin days when the sky can't decide if it wants to storm or sleep. She was curled in my old college hoodie, her hands wrapped around a chipped mug, eyes distant in that way that always meant something was coming.

"We should take your dad," she said softly.

I looked up from the emails I hadn't been reading. "To Maui?"

She nodded. "It's on his bucket list, right? I remember you saying he saw Hawaii once—just from the airport. Headed to Vietnam."

The memory came back, slow and uninvited. A conversation from years ago. We were in the garage, fixing something on the car—or pretending to. He'd mentioned it almost offhand, like it was just logistics. "They dropped us in Honolulu. Never left the terminal. Straight to another gate. Then the jungle."

He hadn't said it bitterly. But there was something in his voice. A flattening. Like the story wanted to mean more, but he wouldn't let it.

"I don't think he's ever talked about going back," I said.

"Maybe not," Danette said. "But maybe he should."

Her eyes met mine across the table, and I could see the island still in them. Not the place, exactly, but the feeling. The stillness. The possibility. That maybe something good—something whole—could still come from a place once marked by waiting and war.

"He might not go," I said after a pause. "Even if we offered."

"Maybe," she said. "But maybe he needs to know the offer's real."

XV: One Gift

She reached across the table then, rested her fingers on mine. "I think it could be healing," she whispered. "For all of you."

And something shifted. Not a decision. Not yet. Just the first brush of purpose. Like a door had creaked open—not fully, but enough to feel the light pouring in.

And just like that, something started. Not a plan. Not yet. Just a possibility. A whisper of what could be—if we dared to believe he deserved something beautiful.

We dove into planning that night. The kitchen table became our war room. My laptop open to half a dozen tabs—flight aggregators, hotel reviews, military history sites. Danette had a yellow legal pad where she scribbled notes in the margins like she was charting coordinates for something sacred. It felt almost holy. Like maybe, if we could just piece it together right, offer him something that might not just touch the sand—but untangle something deep inside.

We mapped it all out. Where we'd stay. What he'd see. The old WWII hangars still standing. The memorials tucked away in quiet corners. The black sand beaches he never got to walk. The hikes we knew he probably wouldn't attempt, but we still circled them on the map—just in case. Every little detail felt like stitching a new chapter into his story, thread by thread.

It felt like a mission. A quiet one. Not dramatic or loud, but deliberate. A gift we were supposed to give. Not just to him—but maybe to ourselves too. Maybe to the version of him that came home from Vietnam and never asked for anything more.

But reality pressed in fast. Airline prices weren't kind. Hotels were worse. The numbers on the screen didn't lie. But the spreadsheets soon started to look like barriers instead of bridges. We budgeted and trimmed and cut things from our own expenses—nights out, new clothes, even gifts we'd planned to give others. Birthday plans became hand-written notes. Dinners became shared appetizers.

Our honeymoon glow slowly gave way to financial reality.

The math still didn't work.

We tried everything. Quiet conversations with family—soft pitches over coffee or during Sunday calls. "We're thinking of taking Dad to Hawaii," we'd say, as lightly as we could, as if it wasn't everything. Discreet texts to a few close friends, seeing if they might want to help. Not asking for the whole thing—just a little push. Something to close the gap.

But nothing came.

Not from lack of love. Just… timing. Everyone had their own obligations. Everyone was stretched. We understood—medical bills, kids in school, surprise repairs. Life, doing what it always does—showing up with hands already full.

At night, Danette and I would sit in the dark, a laptop glowing between us. "Maybe in a few months," she'd say. "Maybe we wait until next year." I'd nod, because what else could we do?

Every time we almost let go of the idea, something small would tug it back. A photo of the island. A memory Dad shared without realizing it. A glimpse of what could be.

We didn't talk about giving up. Not really. But the silence between us some nights said what words couldn't. That maybe this was too much. Too big. Too far from where we were.

Still, we held on. Barely.

Then came the GoFundMe.

At first, it felt like the logical next step. We had exhausted the quiet channels—family, friends, polite inquiries couched in conversations about weather and weekend plans. But nothing had come. Not because people didn't care, but because everyone was already giving somewhere—to medical bills, to tuition, to rent. We knew that. We honored that. But we also still believed this mattered.

On Friday night, I sat at the kitchen table and started writing. This wasn't just a plea—it was a tribute. A thank-you, decades overdue.

I spent two days carefully shaping the story, trying to capture the truth, not embellish it. I opened with a photo of Dad from the seventies—standing in the backyard in a navy windbreaker. Solid. Unyielding. A quiet pillar.

Then I told the story—how he'd passed through Hawaii once, en route to Vietnam. No sand. No ocean. Just concrete. Just war.

He never asked for anything. Never complained.

Now, all these years later, we just wanted to give him something back: a memory that didn't hurt.

I wrote it all.

Danette helped me edit.

We chose our words like bricks, laying them carefully, hoping they would build something strong enough to carry the weight of what we were asking.

And then we launched it.

GoFundMe. The fundraiser went live.

We shared it with friends on Facebook. Emailed it to our church group. Texted it to a few people we knew were good at spreading the word.

We watched the screen.

The first day, nothing.

The second day, a few "likes." A couple of hearts. Well-meaning emojis that felt more like polite nods than open hands.

A week passed. Still nothing.

Then, finally, a small donation. Ten dollars. Anonymous.

We stared at it like it might grow.

Danette checked the page every morning, her face a mix of hope and resignation. She never said it aloud, but I could see it in the way her finger hovered before refreshing the screen—as if willing the numbers to change.

I stopped checking altogether.

Every time I thought about that empty donation bar, it felt less like a lack of support and more like a verdict. Like the world was telling us: nice idea, but not urgent. Not necessary.

But it was, to us.

XV: One Gift

Every dollar we didn't raise echoed a question I hadn't known I was asking: Was my father's story worth honoring in this way? Had we made it too much about sentiment, too little about scope? Had we failed to make people feel what we felt?

Danette never blamed anyone. She just got quieter about it. She folded laundry while staring at her phone. Cooked dinner without humming like she usually did. Once, I caught her scrolling through our honeymoon photos—images of the Maui trip that had planted this whole dream—and then quietly closing the album without saying a word.

By the end of the second week, we stopped mentioning it. The link sat buried in our social feeds, untouched. The campaign had raised exactly ten dollars.

Just my ten dollars—meant to get the ball rolling.

The dream, it seemed, was over.

We both started looking for alternatives. Maybe a road trip instead. Simpler. Smaller. Less costly.

Maybe one day, we told ourselves. Just not this year.

The day we decided to cancel, it wasn't even a big moment. Just Tuesday. Rain on the windows. We were having leftover pasta.

And that's when the phone rang.

Aunt Janice.

Her name lit up my phone screen like a flare—familiar, unexpected. She didn't call often. Not because we weren't close, but because we both understood each other's silences. We came from the same stock—say less, mean more.

I answered. "Hey, Aunt Janice—"

She didn't respond right away... Then she said, "Jeff, it's your Aunt Janice. Are you still trying to raise money to get your dad to Hawaii?"

No pleasantries. No easing into it. Just the question. Direct. Unfiltered. Janice never wasted words.

I exhaled, rubbing the back of my neck. "Honestly? We're about to cancel. The fundraiser flopped, and we're tapped out." My voice cracked a little—not from sadness, but fatigue. It had been a long few weeks of pushing against doors that wouldn't open.

She didn't respond right away. Just breathed on the other end of the line. I imagined her pacing in her living room, cordless phone tucked under her chin, slippers shuffling against tile.

Then she said, soft but steady, "Well... I want to help. I love my brother. I want him to see Hawaii."

Her voice caught slightly, and I felt my chest tighten.

"I'm going to give fifteen hundred dollars," she said.

A pause.

Not like she was waiting for my reaction—but like she was trying to understand her own words.

Then again, firmer this time: "Yep. Fifteen hundred."

A small chuckle slipped out, almost sheepish. Like she'd surprised herself.

XV: One Gift

I blinked, completely still in the kitchen. Danette looked up from the table, sensing something had shifted. I put the phone on speaker.

"Janice…" I said slowly, "are you sure?"

She let out a breath—half sigh, half prayer. "I was going to give a thousand. That's what I had in mind."

She went quiet for a breath.

"But before I called, I asked God to help me say the right thing. I didn't know how to offer it. I just… I didn't want it to come out wrong."

Her voice warmed.

"And when I opened my mouth, fifteen hundred came out." She laughed—half incredulous, half obedient. "So that's what I'm doing."

Danette's breath caught. "That's exactly what we needed," she whispered, tears forming without falling.

I stared at the phone, dumbfounded. "Janice… that's exactly the amount. Down to the dollar."

There was a pause on the other end. Then she said it again, softly this time: "fifteen hundred. I don't know why. I just knew I was supposed to."

We met at Abbyland Truckstop off Hwy 29—comfort food, a window seat, semis rolling by.

Janice was already seated when we arrived. Danette and I slid into our chairs across from her, the air still carrying that mix of fryer grease and road trip stories.

Janice smiled, reached into her coat, and handed me the check. No buildup. No speech. Just a quiet gesture that carried the weight of something far more than numbers.

She passed it across the table like it was a receipt, not a miracle. Danette's eyes welled up—she didn't need to speak. We all felt it.

We ordered lunch and talked about everyday things—weather, work, the usual weekend shuffle.

But beneath it all, something else was happening.

That check wasn't just money.

It was permission. A green light. A bridge.

She didn't walk us through the gate, but she built it—and trusted us to cross.

We covered the rest—meals, tips, souvenirs, things Dad would never ask for but always quietly appreciated.

But Janice?

She gave us the part we couldn't reach alone.

She gave us the bridge.

And we walked across it together.

The room didn't leap to comment. It exhaled. That quiet kind of breath that only happens when people realize they've been holding something tight inside—doubt, hope, disbelief.

Reid broke the silence first. "That's… a miracle," he said. Not with awe, but with certainty.

Aisha nodded slowly, her hand still resting near her cross. "Not just the money. The timing. The way it lined up."

Bree leaned forward slightly. "Maybe grace doesn't always change the moment," she said quietly. "Maybe it just gives us a way across it."

Wright looked at her, but didn't respond. The silence was agreement.

Kai leaned back, arms behind his head. "You didn't force it. You just waited… and it came. That's not strategy. That's something else."

Even Diego, who usually met everything with a smirk or a scoff, didn't offer a punchline. He sat forward this time, elbows on his knees, staring at the floor. "You said you were about to cancel," he said. "Like… it was over."

"It was," I said. "And then it wasn't."

He nodded slowly, then looked up—eyes red-rimmed but dry. "Something like that happened to me once. Not money—just…" He shook his head, searching for words. "It's like… you're standing at the edge, and something pulls you back."

It caught Bree off guard. She turned toward him, brows raised. Not in judgment—more like surprise. Like maybe she'd never seen him like this before.

Diego noticed, too. "Yeah, don't look so shocked," he said, softer than usual. "Even sarcasm has a breaking point."

Bree's pen had stilled. She glanced down at her notebook, where she'd drawn small, tight circles in the margin—nervous movement without direction. "She didn't even plan to say fifteen hundred," she murmured. "That's the part that gets me." Her voice cracked slightly on *plan*, and she blinked like it surprised her.

She looked up, hesitated, then said, "I had a friend once. We stopped talking after she got religious. I thought she was... delusional. She told me God had answered a prayer and saved her dad's life. I told her it was luck. Medical timing. Nothing more." Bree's eyes didn't quite meet anyone else's now. "I told myself it was for her sake—to keep her grounded. But if I'm honest, I think it was for mine."

The silence in the room grew denser, expectant.

"I think I've spent years making peace with the idea that things just... happen. That there's no hand behind it. No reason. Just chaos, and recovery, and whatever you build from the rubble." She exhaled slowly. "It was easier than believing someone was watching... and let it happen anyway."

Her words didn't land with a thud—they hovered. Heavy. Honest.

Diego glanced over at her, but didn't speak. No one did. Because everyone heard what she hadn't said. Her voice was composed, but her fingers twisted the edge of her sleeve—like she needed something to hold onto.

"And maybe," she said, "I was afraid grace could still find people. Because if it could find them..." Her sentence trailed off. She looked away, blinking hard, then shook her head lightly. "Forget it. It doesn't matter."

"It does," Aisha said gently. "Maybe more than you think."

Bree didn't reply. But she didn't argue either.

And that—not the silence, but the lack of resistance—felt like the crack.

Professor Wright shifted in his chair, a reflex born of discomfort. He opened his mouth, but whatever retort he had caught in his throat. He closed it again.

Because once you see something as a miracle, it's hard to file it back under 'coincidence.'

I gave them space to process it. Then, quietly, I added, "That was the trip we took… right as this class started."

That got their attention.

"I missed a week in February—February sixteenth to the twenty-fourth, to be exact."

A few brows furrowed, some checked phones or notes, trying to remember if they'd noticed.

"You probably didn't notice," I said. Not bitter. Just honest. "Back then, I was just another seat in the room. Easy to miss."

Bree looked straight at me now. "Not anymore," she said, without blinking.

I looked down at my notebook for a second, then back at them.

"We booked that week because the tickets were cheaper. And someone had canceled last-minute on an Airbnb right next to the Maui Ocean Center—Maalaea Kai Condominiums. Right on the beach."

Diego let out a slow breath. "I don't believe in fate," he said. "But I think I might believe in… timing."

Lena smiled faintly. "Sounds like grace doesn't care what week it is."

I nodded.

Wright finally exhaled. "Maybe grace doesn't follow logic. Maybe it just shows up."

I didn't answer out loud. But in my chest, something settled.

Maybe grace *had* just shown up.

XVI: Turning Tables

The silence after Bree's last words hadn't just settled—it had claimed the room. Even the fluorescent hum seemed subdued—as if the room knew not to intrude.

Professor Wright leaned slightly forward, elbows on his knees, eyes narrowed—not in skepticism, but in calculation. He wasn't finished—not by a mile.

"Coincidences…" he finally said, his voice deliberately even, "are often mistaken for miracles because we prefer comfort over ambiguity. It's a human impulse—to ascribe purpose where there may be none."

A few students shifted in their seats, not from disagreement, but from the discomfort of someone turning the lights on too fast after a long dream.

Reid leaned forward, his voice lower now. "What's more comforting, a world where something meaningful happens out of nowhere, or a world where nothing is ever more than random noise?"

Professor Wright tilted his head. "That depends, on whether you value truth more than narrative."

Aisha frowned. "Are they mutually exclusive?"

Wright let that question hang for a moment. "Not always," he conceded. "But often."

He stood and took a few steps toward the board, as if needing motion to stabilize his thoughts. "We like stories," he said. "We're hardwired for them. They give structure to memory, purpose to pain. That makes them meaning. Not necessarily truth."

He turned, marker in hand but unused. "It's not wrong to need stories," he continued. "But maybe their power isn't in their fact—but in their function. What they accomplish emotionally. Socially. Psychologically."

"I've read papers," Wright went on, "where people found spiritual meaning in everything from lottery wins to missed buses. They drew significance from things that, on a statistical level, were unremarkable. But the meaning they felt? That was real. For them."

"And maybe that's what matters," Aisha said.

Professor Wright nodded, "Perhaps. But we still have to ask—what is a miracle, if everything meaningful becomes one? Doesn't that strip the word of its weight?"

The question hung there. Instead, they looked at me.

I didn't expect it. But when the moment came, I didn't flinch.

I cleared my throat. "I told you we went to Maui," I said. "What I didn't mention was that we didn't start there."

Wright turned slightly, curious. "Where did you start?"

"Oahu," I said. "Thirteen hours. A direct flight. Minneapolis to Honolulu."

"Long trip," Diego murmured.

"Longer if you can't sleep," I said. "My dad didn't shut his eyes once."

Reid raised a brow. "Jet lag?"

"No," I said. "Anticipation."

The class was quiet again—not with disbelief, but with the lean-in kind. The kind that says, keep going.

"My dad had landed in Honolulu once before," I continued. "On the way to Vietnam. But he never left the airport. Never touched the sand. Never saw the ocean. Just one gate to the next, then gone. War."

That word didn't echo. It dropped.

"But this time," I said, "he wasn't on his way to war. He was on his way to rest."

Bree looked down, pen tapping lightly against her desk.

"I watched him sit there on the flight," I said, "staring out the window into the dark, like he was afraid to blink. Afraid the dream might reset."

"You could see it?" Lena asked softly.

I nodded. "He didn't say much. But his hands wouldn't sit still. He kept shifting. Tapping his fingers on the armrest. Not nervous—just... lit up inside. And trying not to show it."

There was a pause before I added, "I think that was the beginning of it. Not the miracle. Not yet. Just the beginning of the letting in. The idea that maybe this was really happening. That maybe he didn't have to carry it all anymore."

Professor Wright leaned against the desk again, arms crossed now—not in authority, but in thought.

"And when we landed," I said, "he didn't smile. Not at first. He just stood still on the jet bridge, like he needed a minute to trust the ground."

Reid leaned in. "That sounds like church," he said with a faint smile.

I gave a half-smile. "It was."

"Was he different?" Bree asked. "After you landed?"

"He was... lighter," I said. "Not suddenly. Not completely. But it was like someone had cracked open a window inside him. And for the first time in a long time, he was letting air in."

Kai exhaled through his nose. "That'll do it. Islands do that."

"Yeah," I said. "But it wasn't the island, not yet."

"Then what?" Aisha asked.

I paused.

"There was this moment," I said, my voice steady but lower now. "We spent the morning at Pearl Harbor. Did everything—Arizona Memorial, the aviation museum, and the Missouri. Dad didn't talk much. Just observed. Took it all in like he was scanning the past for something only he could see."

Wright studied me. "Was he... moved?"

I nodded. "Yeah. Quietly. But deeply. You could see it in the way he carried himself. Like he was letting the place speak to him."

"And what did it say?" Lena asked.

"Not words. But something like acknowledgment," I said. "Like the ground itself had a memory—and for once, he felt seen by it."

I didn't expect to say that. But once I did, it felt true.

And it was only the beginning.

We arrived at Pearl Harbor under a sky that seemed to hold its breath. The clouds hung low, not heavy, but waiting—like they knew the ground below was sacred and didn't want to interrupt.

The whole place felt designed to keep you aware of time—not just minutes, but the kind that stretches backward into memory and forward into meaning.

The air smelled like salt and steel, old paint and water that's seen too much. It wrapped around us as we stepped through the gates—soft, but not gentle. You could feel the weight of history pressing in from every side.

Dad wore his Vietnam Veteran hat, like always. No ceremony to it. Just part of him—sun-faded, sweat-ringed, edges curled from years of wear. He wore it to the grocery store. To church. Around the house. But here, it looked different. Not because it changed—but because it was seen.

People noticed. Nods from strangers. Quiet acknowledgments passed without words. The kind of recognition that only comes from those who know what it means to carry something for decades and still stand up straight.

We walked the grounds slowly, pulled toward something unspoken. Dad kept a steady pace. Not rushed. Just forward. Like he was being drawn toward something he hadn't named but knew he needed to find.

As we approached the USS Missouri, that's when it happened.

One of the veteran volunteers—gray-haired, sturdy, eyes like he could still see things that had happened decades ago—looked up from his post and caught sight of Dad. "You served?" he called out.

Dad didn't say anything right away. Just gave a small nod. That was enough.

The man waved him over. "Come with me."

There was no fanfare. No explanation. Just a clear invitation.

Danette and I instinctively stepped back. There was no invitation for us—just for him. And that was okay. We knew this was his moment. A moment that didn't require witnesses.

The volunteer didn't take him along the normal route. He didn't hand him a brochure or walk him through the public walkway. Instead, he opened a side gate, ducked under a chain, and with a simple gesture, led Dad into the heart of the ship.

We watched them disappear inside, then found a bench near the rail. The harbor stretched out in front of us—wide, blue, and silent. The water glinted under the sun like it had secrets, like it was remembering.

We didn't say much. A few comments here and there. But mostly we sat in quiet. It felt sacred. Like a space we weren't meant to fill with noise.

Dad was gone for over an hour.

We later found out that the volunteer took him through parts of the ship most people never saw. The underbelly. Engineering. Officers' quarters. Comms rooms. Spaces sealed off from the standard tours. Rooms that still held the echo of orders given and lives changed.

They didn't just tour. They talked. About service. About the strange weight of coming home. About ships and silence and the years that stretch between what you survive and what you remember.

When Dad came back into view, he walked slower—not from exhaustion, but from something deeper.

Reverence, maybe.

Or resolution.

He didn't speak right away. Just came up to us, nodded once, and looked out at the harbor.

But something in him had shifted.

His shoulders, usually drawn slightly in from years of carrying invisible weight, were looser now. His posture was taller. His eyes didn't dart—they rested. Looked. Took in. They had a kind of brightness to them that I hadn't seen in a long time.

Danette leaned close and whispered, "He looks taller."

I watched him walk. The same man—but something about his shadow felt... unburdened.

We moved through Pearl Harbor with quiet purpose, each stop shaping the day in its own way. The Arizona Memorial left us somber—its stories heavy with sacrifice. The battleship Missouri echoed with resolve, its corridors thick with history. Slowly, these moments were building toward something—something we couldn't yet name.

Then, almost naturally, we reached the Pacific Aviation Museum. It wasn't joy. Not yet. But it was something close. A beginning. Like something inside Dad had finally let go—something clenched for decades now breathing again.

The museum had a different rhythm than the rest of Pearl Harbor. Where the Arizona was reverent and the Missouri monumental, this place felt like memory in motion—restored planes frozen mid-flight, placards of dates and missions, engines gleaming under soft spotlights. It smelled of oil, dust, and old ambition.

Dad moved slowly, but not from fatigue. His steps were deliberate. At every exhibit, he paused—not just to read, but to linger. He touched the edge of a propeller, the nose of a Mustang, the frame of a display board like each might respond. Danette and I hung back, giving him space. He wasn't just seeing planes. He was seeing moments. Eras. Maybe people he once knew. Maybe people he couldn't forget.

Then came the commotion.

We were near the section with helicopters when we heard it.

Then, suddenly...

"Carl! Carl, Carl, Carl!"

A young museum staffer—early twenties, at most—was hustling toward us. He looked panicked, his lanyard flapping against his chest as he jogged. At first, we thought he must be calling for a supervisor. Maybe something had gone wrong. An alarm? A spill? A guest in trouble?

"Carl!" he called again, eyes locked on my dad.

Dad turned slowly, confused. He didn't respond at first—why would he? His name wasn't Carl. But the guy kept coming, urgency in every step.

Then Dad stopped. Turned to face him fully.

The young man pulled up short, skidding a little on the polished floor, eyes wide.

"You're not Carl," he said.

It was such a deadpan delivery, so abruptly disappointed, that for a second none of us knew how to react.

Dad looked him square in the eyes and, with the gravity of a war hero accepting one last mission, said, "I can be Carl if you need me to be Carl."

XVI: Turning Tables

Then, as if he'd just cracked the greatest joke of his life, he chuckled—a deep, satisfied sound that seemed to come from somewhere ancient.

Danette snorted so hard she startled a nearby docent. I doubled over, wheezing. Even the young man, mid-sprint, glanced back with a puzzled grin before disappearing into the next hangar.

The guy, flustered but good-humored, offered a quick "Sorry! I really gotta find Carl," and jogged off again in another direction, his sneakers squeaking.

We never found out who Carl was. Or what the emergency was. Or if there was one at all. But it didn't matter. Because from that moment on, Dad wasn't "John" anymore.

He was Carl.

Later, in the gift shop, Danette found a little keychain with the name "Carl" engraved in bold white letters. She bought it without a word and handed it to him on the sidewalk outside.

He didn't say much—just slipped it into his pocket with a grin. But after that, whenever we'd ask a question—where do you want to eat, are you tired, need a break?—he'd reply, deadpan, "Ask Carl."

The transformation wasn't dramatic. He didn't start dancing in the streets or suddenly become extroverted. But the shift was unmistakable.

He smiled more.

He walked taller.

He joked with strangers.

That night, over dinner on the balcony of our condo in Maui, he lifted a glass of pineapple wine, looked out over the dark ocean, "Carl's doing alright," he said, raising his glass with a twinkle in his eye.

And in that laugh, in that moment, I saw the man who'd been buried under decades of weight finally come up for air.

Dinner that night was takeout—nothing fancy. Teriyaki plates from a little roadside grill with sticky rice and tangy slaw, eaten out of Styrofoam containers on the lanai of our hotel room.

The sky had darkened to deep indigo, the kind that feels heavier than night, like the world is wrapped in velvet. A few stars blinked through, and down below, the harbor lights cast gold reflections that wobbled across the surface of the water like they weren't quite sure they belonged.

Dad was quiet, but it wasn't the kind of quiet we were used to. Not the brooding or withdrawn silence he wore so often at home. This was... presence. Not silence to hide in, but space to breathe. Stillness, not avoidance.

Danette handed him a fork. "Don't let it get cold."

He smiled faintly. "Tastes better outside anyway."

We ate without much talk. Just the sound of plastic forks, the low hum of distant cars, and waves slapping gently against the seawall.

Halfway through his meal, Dad looked out across the harbor and said, "I needed this." He didn't look at us when he said it. Didn't say more. Just those three words.

But they hit like gospel.

It wasn't just the place. It was the culmination—of everything. The Pearl Harbor visit. The laughter at the museum. The silence of the memorial. The gift that made the whole thing possible. It all folded together into something that didn't need unpacking.

That night, we slept with the windows open. The air was soft and full of salt, and even the birds seemed to speak in whispers. Dad snored a little in the next room. A content kind of snore.

The next morning, February 17th, we boarded a short flight to Maui. It was only about thirty minutes in the air, but it felt like we were crossing a border—like we were leaving behind the ghosts of history and stepping into something more personal. Something alive.

Dad sat by the window, eyes locked on the ocean below. His hands rested lightly on the armrests, no white-knuckled grip, no fidgeting. Just stillness. Peace.

When we landed, the air felt warmer, rounder. Maui was greener than Oahu—less about monuments, more about moments. As we drove to the condo, Dad kept the window cracked, letting the breeze touch his face.

The Maalaea Kai Condominiums were modest, but perfect. Right on the edge of the bay, close enough that the crash of the waves was a constant, soothing presence. Palm trees swayed like metronomes. The water sparkled like it wanted to be watched.

We checked in, hauled our bags upstairs, and opened the sliding doors to the lanai.

Dad stepped outside first. Didn't say anything—just stood there, hands on the railing, breathing like someone who finally remembered how.

That afternoon, we walked down to the beach. It was quiet, sparsely populated. A few sunbathers. A couple playing catch with their dog. And just beyond the break, whales. Breaching, diving, exhaling mist into the air like punctuation marks.

"Whales," Dad said softly. "Incredible."

He sat down in the sand, cross-legged, like a child watching fireworks. Danette and I sat nearby, but we didn't speak. We just watched him—watched the stillness, the way his face softened with every breach.

Then came the turtles. Two of them, massive and slow, crawling up onto the shore like they had no fear of the humans nearby. Dad turned to us, smiling. "Even the turtles take a vacation," he said.

We laughed.

We stayed there for hours, watching the light shift from gold to amber to that deep blue that always comes before true darkness. The air cooled, the sand held its warmth. Dad didn't move much. Just sat, watching, taking it in like he was afraid to blink.

Later, back at the condo, we sat on the lanai again. No meals this time. Just water and the sound of waves.

"You know," Dad said, his voice low, "I thought I came here to see something," he said. "To cross it off the list."

He paused.

"But I think… I came here to be seen."

We didn't interrupt.

XVI: Turning Tables

"I've spent years…" He trailed off, then smiled gently. "Never mind. I don't need to explain it. I just know this—right now, right here? I needed this. More than I thought."

His words lingered in the quiet. Sometimes it takes thousands of miles to let go of what you never knew you'd been carrying all along.

XVII: The Sign

The condo was quiet, the kind of quiet that usually brought sleep easy. The waves whispered against the shore like they had every night since they'd arrived—soft, rhythmic, eternal. But sleep didn't come. Not for Dad.

He had tried. He really had. Laid flat on the mattress, eyes closed, breathing steady. But even with the windows open and the night air cool on his skin, there was no drifting off. His body was still. His mind, anything but.

He turned on his side. Stared at the ceiling. Then the wall. And finally, the shadow of the fan, barely moving in the dark.

Beside him on the nightstand sat his wallet, the VA card still tucked inside, and a paperback he hadn't touched since the flight. His hat hung from the back of a chair, its sun-bleached brim slightly curved from habit. He reached for it, fingers curling around the crown like muscle memory.

He slipped it on.

It wasn't discomfort that kept him up. Not anxiety either. It was something quieter. More persistent. A hum, deep inside, like unfinished business. Like a phone vibrating with a call you couldn't ignore.

So, he got up.

He moved slowly, not wanting to wake anyone. The floor creaked under his heel just once. He paused. No one stirred. He crossed the living room and slid open the patio door. The air outside was salt-rich, still warm from the afternoon sun but now laced with a midnight coolness. Somewhere in the distance, a palm frond rustled, but otherwise, it was still.

Dad stepped outside.

The moon was high, casting a wide silver path over the water. The kind of light that made the ocean look like it was alive—its ripples like breath, its shimmer like thought. He watched it for a minute from the lanai, then decided he needed to be closer.

Cool sand gave under his steps, and the wind moved only enough to whisper—not push. He walked along the edge of the water where the tide slid in with a hush and slipped back again without argument. There were no footsteps on the beach but his. No one else awake, or so it seemed.

He kept moving.

Up above, stars held their ground. The moon, full and wide, painted everything in silver. Even the waves sparkled. They breached occasionally out beyond the reef—whales, still at play, their heavy bodies emerging in arcs before disappearing again into the black.

Dad stopped walking.

He stood there, eyes fixed on the horizon. Somewhere behind it was Oahu. Behind that, the mainland. Behind that, Vietnam. And behind all of that—memories too heavy to name.

He pulled his jacket tighter.

He told me later—it wasn't just a sleepless night. It was a summoning.

Something in the air. Something in the light. Something he couldn't name but couldn't ignore. He wasn't out here for peace. He already had that. This was something else.

The condo had settled into stillness. The kind that only comes after the day has given all it has and the night stretches wide and still, like it's holding something sacred.

Danette had gone to bed hours earlier. I could hear her even breathing through the thin walls.

But Dad... Dad hadn't even tried to sleep.

He sat on the lanai for a long time after we said goodnight, just staring out over the bay. He was motionless for the most part, one arm hooked over the back of the patio chair, the other resting lightly on his knee. Every so often, the silhouette of his head would tilt—left, right, then center again. Not restless. Just present.

Eventually, he stood.

XVII: The Sign

I heard the sliding door hush open, the creak of the screen, then the soft fall of his footsteps down the wooden stairs that led to the narrow path beside the water. I slipped out of bed and peered through the curtains, just enough to see his figure heading toward the beach.

I wasn't sure what pulled him out there. But something had.

He didn't take a flashlight. Didn't need one. The moon was nearly full, casting the shoreline in a cool silver glow. It painted the sand in long white ribbons and turned the slow roll of the waves into something dreamlike—like the ocean had agreed to calm itself just for him.

He walked barefoot, shoes in hand, his feet sinking slightly into the sand with every step. The tide had pulled back just enough to reveal smooth, wet sand, still warm from the day's sun. A breeze moved gently through the palms, rustling fronds like old paper turning in a book.

Out on the water, the whales were still active—occasional breaches broke the surface with slow, powerful grace. You could hear the distant splash, the pause, the exhale. Even from shore, it felt close.

Dad stopped for a long moment near the waterline, the hem of his jeans darkening slightly where the tide kissed the fabric. He stood with his arms crossed over his chest, shoulders hunched just a bit forward—not in tension, but in thought. Like he was holding something close inside. Something not yet ready to be released.

The moonlight bounced off the ocean in shifting patterns. It looked like the water was covered in moving glass—reflective, alive. Dad stared at it, unmoving, like he was trying to understand something it was trying to say. Maybe he was.

The whole beach was quiet. The kind of quiet that doesn't ask anything of you. The kind that gives more than it takes.

He walked slowly down the curve of the shore, each step measured. He wasn't in a hurry. There was no place he needed to be—except here.

That night, something in the world felt aligned. Like this beach, this moonlight, these whales... like they weren't just background. They were part of something else. A moment with edges. A memory in the making.

And Dad was exactly where he was meant to be.

Further down the beach, a shape came into view.

At first, Dad thought it might've been driftwood or a cluster of rocks—something left behind by the tide. But as he walked closer, the shape took on form. Shoulders. Arms. A man.

The figure was sitting in the sand, knees drawn up, head bowed so low it looked like he was trying to fold himself out of the world. His hands were clasped around his shins, knuckles pale, as if he were holding himself together by force.

Dad slowed his steps. Not cautious—just respectful.

The man didn't move.

Only when Dad was about twenty feet away did the figure glance up. The moonlight caught his face—lined, weathered, probably in his sixties. Eyes glassy. Not from tears exactly, but from something heavier.

Then the man's gaze dropped to the cigarette between Dad's fingers.

"You got another one of those?" he asked, voice low and raw.

XVII: The Sign

Dad didn't hesitate. He reached into the front pocket of his jeans, pulled out a soft pack of Marlboros, and tapped it gently against his palm. One cigarette slid free. He held it out.

The man took it with quiet gratitude.

Dad struck his lighter, leaned forward, and cupped the flame against the wind. The man bent into it, inhaled, and let the first drag out like it had been holding his lungs hostage.

They stood there a moment—two silhouettes in the moonlight, smoke curling upward in lazy spirals.

No questions.

No introductions.

Just one man recognizing the storm inside another... and offering a match.

"Thanks," the man said, exhaling slowly. "Couldn't sleep either?"

Dad shook his head. "Nope. Sometimes the past doesn't let you rest."

The man glanced sideways, eyes catching the worn fabric of Dad's ever-present Vietnam Veteran hat. "What year?" he asked, his voice quiet, but heavy.

Dad exhaled slowly. "Sixty-six to sixty-seven. First Infantry Division. Big Red One."

The man let out a long, low whistle and nodded. "Yeah... I was in-country then too. Sixty-six to early sixty-eight. Graves Registration detail. We worked mostly out of Tan Son Nhut but got pulled everywhere—

whenever the numbers got bad. I was in Tay Ninh during Junction City. Spent more time in the Iron Triangle than I ever wanted. Some of those recoveries..." He paused, jaw tightening. "We pulled three dozen out of a tunnel complex during Cedar Falls. Took us two days. The heat down there—Jesus. Felt like the walls were sweating blood."

Dad's head tilted slightly, eyes narrowing in recognition—not just of the place, but of the experience. There was a shared weight there. This man knew the terrain—not just physically, but emotionally. He'd carried the same ghosts.

"Cedar Falls," Dad said finally, voice low. "That was a mean one. We went in right before you. Spent a week clearing those tunnels. They were so deep, so dark... hadn't seen daylight since the French were there."

The man turned his full body toward Dad now, the cigarette between his fingers forgotten. "You were a grunt?"

Dad nodded once. "Big Red One. Iron Triangle. Junction City right after. We walked into ambushes so thick, I stopped counting the dead. Just... kept moving."

The man looked away, his gaze fixed on the dark horizon. "We'd get the call, head out, and start collecting. Sometimes, they were still warm. Other times... the heat and humidity had already taken their toll. The smell... it stays with you. Gets into your skin."

He paused, his hands trembling slightly. "We cataloged everything. Dog tags, letters, photos. Wedding rings, little trinkets. Cleaned them up as best we could before sending them off. It felt invasive—like we were meddling in their last moments."

XVII: The Sign

Dad listened, the weight of the man's words settling heavily between them.

"You had a mission. You fought back. I just picked up the pieces."

Dad's voice was low, steady. "And gave those pieces back to the people who needed them. That matters. More than you'll ever know."

He paused, letting the weight of that truth settle between them. The man's eyes dropped, his shoulders tightening like he was trying to shrink into himself, but Dad wasn't finished.

"You carried us," he said. "When we were too broken to carry ourselves. You think that's nothing? It's everything."

The man blinked hard, his mouth tight, words caught somewhere in his throat.

Dad took another drag from his cigarette, the ember flaring briefly in the dark. "Don't tell me my hell was hotter than yours," he said softly. "We all walked through the fire. Just different flames."

The man glanced over, eyes narrow. "Iron Triangle... you see what was underneath that jungle?"

Dad's lips tightened. "Tunnels. Miles of them. Rooms. Weapons caches. Hospitals. They called it 'Black Echo'—the silence down there. You'd crawl in, flashlight barely cutting through, not knowing if the next bend had a tripwire, a spider hole, or an entire company waiting."

The man winced. "Jesus."

"Sometimes it felt like we weren't fighting people," Dad said. "Just shadows that never ran out. You'd think you cleared a section and the next day they'd be back like nothing happened. Like the jungle itself was fighting us."

The man stared out at the water. "That's why they sent you guys in first. Big Red One softened the ground before we ever showed up."

Dad nodded. "Softened. That's a funny word for it."

They sat in silence, the waves breaking rhythmically like distant artillery. Then Dad said quietly, "You know, I used to hate you guys."

The man blinked, startled. "Us?"

"Not you personally. But Graves Registration. It meant someone didn't make it. Meant another name in a bag. Another hole in the squad. I saw you coming and I knew I'd lost a brother."

The man nodded slowly, understanding. "And I used to envy you."

"You know," Dad began, "there's a verse in the Bible about soldiers. It talks about how there's no greater love than to lay down one's life for one's friends. We all did that in our own ways."

The man's gaze drifted toward the horizon, where the moonlight shimmered on the restless waves. "Maybe," he murmured. "But sometimes I feel like I didn't do enough. Like I was just a shadow on the edges of the war, watching everything fall apart."

Dad turned to him, his own face etched with the memories of battles he could never quite leave behind. "I used to think like that, too. For years after I came home, I carried the weight of every man I couldn't save, every brother I saw fall. It nearly crushed me."

The man glanced at him, his eyes weary yet searching. "What changed?"

Dad exhaled deeply, the smoke curling upward into the night air. "Faith. And time. For years, I fought against everything—tried to bury myself in work, in distractions, even in anger. But it wasn't until I hit rock bottom that I realized I couldn't carry it all on my own." He paused, looking down at the cigarette in his hand. "That's when I started praying. Not the kind of prayers you say in church because you're supposed to—but the raw ones. The ones where you yell at God or beg for answers."

The man tilted his head slightly, his expression a mix of curiosity and skepticism. "Did it actually help?"

Dad nodded slowly, his gaze steady. "It did. It didn't happen overnight, but piece by piece, I found peace. I realized that I wasn't meant to carry the weight alone. God stepped in, and I started seeing things differently—not just the war, but life itself."

The man let out a heavy sigh, his shoulders slumping as if the burden he carried had doubled. "I don't think I'm strong enough for that."

"You don't have to be," Dad replied gently. "That's the point. We're all weak in our own ways—broken by the things we've seen and done. But that's why grace matters. It's not about earning it or proving yourself. It's about accepting that you're not alone in this. There's a plan for you, even if you can't see it right now."

The man's lip quivered, and he looked away, his voice barely audible. "I don't know if I believe in plans anymore. My wife—she was my everything. And now she's gone. My son won't talk to me. I walk around every day feeling like a ghost."

Dad leaned forward, his voice steady yet filled with compassion. "I won't pretend to know your pain. But I do know this: You're still here for a reason. Sometimes it's hard to see, but every breath you take, every step you make—it matters. It matters to someone. And it matters to God."

The man stared at him, tears streaming down his face as the words found their way into the cracks of his heart. "I don't even know how to start."

Dad pulled out the card from his wallet again, holding it up. "You start by taking one step. Call the number. Talk to someone who can help. And then, when you're ready, maybe try talking to God. Just say what's on your mind—no filter, no pretense. He's big enough to handle it."

The man looked down at the card in his hand, his shoulders shaking as he silently wept. Dad placed a comforting hand on his shoulder, grounding him in the moment. They sat like that for a long time, the sound of the waves washing over them like a balm.

After a while, the man spoke again, his voice tentative yet resolute. "I think I'll call. And maybe... maybe I'll try praying."

Dad nodded slowly, a soft smile spreading across his face—the kind that comes not from happiness, but from witnessing something sacred unfold. Then, out of nowhere, he let out a deep, warm laugh.

The man blinked at him, caught off guard. "What's so funny?"

Dad shook his head and chuckled again, pointing toward the sky like he was addressing someone directly. "Good one," he said.

The man looked confused.

XVII: The Sign

Dad looked back down at him, his smile now tinged with wonder. "You know what day it is?" he asked.

The man shrugged, still trying to collect himself. "I don't know... the eighteenth?"

"February eighteenth," Dad said, almost to himself now. He leaned back, cigarette trailing smoke into the night air. "2/18. John 2:18."

The man's brow furrowed. "That mean something to you?"

Dad nodded, eyes shining. "After Jesus flipped the tables in the temple—after He cleared out all the mess—the leaders demanded a sign. 'What sign can you show us to prove your authority to do all this?' That's John 2:18. They couldn't see the sign that was already in front of them."

He paused, the silence between them thick with reverence.

"Tonight?" Dad said, gesturing between them. "This conversation. You. Me. This beach. That hat." He tapped the brim of his cap. "That card. That laugh. You think it's all coincidence?"

The man swallowed hard, his voice barely above a whisper. "I don't know what I think."

Dad leaned in gently. "That's okay. You don't have to understand it all right now. But I'm telling you, there's a sign in this. This moment isn't random. God didn't bring you all the way here just to break. He brought you here to begin."

The man's lip trembled. His eyes flicked skyward, as if trying to see the sign Dad spoke of.

"You said earlier," Dad continued, "that you didn't believe in plans anymore. But brother... there's a plan. You were meant to walk this beach tonight. You were meant to find me."

The wind stirred again, soft as breath.

"Not because I have the answers—but because He does. And He knew you needed someone to remind you of that."

The man's voice cracked. "I just feel like I've already lost everything."

Dad nodded, his gaze steady. "I know that feeling. I've been through the fire too. Lost my daughter. Lost my wife. Thought I lost myself. But you know what I found, standing in all that ash?"

The man looked at him, eyes wide and wet.

"Grace," Dad said. "Not because I deserved it. Not because I was strong enough to reach for it. But because God put someone in my path when I needed it. And now, maybe, I'm that someone for you."

The man covered his face with one hand, overcome.

Dad didn't speak for a while. Just let the waves do their work.

Then, finally—after everything—they sat in a stillness so complete it felt sacred. The tide had begun to change, pulling back ever so slightly, the moon's reflection rippling in soft silver threads.

The man looked up.

"My name's Carl," he said, voice hoarse but steady.

Dad froze. The name hit him with such force that for a moment, he couldn't speak. Then it broke—first into a grin, then into a full-blown, belly-shaking laugh. He doubled slightly, one hand resting on his knee, the other wiping away tears that now came not from grief but from sheer disbelief.

Carl blinked, startled. "What's so funny?"

"That's what they've been calling me too!" Dad finally managed to say, laughter tumbling out of him like water over rocks.

Carl stared, confused. "Wait… what?"

Dad waved a hand, trying to catch his breath. "Not really. My name's John. But man… you're not gonna believe this."

Carl tilted his head, clearly intrigued now.

"A couple days ago," Dad began, the smoke from his cigarette curling lazily in the moonlight, "we were at the aviation museum on Ford Island. Out of nowhere, this guy comes charging through the hangar yelling, 'Carl! Carl! Carl!' like he was looking for a fugitive. He stops right in front of me—dead serious—and just stares."

Carl chuckled. "What happened?"

"He looks me in the eye and says, 'You're not Carl,' then runs off without another word." Dad shook his head, still grinning. "Since then, my son and daughter-in-law—Jeff and Danette—haven't let it go. Been calling me Carl all week."

Carl laughed louder, a rich sound that felt like it hadn't been used in years.

Dad reached into his pocket and pulled out the keychain. He held it up between them, catching the starlight. The metal tag gleamed softly: **CARL.**

Carl stared. Then he doubled over laughing, hands on his thighs. "You're serious? That's insane."

Dad nodded, eyes still twinkling. "At first, I thought it was just funny. But now? Now I think God's just showing off."

They laughed until the waves seemed to echo with it—until all that heaviness lifted, not vanished but lightened, shared.

Then Dad went quiet. He looked down at his hands, then at the sky. Something about the moment shifted again—like the laughter had cracked open something deeper.

"Can I pray with you?" he asked.

Carl hesitated. His eyes dropped to the sand, then lifted—just briefly—toward the sky, as if searching for something he didn't yet believe in. For a moment, it looked like he might say no. Might walk away.

But then he nodded.

They stood, shoulders just touching, two silhouettes carved out by moonlight.

Dad closed his eyes and began.

"Father, thank You for this moment. Thank You for the grace that brings light into the darkest corners. Thank You for Carl—thank You that he's still here. That tonight, he found someone who sees him. You've already met him here—thank You for that. Now show him he's not alone. Remind him he still has something to live for. Help him find his way back to the people he's lost. Heal the hurt with his son. Open a door back to his family. To hope. To peace."

"And Lord, remind him—like You reminded me—that we don't have to be strong to be loved. We don't have to have it all figured out to start over. You take broken things and make them beautiful. Do that now. In Carl's heart. In his life. Amen."

Carl didn't move. Not right away. But then, slowly, he lifted his head.

Tears streamed down his cheeks again, but these were different. Not collapse. Not despair. These were the kind that come after something begins to rebuild.

He looked down at the card in his hand, fingers tightening around it.

Wordlessly, he extended it back toward Dad.

But Dad gently pushed it back. "Keep it," he said. "It's yours now."

Carl stared at it a moment longer, then nodded and slipped it into his pocket like it was something sacred.

He looked over at Dad and whispered, "Amen."

Dad smiled, then looked at the stars.

Carl whispered again, almost to himself, "Maybe I wasn't forgotten after all."

The night didn't answer. It didn't need to. The ocean had already spoken, and the stars hadn't looked away. The waves kept their rhythm. The stars held still.

Dad squeezed his shoulder.

"*You never were.*"

XVIII: The Call

The room felt different now. Same walls. Same seats. Same mid-morning light streaking through the narrow windows. But the air had weight now—like the room had listened…and would never forget.

Some students hadn't moved, but their expressions had: slouched backs now upright, heads cradled in hands, eyes wide.

One girl, I noticed, hadn't blinked in nearly a minute. A guy in the back had slid his chair forward, arms on his knees, posture like he was trying to get even closer to what he'd just heard.

No one spoke—not even those who'd scoffed when I first began—especially them—sat stunned. Not because of what I was saying. But because it was undeniable.

XVIII: The Call

There was power in truth. And this felt true—truth that seeped into skin and soul.

I walked slowly back to the front of the room. I didn't look at Professor Wright. Not yet. He hadn't moved since I started talking. Hadn't interrupted. Hadn't even breathed loud enough to notice.

His silence had been permission.

"All of this…" I said, voice softer now. "It unfolded in the spaces between breaths."

A few heads nodded, slow and reverent.

The room—once a space for questions—had become something else entirely.

A witness stand. A chapel. A sacred pause in the rhythm of ordinary life.

If you take one thread out of a story, you don't always notice. At first.

But pull enough, and the whole fabric falls apart.

"That's what I've been trying to say to you all—what I finally realized myself.

Every detail, every decision, every regret and moment of grace in my dad's life… it wasn't random. It was a tapestry. A pattern you could only recognize if you stepped far enough back. And now, I can see it. Every frayed edge. Every hidden knot.

And it didn't start on that beach. It started *long* before Carl. Before the keychain.

That's when I saw it—not only the beach miracle, but a hundred small miracles…threaded together.

If my dad hadn't grown up in a house full of silence and scars, passed down like heirlooms—he might not have survived Vietnam. And without Vietnam, he wouldn't have known how to reach Carl. He wouldn't have understood what that man's silence meant, or how to answer it with something more than clichés.

Without my mom—her strength, her loyalty—he wouldn't have made it home, not really. My brother, my sister, me—we're here because she held him together while he fell apart and stitched himself back again.

If not for that VA visit—Keith, Dr. Palmer, group therapy, flashbacks—he wouldn't have known how to carry it forward.

And if Jeff hadn't called that night—when Dad sat in his recliner at the edge of despair—there might never have been a return to church. No whisper in the dark. No kneeling moment. No "FEW."

If my aunt hadn't scraped together money we didn't have—because she sensed something sacred about the timing—none of us would've been in Hawaii. Dad wouldn't have walked that beach. Danette wouldn't have bought the keychain that turned into a running joke and a sacred token. We wouldn't have laughed. And I wouldn't be standing here talking to you.

And if that guy hadn't come barreling through the aviation museum yelling "Carl!"—Dad wouldn't have been given the name. Wouldn't have carried that joke in his pocket. Wouldn't have had the sacred moment with a stranger who needed exactly what he had to give.

XVIII: The Call

It was all connected. Every sleepless night. Every whispered prayer—angry or desperate. Every seemingly wasted moment. None of it was wasted.

All of it... mattered.

He didn't know that at the time.

How could he?

He didn't know that when his own father screamed or hit him, it was building something in him—something painful, yes—but something that would later help him endure things darker than anyone should face.

He didn't know that when he buried his daughter, one day he'd hold a stranger's pain like a pastor at a funeral.

He didn't know that the stories swapped in a circle of broken veterans would one day echo in the ears of a man on a beach, at the very edge of choosing life or death.

He just lived. Endured. Rebuilt.

And somehow... that was enough.

My dad wasn't perfect. Life cracked him in places no one could see. But he didn't fall apart. He carried it all forward. And when he handed Carl that card and said, 'Keep it,' he wasn't just giving him a number.

He was giving him *everything* he'd fought through. Every ounce of pain turned into purpose. Every lesson grace had to teach."

"I used to think," I said, my voice gentler now, "that the miracle was what happened on that beach. That Dad helped save a life. And maybe that is the miracle. But maybe not."

I paused. Swallowed.

"Maybe the miracle is everything that came before. Everything that led to that one night. The kind of miracle that looks like pain. Like loss. Like ordinary days that stack up until you look back and realize they weren't ordinary at all."

I turned slowly toward the whiteboard, the remnants of Professor Wright's earlier lecture still visible—half-faded words about "**historical context**," "**ancient texts**," "**metaphor over miracle**."

And I thought: no metaphor explains this.

This was real.

This was holy.

This was every breath my father ever took leading to one sacred inhale shared with another man under the stars.

And if it weren't for everything... then none of it would've happened.

The silence that followed felt sacred—like the room had just witnessed something true. The air was thick with emotion, each student grappling with the weight of what they had just heard.

The room stayed hushed—caught in the weight of the moment.

Then, from the second row, Bree shifted forward in her seat. She didn't look around for permission or acknowledgment. Her eyes were locked somewhere far off—on memory more than present company.

"I never used to believe in miracles," she said quietly. "Not because I didn't think they were possible… but because I didn't think they were for people like me."

The silence deepened.

"I used to pray. When I was little. After it happened…" Her voice caught, just for a moment. "After my uncle." Her hands clenched in her lap. "I begged God to take it away. To fix it. To make someone see. But no one ever did. So I stopped praying. I figured either He wasn't there… or He didn't care."

"I've never said that out loud before," she added quietly. "But maybe it was time."

Every eye was on her now. No shock. Just stillness.

"But listening to all this?" she continued, voice gaining strength. "Your dad. That man on the beach. The coincidence that wasn't a coincidence. The way one moment rippled into the next like it was all leading somewhere…"

She looked up, finally, eyes glistening but fierce.

"Maybe miracles aren't about stopping the bad. Maybe they're about what happens after. About not being buried by it. About surviving long enough to be part of someone else's healing." She exhaled shakily. "Maybe God wasn't ignoring me. Maybe He was preparing me."

No one said a word. Not even Wright. Bree's gaze dropped again, but not in shame—just in exhaustion, like something long-carried had finally been laid down.

Aisha spoke next—not loudly, but with the same calm clarity that always seemed to center the room.

"When my cousin died," she began, "I thought it would break me."

Her voice was gentle, but it carried like wind through glass—quiet, but impossible to ignore.

"She was more like my sister than anything else. We did everything together. And then... one day, she was just gone. Drunk driver. Wrong lane. Wrong second." A pause. "I prayed. I really did. I asked God to save her. But He didn't."

She looked down at her desk, fingers brushing the edge of her notebook. "For a while, I thought maybe I wasn't praying hard enough. Or right enough. Like faith was some formula and I had missed a step."

Then she looked up, and her eyes weren't just tearful—they were glowing with something remembered, something sacred.

"The last thing she said to me before she got in the car... she squeezed my hand and said, 'You're going to help someone live one day. And when you do, you'll know it was me who sent them to you.'"

A hush fell over the room.

"She didn't say it like a goodbye. She said it like a promise. And I didn't understand it then. But now..." her voice caught. "Now I'm in nursing school. During my clinicals last week, I sat with a patient who was scared, and I told her she wasn't alone—and she looked me in the eye and said, 'You're the reason I'm not afraid.'"

Aisha swallowed. "That's when I knew. My cousin's prayer wasn't about her own life. It was about mine. About all the lives still waiting to be touched."

No one moved. Not even the clock seemed to tick.

"But then I started thinking about what she believed. About how her faith didn't depend on things going right. She didn't pray because she expected to get everything she wanted. She prayed because she trusted Someone was listening—even when the answer was silence."

Aisha turned slightly toward the center of the room. Her voice didn't shake. It settled like peace in a place that had long needed it.

"I still miss her. That never goes away. But I believe—more now than ever—that God wasn't absent in that moment. He was just doing something I can't see yet." She let the silence stretch. "And maybe all of this... all of us being here right now... is part of that."

"I never thought this class would be where I finally talked about her out loud," she said. "But I think she would've wanted me to."

She looked at me. Then at Wright.

"I believe it," she said simply.

And that was enough.

Across the room, Gabe let out a long breath. He didn't raise his hand—just started speaking, his voice lower than usual. Not sharp. Not guarded. Just... honest.

"I remember sitting in this room at the start of the semester thinking I had most of it figured out. That belief was for people who couldn't handle reality. That faith was just... a kind of emotional crutch."

He looked at me, but not with challenge. With something softer.

"My brother came back from Afghanistan different. Not just shaken—haunted. He didn't talk about it much, but you could see it in his eyes. The way he'd stare at the floor when the news was on. The way he flinched at fireworks. I remember one night, I heard him whispering in the dark—like he was begging someone not to leave him alone."

Gabe's jaw tightened. "Back then, I just thought it was PTSD. Brain chemistry. A thing to be fixed with meds or time. But now..."

He shrugged, then rubbed the back of his neck. "Now I wonder if maybe... maybe he wasn't talking to himself. Maybe he was talking to God. And maybe God was listening."

"I still don't know what I believe," he admitted. "But today made me want to believe he wasn't alone."

He didn't offer a conclusion. He didn't need to.

Beside him, Lena shifted slightly in her chair. She glanced at Gabe, then at me, and then—slowly—spoke up too.

"When I was little, my grandma used to pray over me before bed. I always thought it was sweet, but silly. Like something people did because they didn't have anything better."

She swallowed hard. "But this class... this hour... I don't know. Something's shifted. I still don't know what I believe. But I keep thinking about your dad. About Carl. About all the things that had to line up just right for that moment to happen."

Her voice trembled just slightly. "Maybe it's not about having it all figured out. Maybe it's about being willing to ask the questions."

She looked down at her hands, then gave the smallest smile. "That's where I am right now. Still asking."

"And I think that's okay."

Reid leaned forward in his chair. His elbows rested on his knees, hands clasped loosely, eyes fixed on the floor as if the right words were hidden in the tile.

When he finally spoke, it was quiet—so quiet we had to lean in.

"You know," he said, "I used to think the point of all this was to prove something. Or disprove it."

He looked up, his gaze sweeping across the room.

"But today... I don't know. It felt more like we were just... witnessing something. Like we were supposed to be here for it. Like it was never about proving anything—it was about seeing it."

He sat back again, the chair creaking beneath him.

"Maybe that's faith. Not answers. Just... presence."

Beside him, Liam nodded. He hadn't said much during the semester either, but when he did, it always landed like a stone dropped in still water.

"I get that," Liam said. His voice was deeper, slower—like he carried the weight of experience behind every syllable.

"My dad used to say that life doesn't make sense in the moment. You have to live enough of it to see the thread. I saw it today. In your dad. Even in Wright."

"My dad wouldn't have called it a miracle. But he'd have known what it was."

He glanced toward the professor, whose face was still unreadable.

"That kind of thread? You don't make that up."

And then, simply: "That's how I see it, too."

Kai, who early in the semester had been the loudest voice of skepticism—mocking, scoffing, always ready with a jab—was now leaning forward, elbows on his thighs, hands clasped between his knees. He stared at the floor for a long moment before he spoke. When he did, his voice was low, not uncertain, but careful.

"I used to think this stuff was just... stories," he said. "Things people tell themselves to feel better when life gets hard."

He looked up, scanning the room—not to challenge, but to connect.

"But hearing all of that just now—your dad, the war, the beach, the name... I don't know, man. I kept waiting for it to fall apart, like there had to be some explanation. But it didn't. It just... held."

He let out a slow breath.

"Maybe that's what it is. Maybe it's not about whether it's true in the way we usually measure truth. Maybe it's about what holds when everything else falls."

He paused, glancing toward Bree, toward Reid, then finally toward me.

"I still don't know if I buy all of it. But I get why people do."

And for the first time, there was no sarcasm in his voice. No sideways grin. Just respect.

At the back of the room, Diego—who had spent most of the semester sharpening words into weapons—was unusually still. No smirk. No raised eyebrow. Just a long, steady stare toward the front of the room.

He cleared his throat, and when he spoke, his voice had lost its edge. It was… slower. Measured.

"Look," he said, "I still don't buy all of it. Miracles. Divine timing. God playing cosmic chess."

He gestured vaguely toward the board, toward the space we'd all been breathing in for the past hour.

"But I can't argue with what I saw today. Not just what happened with your dad, or this guy Carl, or even Wright. It's the whole thing. The way every detail connected. Like… like it was written."

Diego tapped his pencil once against his notebook, then stopped.

"I used to think belief was a kind of surrender. Like giving up on reason. But now, I'm not sure. Maybe… maybe belief isn't about surrender. Maybe it's about accepting that not everything's supposed to make sense right away."

He sat back, exhaled.

"I came into this class trying to win arguments. Now I'm just trying to figure out what it all means."

"I guess… I came here for credits. I'm leaving with questions."

He didn't say more. He didn't need to.

Because the room didn't need winning anymore. It needed wonder.

Professor Wright had sunk lower in his chair as the students spoke. He hadn't moved, hadn't looked up. But something in his posture was changing—like gravity had gotten heavier, like the weight of the room had finally found its resting place on his shoulders.

And then, in the silence that followed Diego's words, he spoke.

"My dad's name is Carl," he whispered. "A few weeks ago, I got a call. Out of the blue. Number I didn't recognize. I almost didn't answer it. But I did."

He swallowed hard. "It was my father. I hadn't heard from him in years. Not really. We talked once, maybe twice, in the past decade. But that day… he sounded different. Not tired or bitter like before. He sounded… whole."

He hesitated. Looked down at the desk like something holy had landed there and he wasn't sure he was worthy to touch it.

Wright finally looked up. His eyes were glassy, rimmed red. "He told me he was in Hawaii. Said he'd met someone. Someone who helped him find himself again. He said he'd found God." He paused, voice cracking. "He said he'd seen a miracle."

XVIII: The Call

"He said he wanted to talk. Really talk. Said he didn't want to die without making things right between us. He kept using these words I wasn't used to hearing from him—grace, forgiveness, peace. He said he wasn't the same man anymore. That he was finally ready to be my dad."

Wright blinked hard, as if fighting the part of himself that still didn't know how to receive love when it came unannounced.

Wright leaned back, hands shaking just slightly as they gripped the edge of the desk.

"I hung up on him."

The words landed like thunder in a room already aching with silence.

"I told him he was too late. That miracles don't happen. That change like that doesn't happen overnight. I told him... I didn't believe him."

The silence felt alive. Like even the air was holding its breath.

He took off his glasses, rubbing his eyes. "I thought it was a joke. Some phase. I told him he was delusional. And I haven't heard from him since."

There was a long pause before he added, "But now... now I think I know who that 'someone' was."

I let out a short, stunned laugh—sharp and sudden, breaking the reverent stillness like a breath held too long. Not mocking. Not disbelief. Just awe cracking through the silence.

"You've got to be kidding me," I muttered, almost to myself, shaking my head.

Every eye in the room turned my way.

I smiled—just a little—and felt something deeper behind it. Something like fire.

"If you can't see now that God can do whatever He wants—when He wants, how He wants—then I don't know what else to tell you."

A couple of students exhaled softly, the kind of sound people make when awe meets disbelief. Others just stared, jaws slack, silence stretching like a held note in a song.

Wright stared at me. Really stared. And for the first time all semester, he didn't look like the professor. He looked like a man stripped bare. No pretense. No armor. Just questions and a face full of longing.

"It was him, wasn't it?" he asked quietly. "Your dad."

I nodded. Slowly. "Yeah. It was him."

His head dropped into his hands.

"I thought I missed my chance."

I kept my voice soft. "You didn't. The fact that you're sitting here? That he called you before you even knew what he was walking into? That you heard all this today? That doesn't feel like a coincidence."

Wright's voice barely broke the silence. "I shut him down when he finally opened up."

I looked at him with something gentler now. "Yeah. And maybe now it's your turn to open up."

He looked up again. His eyes brimming.

XVIII: The Call

"I don't even know what to say to him."

I shrugged, a quiet smile tugging at the edge of my mouth. "Maybe just start with, 'Hi, Dad.'"

For the first time, Wright didn't argue. Didn't lecture. Didn't hide behind logic or intellect or control. He just nodded.

He sat there, staring past us, past the board, past the moment—like trying to rewind something with his mind. His thumb traced a circle on the desk. One breath. Then another. Like he was practicing for something sacred.

Wright glanced at the clock, then back at us. No one moved. No one packed up. The silence wasn't awkward—it was reverent. Like the room itself didn't want to be dismissed.

And then, from the corner of the room, a low vibration hummed across the desk.

Heads turned.

Wright glanced down.

The caller ID lit up: "Dad."

He stared at it like it was something out of a dream—unbelievable and undeniable. Like grace had a ringtone.

His eyes widened, just slightly. His hand hovered over the screen, then pulled back. Then hovered again. The moment stretched like a prayer on the edge of being spoken.

His hand moved slowly toward the phone.

The second hand on the wall clock ticked louder than usual. It was technically time to go. But nobody stood. Not yet.

A zipper sounded. Then a shuffle. But no one made for the door. It was as if the weight of what just happened anchored everyone in place.

Wright didn't say, 'Class dismissed.' He just nodded once—slowly—and stepped back. Like he knew whatever lesson needed teaching had already landed.

Diego had gone quiet, but I caught the look in his eyes. It wasn't just analysis anymore. It was something deeper—like maybe, for the first time, he saw presence as more than a treatment plan. Like maybe this was something he'd carry forward into the work he was already meant to do.

Liam stood halfway. Then sat back down. No one said anything. No one had to.

I rose from my chair, walking slowly toward the door. Then I paused. Turned back.

Wright was still staring at the phone.

I tilted my head.
"Are you going to answer it?"

He didn't speak. Just looked down again—like the phone had become something sacred.

And maybe it had.

After all the silence, all the doubt, all the missed years—here it was. Not a trumpet. Not a burning bush. Just a vibration on a desk.

I didn't need to hear the conversation.

XVIII: The Call

The miracle wasn't in the words.

It was in the willingness... to answer.

XIX: Born Again

Time moved on. The class ended. Semesters changed. People graduated.

And then—November 3rd, 2024—everything changed again.

Dad had just moved in with my son's family in Antigo after putting his house on the market. Said he was just tired. "Off." We thought maybe it was stress.

Then came the confusion.

Then the color drained from his skin.

Then the ER doctor in Antigo said the seven words that cracked the floor beneath us: 'He needs to get to Madison. Now."

XIX: Born Again

They rushed him to the Madison VA Hospital. Blood drawn. IVs started. No time for fear, just triage. Within hours, the name dropped: Acute Myeloid Leukemia.

Fast. Aggressive. Brutal.

They stabilized him as best they could. Then wheeled him through connecting corridors into the UW Hospital's oncology wing—same building, different battlefield.

For weeks, it was machines and murmured prayers. Beeps in the dark. Sleepless nights waiting for blood counts to climb. By mid-December, we thought maybe—maybe—he'd be home for Christmas.

But then came neutropenic fever. Back to the VA. No tree. No laughter. Just distance, dread, and a hospital blanket where a plate of stuffing should've been.

We'd had empty seats before. This one felt permanent. But he made it. Again.

By January, he was home—with us. Weak, but alive.

Now he sat in his old recliner—creased brown leather, familiar as breath. The sunlight cut through the blinds, laying gold across his shoulders. Not the kind that ends a day. The kind that begins one.

Not a memory.

A beginning.

I sat across from him, not saying anything at first. We didn't have to fill the silence anymore. Years had stripped away that urgency. What mattered now was being here—together, breathing in the same room.

His skin looked thinner than it used to. Paler, too. But his eyes were the same. Steady. Searching. Still trying to solve things with the quiet kind of wisdom that didn't need applause to exist.

"You ever feel like you're on borrowed time?" he asked.

The question hung in the air like dust in sunlight.

"Most days," I said.

He nodded slowly, eyes drifting toward the window. "Some mornings I wake up and forget for a second. I stretch, I breathe... and then I remember. The pills. The appointments. The tubes. The weight of it all."

"Leukemia's a cruel thing," I said softly.

He smiled, but it didn't reach his eyes. "Yeah. It is."

There was a long pause before he spoke again.

"I think about everything sometimes. Vietnam. Your mom. The beach. Keith. Dr. Palmer. Nicki. That classroom you talked about. Carl. Wright." He chuckled under his breath. "Even the stupid belt buckle."

His voice cracked just a little on the last word. Not enough to shatter the moment. Just enough to mark it.

"And I wonder," he continued, "if all that was building to this. Not just to the cancer. But to something I can't see yet."

I leaned forward, elbows on my knees. "You don't really think God gave you leukemia, do you?"

He looked at me then. Really looked. And when he spoke, it was without an ounce of bitterness.

XIX: Born Again

"I think… maybe He allowed it. Like everything else. Like Vietnam. Like losing her. Like everything that's broken me and held me together all at once. Maybe He knew this was another road I had to walk. Another place I needed to be."

"To teach someone? Or reach someone?" I asked.

He shrugged. "Or maybe just to be present. To show up in the middle of it, and prove that faith can bleed and still be alive."

I swallowed. Hard.

"You've already done more than enough, Dad."

His hand reached over, gripping mine with a strength that still surprised me.

"Maybe," he said. "But maybe there's still one more story I'm supposed to be part of."

We sat like that for a moment, the stillness heavy, sacred.

The Brewers game played low in the background—volume down, but still audible. Just the cadence of the announcer and the soft thump of the ball hitting the glove.

Dad had watched the first couple innings while I made coffee.

The game wasn't even that good. Missed swings. Sloppy fielding. But the sound of it—the rhythm of it—was steady. Familiar.

Dad sipped his water. His hand trembled just slightly.

"Mathews would've knocked that one to Lake Michigan," he muttered.

I smiled. "You're not wrong."

He didn't say more. But I knew he was thinking about that summer. The hayfields. The porch. Earl.

He knew I still had the glove—the Eddie Mathews model he saved up for when he was twelve.

It sat in a shadow box in my office now. Preserved, not because it was perfect, but because it had survived.

Like him.

Then I glanced at the clock. "We have to go."

He sighed, the kind of sigh that came from somewhere deep—exhausted, yes, but not defeated.

"Let's go," he said, easing himself up with slow, careful movement. "Time for me to hate leukemia up close again."

I smiled, but he didn't stop there.

"Still," he added, grabbing his coat, "maybe God gave it to me for a reason. Like He did with everything else."

He looked back at me, something half-hopeful, half-defiant in his eyes.

"Wouldn't be the first time He turned my mess into someone else's miracle."

The cancer center didn't feel like a place of hope when we first started coming.

XIX: Born Again

At first, it smelled like antiseptic and resignation. White walls. Quiet televisions mounted too high. Magazines no one touched. A fish tank that bubbled endlessly but never seemed to soothe. That's what I remembered from those early visits—this creeping sense that time was being measured in drips and beeps, not seconds.

But now, somehow, it felt different.

Because of him.

From the moment we stepped through the automatic doors, he changed the space.

Nurses glanced up from behind their stations and smiled—not out of politeness, but recognition. A tech offered a casual wave, hand lifted like they were greeting someone who mattered. One of the custodians nodded in his direction as we passed—not saying a word, but with a look that said, *"He's one of us."*

He never wore a title. But he didn't need to.

People greeted him with a quiet respect, the kind reserved for someone who had become an anchor in uncertain times.

Dad grinned back—small, unassuming, but warm—offering a little salute, the kind soldiers give when words aren't needed.

Everywhere he went, people lit up.

Not because he was telling jokes. Not because he was loud or attention-seeking.

But because he saw them.

Really saw them. And they knew it.

"Danette, honey!" the receptionist called as we approached. "Y'all brought the trouble with you today!"

Danette squeezed Dad's arm affectionately. "He's the trouble. I'm just the chauffeur."

Dad leaned over the counter, whispering just loud enough to be heard, "She drives like she's late to a wedding she didn't want to attend."

The receptionist burst out laughing.

And it was like that the whole walk down the hall.

Smiles. Nods. Little waves. Not a single person called him anything official.

But the way they looked at him told you everything.

Like he was the steady presence in a place full of unknowns.

And without missing a beat, Danette pushed his wheelchair forward, and every few feet, he'd grin and call out, "Wanna race?"

Most laughed.

A few played along.

When we reached the treatment room, a young nurse met us with a clipboard in hand.

"Your chair's ready, John. You want the window or the wall today?"

"Window," he said. "So I can keep an eye on the trees. They're good at listening."

She smiled. "Trees and nurses—we're both used to hearing a lot."

XIX: Born Again

As he settled into the recliner, Danette and I exchanged a glance. She gave me a small nod, reading the unspoken plan between us.

"Want us to grab coffee?" I asked.

He waved a lazy hand, already settled deep into his chair, blanket draped over his lap like a king surveying his domain. "Only if it's black as a moonless night and hot enough to scorch the unworthy."

"Got it," I said. "One molten cauldron of liquid fire, coming right up."

We turned to go, our footsteps soft against the linoleum.

But just before we rounded the corner, I heard his voice again—low and steady. Not praying. Not yet. Just talking. Gentle, warm.

"Name's John," he said. "What's yours?"

There was a pause. Then a voice answered, gruff, guarded.

"I don't want to hear about God."

The voice hit like a slow echo. I couldn't place it—but the rhythm pulled something loose from memory. A classroom. A desk by the window. Room 304.

Danette paused beside me, glancing over with a raised brow.

I looked back.

Dad hadn't moved. Still calm. Still smiling.

"I hear that a lot," he said. "But I'm going to talk anyway."

Danette raised an eyebrow, amused. "He never stops," she whispered.

I grinned. "That's the problem with preachers. They're like jazz musicians. Always improvising."

Then, just as we stepped into the hallway, I heard the other voice again. Lower now. Softer.

Something about it stopped me cold.

I turned.

Dad leaned slightly toward the young man in the next recliner, his hands folded over his stomach, eyes warm and relaxed. Like they were just two guys chatting about the weather.

"You mad at Him?" Dad asked, not unkindly.

The man didn't answer right away. His arms were crossed tight over his chest. A band of tape peeked out from under his sleeve—fresh from an IV.

"Mad at everything," he muttered. "Life. God. Cancer. People who say everything happens for a reason."

Dad chuckled. Not to mock him, just because he understood.

"Yeah," he said. "That line used to make me furious too."

The man shot him a look. "So don't say it."

"Wouldn't dream of it," Dad said. "I've earned the right to hate that phrase, too."

There was a stretch of silence. Then the man's voice, bitter. "I used to be healthy. Played sports. Ran five miles a day. Now I'm fighting to stand up without throwing up."

Dad nodded. "Cancer'll do that. It's a thief."

Another pause. Then: "So where's your God in all that?"

Dad didn't rush the answer. He never did. He just let the question hang there in the quiet.

"He's right here," he said finally. "Sitting in a plastic recliner next to a kid who's hurting. Crying with him. Holding the IV bag when the nurse's hands shake. Whispering through strangers who know what pain feels like."

The man scoffed. "Sounds convenient."

"No," Dad said gently. "It's not. It's costly. It cost Him everything. But that's the thing about grace—it never looks convenient when it's real. It looks like blood and sweat and breathless prayers at two a.m."

The man didn't speak for a long time. Just stared ahead at the wall.

Dad kept going. "I watched my daughter die. Watched men die in war. Watched parts of myself break that never fully healed. And I used to scream at God for letting it all happen."

"Then why still believe in Him?"

Dad leaned his head back, closed his eyes for a beat. Then opened them again, meeting the young man's stare.

"Because He didn't let it all happen to hurt me. He let it happen so I could be here. With you. Right now."

The man blinked. Once. Twice.

Dad kept going, his voice low and steady.

"You don't have to believe that yet. I get it. But I've been where you are. Angry. Scared. Certain that life had cheated me. And then, one day, someone sat next to me and didn't try to fix it. They just stayed. Reminded me I wasn't alone."

His voice softened even more.

"So that's what I'm doing now. Staying."

The man didn't look at him. But he didn't pull away either.

"Why?" he asked finally.

"Because someone did it for me," Dad said. "And because it changed everything."

I froze in the hallway. The voice had shifted. Less bark, more break. Like anger had been a wall and Dad's calm had found a crack.

Danette touched my arm, but I stayed still, listening.

"Don't start preaching at me," the man was saying. His voice trembled—not with fear, but with fatigue. "You don't know what it's like to be twenty-seven and dying."

Dad didn't flinch. "No," he said, "but I know what it's like to wish you were."

A beat of silence followed. Thick. Heavy.

"What?" the man said, thrown.

"I buried a daughter," Dad continued, voice even. "Held my wife's hand while we said goodbye to a child we'd prayed for. Spent a decade coming home from a war I left twenty years before."

XIX: Born Again

"You don't—" the man began, but Dad didn't let him finish.

"I've begged God to take the pain. Screamed at Him in the middle of the night. Cursed Him for being silent. I know what it's like to bleed in ways doctors can't see."

Another pause. Then a sigh from the stranger.

"I stopped praying when I was a kid," he said, quieter now. "When Mom died. I figured if there was a God, He either hated me or forgot I existed."

"I used to think the same," Dad replied. "But what if He hadn't forgotten? What if He was just waiting for the right moment?"

The man scoffed. "And now's the right moment? When I'm bald and puking up chemo and can't even take a leak without help?"

Dad chuckled, not unkindly. "Sounds like the kind of moment Jesus would show up in. He was always showing up in messes."

"That supposed to comfort me?"

"No," Dad said. "It's supposed to make you think."

There was a long pause. I imagined Dad just sitting there, hands folded over that ridiculous hospital blanket, looking at this man like he was already family.

"I've seen a lot," Dad went on. "Buried more than I've baptized. Lost years I can't get back. But I've also seen a woman hold her abusive husband's hand in forgiveness. Watched a Marine hug a stranger on a beach and say, 'I think I'll call.' I've seen grace show up in places too dark for light."

The man didn't respond.

Dad lowered his voice. "You being here isn't random. Me being here isn't either. You think you're forgotten, but I promise you—God knew you before you were born. He knows your name."

The stranger laughed bitterly. "Yeah? Then what is it?"

There was a beat. Then Dad answered—not with the name. With something better.

"I don't need to know your name to see you," he said. "Really see you."

And that—something in that—broke whatever defenses had been left.

The man's voice cracked. "It's Diego."

The name hit me like a cymbal crash.

I turned to Danette, wide-eyed. She mirrored the look.

Then I stepped back into the room.

Diego saw me—and crumpled.

He didn't cry. Not exactly. It was something deeper. A collapse of disbelief and memory, the kind of recognition that strips you bare.

"You—" he started. "You were in that class."

I nodded, walking slowly toward him. "Yeah. You were, too."

He laughed through the ache. "I didn't think you'd remember me."

"How could I forget?" I said.

He looked from me to Dad, and back again. "He's your father?"

"He is."

Diego blinked. "Of course he is."

He wiped at his eyes. Then looked down, the weight of it all folding into his lap.

"This… this is insane."

Dad grinned. "Nah. This is grace."

Diego shook his head, still staring at Dad like he was trying to make sense of a cosmic joke that had landed in his lap.

"I thought you were just… some old guy in a chair," he said, voice shaky. "Then you start talking, and I hear your voice, and it's like—" He stopped himself, overwhelmed.

"It's like the semester never ended," I offered.

Diego nodded. "Exactly that."

Dad leaned forward, the IV line tugging gently at his arm. "You were in my son's class?"

Diego gave a half-smile. "I was the one always arguing. Thought I was smarter than everyone else."

"Weren't we all, at some point," Dad said.

Diego let out a soft laugh. "I remember thinking that whole last day… the way everyone shifted. The stories. The weight in that room. It was like the walls were listening."

"They were," I said.

He looked up. "You know what stuck with me the most?"

"What?"

"Wright," he said. "He was the biggest skeptic in the room. Bigger than me. But after you told talked about your trip to Hawaii… after he saw that phone call from his dad… something changed in him. You could see it. The armor just… dropped."

I nodded slowly. "Yeah. I saw it, too."

"He came to see me once," Diego said. "Right after I got my diagnosis. Brought a book of poems. Didn't say much. Just sat with me."

Dad's eyebrows lifted. "Really?"

"Yeah," Diego said. "I think it messed him up more than he expected. Seeing someone from that classroom here, like this."

Danette returned with the coffee, holding it carefully as she stepped inside. She saw Diego, then caught the look on my face, and didn't ask a thing. She just handed Dad the cup and sat in the corner, her eyes scanning the room like it was sacred ground.

Diego ran a hand through what little hair he had left. "I've been in room 304 for the past two weeks," he said. "That's my number here. It's weird—I kept thinking about it. Like maybe that room had something… extra. Some meaning."

I blinked, then looked at him more closely. "You remember our classroom?"

He nodded slowly. "Yeah. Why?"

I hesitated, almost not wanting to say it aloud. "That was 304, too."

XIX: Born Again

His head turned, eyes narrowing slightly as if trying to remember something just out of reach. Then they widened, like puzzle pieces clicking into place.

"No way..."

"Feels like an echo," Diego murmured, glancing around the sterile room. "That class. This room. Your dad's voice."

Dad chuckled, low and deep, a sound full of wonder more than amusement. He looked up, toward the ceiling like he was addressing someone invisible.

"Good one again," he said, half-laughing.

Diego glanced between us. "What?"

Dad leaned forward, the cup cradled in his hands, still warm. "You ever read the Gospel of John?" he asked.

Diego shrugged. "Bits and pieces."

"There's a verse—chapter 3, verse 4. Nicodemus is talking to Jesus. Trying to understand what it means to be born again. He says, 'How can someone be born when they are old?'"

Diego's shoulders slumped slightly. "Feels like he's talking to me."

Dad nodded. "He is. Jesus told him that spiritual birth doesn't follow our rules. It's not logic. It's grace. It's not too late."

He leaned in just a little more. "You're sitting in 304 again, Diego—same number, same question. Different kind of night. Nicodemus asked it at night. I asked it in war. You're asking it with IVs in your arms. All of us wondering... is it too late to start over?"

Diego looked down at his hands—the IV line, the tape, the bruises blooming beneath translucent skin. For a long moment, he was silent.

Then, voice low and rough, he said, "I used to think new life was only for the people who hadn't already been wrecked."

His fingers fidgeted with the blanket edge.

"But maybe… maybe it starts here. In the wreckage. When nothing feels possible."

He looked up. Not with certainty, but with something close—an ache trying to become belief.

"Maybe this is what rebirth feels like."

The room held the moment like breath held in a prayer.

Then Diego exhaled, soft as confession. "Okay."

Like Nicodemus, he didn't find the light by understanding it—He found it by stepping into it.

I watched them—my father and this once-angry boy—and realized something I hadn't before.

This was church. Right here, in the middle of IV lines and broken things.

I thought back to the classroom. To the conversations we had. The lives that shifted that day. I thought about how the Gospel of John didn't begin with thunder.

It began with *light*. With a voice that whispered through the dark—and a witness who stayed long enough to see it.

XIX: Born Again

I smiled.

Then Dad leaned forward and said something that felt strangely familiar. Like I'd always known the words. Like I knew what he was going to say before he said them.

Not because I'd heard them.

But because I'd lived them.

Because, once, I'd spoken them.

Like his voice had once come from my mouth.

That was how he changed me.

And everyone he met. In every quiet act. Every long night. Every second chance. Now he was speaking those words—to Diego.

Maybe that's how faith works—not with thunder, but in moments like this.

I thought again about the classroom. About what started there.

And now, here I am. Another room with fluorescent light. Another Thursday where I still don't know how the story ends.

But I know this much—I saw a miracle. I didn't expect it. I didn't ask for it. But there it was.

And once you see it, once you feel it… it's hard to unsee.

In that moment, Room 304 didn't feel like a hospital wing. It felt like a second chance.

I was still lost in that thought—caught between what happened and what was still happening—when I saw Dad lean forward again, voice low and steady.

"You see? Miracles happen all the time. You just have to see them for what they are."

Epilogue: The Ones Who Saw

Classrooms never really close.

The bell rings. The lights dim. The chairs get stacked in quiet corners. But the stories? They linger. They follow you home. Into your thoughts when the house is quiet. Into hospitals, job interviews, dinner tables. Into the places where faith isn't discussed, just lived.

That room—Room 304—should've been just another semester. A three-credit elective. A checkmark on someone's degree plan. But instead, it cracked something open. Something sacred.

I'd signed up expecting a class on the Religions of the World—just another requirement on the path to graduation. But in that one hour, just a few weeks in, it became clear: this wasn't about textbooks or lectures.

Epilogue: The Ones Who Saw

This was something else. Something deeper.

Something that wouldn't stay in the classroom.

Reid was the first to reach out after graduation. He sent a postcard from D.C.—said he's working in the archives at the Smithsonian, curating an exhibit on faith in wartime letters. He said something I've never forgotten:

I'm still not sure what I believe in. But I know what I saw in that room. Some moments leave fingerprints on your soul.

He signs his letters now with just one word: *"Searching."*

Bree—the sharpest critic, the bravest student.

Last I heard, she was traveling between churches, training them on how to respond to abuse without shame. The work is heavy, she says. But she carries it like it's sacred. And she renamed her nonprofit *Room 304.* Told me she needed a name that felt like a promise. A place where no one's pain was ignored.

She's still fierce. Still writes in all caps when she's mad. But there's peace behind her voice now. A kind of peace that comes from doing exactly what you were made for.

She emailed recently with a photo attached—her standing in front of a church banner that read, *"We believe survivors."* The caption underneath just said: *"Still fighting."*

Wright changed, too. Not all at once. And not in the way that makes for a good movie ending. It was slower than that. Quieter.

He never mentioned our class again—not directly. But the next semester, he cut the unit on comparative mythology. Added one on modern testimonies. A student told me he started the new syllabus with a single question, written in white chalk across the board:

"What if memory is evidence?"

I think about that sometimes—how at the beginning of our class, he'd written:

"Miracles ≠ Evidence."

And now... this.

He still wears the same threadbare tweed jacket, still walks into lectures five minutes late with a coffee that's half foam. But the way he speaks now—there's a reverence in it. A humility I hadn't heard before.

He emailed me last month. Subject line: *"Maybe You Were Right."*

The body of the message just said:

"I still teach the curriculum. Still present the world's religions like a historian. But now I tell them that miracles aren't always ancient. That sometimes, they show up in classrooms. Or chemo wards. Or on a voicemail from a father you thought hated you."

He signs off every email with, *"In Progress."* It suits him.

Carl calls Dad every so often. Sometimes they don't even talk, just breathe together across the line. I think they've both learned that silence, too, can be sacred.

Epilogue: The Ones Who Saw

Last Christmas, Carl sent Dad a gift—an old military coin, polished and mounted in a wooden box. No note, no explanation. Just a coin. Dad held it like it was communion.

He told me later, "Sometimes healing doesn't look like forgiveness. Sometimes it's just showing up. And staying."

Then there's Diego.

Some carry the story like memory. Others carry it like a mission. Diego? He's doing both—helping people hold what broke them, until it doesn't anymore.

He's still stubborn. Still skeptical. Still fighting.

These days, he does telehealth counseling, mostly for young adults navigating trauma. He says he feels more like a translator than a therapist—someone helping others name wounds they thought no one could understand.

We text sometimes, late at night, when sleep feels like a stranger. He sends me quotes—Nietzsche, Kierkegaard, even the occasional Bible verse when he's feeling ironic.

A few weeks ago, he sent one that simply said: "I still don't know if I believe," he wrote. "But I think I trust your dad."

That's when I knew something had shifted.

Because trust—that's harder than belief.

His cancer is stable for now. He's tired a lot, but he still jokes like he's bulletproof. Says the hardest part of therapy is pretending like he doesn't need it himself.

But I think he knows.

He's healing.

Slowly. From the inside out.

And then there's Kai. Still dressing like a tech mogul on vacation. But he's different now, too. He runs a nonprofit startup that helps entrepreneurs in underserved communities. He calls it *Frameworks.*

When I asked him why, he said, "Because you can't change people's lives without giving them something to build on."

He never talks about faith directly. But he always circles back to that semester. To the room. Like it was a hinge his life turned on, even if he doesn't admit it out loud.

I asked him once if he believed now. He just shrugged and said, "Does it matter if I do, as long as I live like I saw something real?"

Lena kept writing.

At first, it was just blog posts—reflective essays about grief, belief, and why neither can be cleanly boxed. Then a publisher took notice. Her book, *Seen Through Smoke: Faith in a Skeptic's Voice*, hit shelves last fall— part memoir, part map, part bridge for those still walking through the fog.

It's honest and unsparing, filled with stories not just from the class, but from the people she met after. Survivors. Doubters. Believers who'd stopped pretending belief was easy.

She still sends me drafts sometimes. One line I'll never forget: *"Pain is the doorway. And walking through it is the miracle."*

Epilogue: The Ones Who Saw

She said she wrote it down the day I first said it in class. Said it haunted her—in the best way. Said it reminded her that staying, hurting, hoping... all of it counts.

That's Lena—still skeptical, but now, more open-handed with the mystery.

Then there's Gabe.

I didn't think he'd stay in touch. Too logical, too driven. But he did. More than that—he built something. Literally.

Now he builds schools in war zones and water systems in drought-ravaged villages—real structures, born of tension. He sent me a photo: a well dug in a rural community, surrounded by children with hands lifted high.

The caption read: "I don't know if this is faith. But it sure feels like hope."

He's still quiet. Still wrestling. But now, he builds with that tension instead of running from it.

Ethan went on to get his master's degree and is teaching now—Theology and Literature—at a small liberal arts college out east. His students love him. They say he doesn't give easy answers—just good questions. He runs a campus group called *Still Waters*, a space for people who've been bruised by belief to talk, breathe, pray, or just sit quietly.

He sent me a poem last month. Said it came to him while sitting alone in the chapel after class. The last line simply read: *"Sometimes the gospel is just an old man in a chair who won't let you hate yourself anymore."*

What he didn't know—what he couldn't have known—is how much that line resembled my father. He doesn't know Dad is sick. And yet somehow, his words landed like a whisper from somewhere deeper. Like grace was connecting threads he never meant to tie.

He's working on a book. Quietly. Gently. Like everything he does.

Liam works in community development now. He moved back to the neighborhood he grew up in—same streets, different eyes. He manages a center for at-risk youth. Soccer fields, after-school tutoring, job training programs. But more than that, he's become a bridge—between what was broken and what could still be made whole.

He told me once that sociology taught him systems—but pain taught him people. And faith... well, faith taught him to stay when it would be easier to walk away.

His mom volunteers with him now. Every Tuesday. She bakes too much and yells too loudly at the boys on the field. But when they win, she cries. Every single time.

Not everyone stayed in view.

Reid, for instance, remains in the shadows—watching, collecting, remembering. He's not writing postcards anymore—he's writing for the world: cataloguing whispered grace in unseen corners, letting his searches illuminate others.

He signs every post the same way: "Still watching. Still wondering."

He once wrote about Wright. Quoted him:

"The most dangerous thing about belief is pretending it's easy. The most beautiful thing is walking into it anyway."

Reid's doubt hasn't left. But now it carries a lantern instead of a sword.

And Aisha?

She's here.

Right now.

I see her every time we come in—blue scrubs, tired eyes, voice like balm. She's still the same. Steady. Quiet. Holy in all the ways that matter. She brings Dad his blanket like it's a sacred rite. Holds his hand like it's prayer.

He calls her "angel" sometimes. She never corrects him.

She was with Diego the day he couldn't stop shaking. Just sat beside him, palm on his knee, whispering verses like lullabies.

"Do you believe?" he asked her once.

She smiled. "I don't have to anymore. I've seen."

There was one moment, during another round of chemo, when I saw her again. Clipboard in hand, checking Dad's vitals. She didn't say much—just looked at me and nodded. Then she leaned in close, adjusting his blanket.

"I remember your voice," she whispered to him. "It still matters."

Afterward, she and I stood in the hallway, where the walls seemed to hum with what they'd heard. Machines murmured behind closed doors, but it wasn't the noise that stayed with me—it was the way her eyes didn't blink when truth passed between us. She said she sees it every day now—

faith arriving right where medicine ends. Not with fanfare. Not with a spotlight. But in the quiet weight of someone who stays.

"It doesn't shout," she said. "It doesn't demand attention. It watches. It waits. It stays when others walk away. It holds people steady when they shake so hard they think they'll disappear. It hears the words they can't form yet. It's there, always, in the space between what breaks and what begins."

Then she said something else. Softer. Slower. Something I haven't been able to stop seeing.

"I used to think miracles were flashes," she said.

"Now I think they're witnesses."

She smiled then—a quiet, knowing kind of smile. "And I think we're only beginning to see."

She walked away down the hallway, not fast, not slow, but sure—like someone who doesn't need signs anymore because she's seen enough to become one. Someone who no longer watches for light at the end of the tunnel... because she's learned to carry it.

And she still does.

One room at a time.

One soul at a time.

One sacred breath at a time.

And Dad?

He's still there. Still in that chair. Still steady.

Epilogue: The Ones Who Saw

Still offering presence like it's the most valuable thing a person can give.

Some mornings stretch longer than others. Some nights are quiet but restless. But he never forgets the question: *"Who needs me today?"*

It's not loud, what he offers. It's not glory-filled or camera-ready.

But it is seen.

He anchors those who are adrift.

He listens when truth is fragile.

He stays when hope needs a witness.

And maybe... maybe that's the whole sermon.

I asked him once, quietly, after a long day, "Do you think we did enough?"

He didn't answer. Just watched the light shift through the blinds— like he was trying to read the story as it unfolded. Not finished. But faithful.

And I thought of Lena's words again: *Pain is the doorway. And walking through it is the miracle.*

Maybe—just maybe—he had walked through it.

Then he turned to me. And smiled.

"Enough?" he said. "Son... we didn't write the story. We just lived our lines."

He squeezed my hand.

"And maybe someone else picks up the next page."

Author's Note

This is a true story.

The events, emotions, and spiritual journey within these pages reflect real people and lived experiences—especially those of my father and myself. While many of the moments happened just as written, others have been blended, reshaped, or imagined to preserve a deeper truth: the truth of what was felt, shared, and witnessed.

I was one of the students in the classroom at the heart of this story. That "classroom," however, wasn't a traditional one. The course was online—but the conversations, shared through discussion boards and private messages, became deeply personal. What you read here captures the weight and meaning of those exchanges, even as the setting has been reimagined as Room 304.

Author's Note

Some names have been changed to protect privacy. Others—like "Diego"—represent composites or fictionalized versions of real people. The cancer ward conversation between him and my father, for instance, didn't happen exactly as written. But it reflects the kind of grace I believe my father would have offered if it had.

The character "Aisha" doesn't work at my father's clinic. But she is a tribute—to the quiet faith, compassion, and steadfast presence I've witnessed again and again in healthcare workers along this journey.

One narrative choice bears special mention: the character of "Carl." In real life, Carl is a man my father met during a trip to Hawaii. Professor Wright, meanwhile, has a real and separate father with whom he reconnected. For the sake of clarity and thematic resonance, I chose to blend those two arcs into one. In this story, Carl becomes both—the man in Hawaii and the father Wright longed for. They are not the same person in real life, but their redemptive journeys ran parallel. Told together, they felt even more whole.

As for the students in the epilogue—some remain in my life. Others have drifted away. Their imagined futures aren't fantasy; they're projections. Glimpses of who I believe they might have become, based on who they were in that unforgettable season.

This book is best understood as **narrative nonfiction**: rooted in truth, told through the lens of story. Every miracle described here is real—even if not all of them happened exactly this way.

And that classroom? It's still with me. Room 304 may have been digital, not brick and mortar—but what happened there was no less real. It was sacred space. A place where faith whispered through doubt, and truth spoke through unexpected voices.

We didn't all believe the same things.

But for one fleeting moment, we all saw something together.

And sometimes, that's miracle enough.

Afterword

If you're reading this and you're in pain—if you've lost someone, lost yourself, or lost the will to believe—this book is for you.

It's not a sermon. It's not a blueprint.

It's a reminder.

A reminder that one life still matters. That one voice, one choice, one act of kindness can echo far beyond its moment.

My father didn't heal anyone. He didn't preach in stadiums. He didn't write books or lead movements.

He just showed up.

Over and over again.

Afterword

In hospital rooms. In classrooms. In living rooms.

He listened. He prayed. He loved without needing anything back. And it changed us.

If you're sitting in the dark, I want you to hear this: **The light shines in the darkness, and the darkness has not overcome it.**

Not then. Not now. Not ever.

So don't give up.

Don't let your pain convince you that God has left the room.

He hasn't.

He's sitting right there beside you—in the chemo chair, in the quiet bedroom, in the whispered prayer without words.

This book is a testimony. Not of a perfect life, but of a faithful one. Not of answers, but of presence. Not of magic, but of miracles—the kind that arrive in conversation, in forgiveness, in grace that shows up late but right on time.

And as the disciple John once wrote: **"These things are written that you may believe... and that by believing, you may have life."**

A real life.

Even in the wreckage. **Especially** there.

Because that's where resurrection begins.

If you're struggling with grief, depression, trauma, or thoughts of self-harm, please reach out.

There is no shame in needing support. There is always someone ready to listen. **You are not alone.**

Don't let anyone tell you otherwise.

Not in this moment. Not in this pain. Not in this life.

Miracles still happen. Healing takes time. You are seen. You are loved. You still matter.

Keep going.

If you need help, please reach out to someone who will stand with you:

- **Veterans Crisis Line (U.S.):** Dial 988, then press 1 or text 838255

- **National Suicide & Crisis Lifeline (U.S.):** Call or text 988 | 988lifeline.org

- **National Domestic Violence Hotline:** 1-800-799-SAFE (7233) | thehotline.org

- **Crisis Text Line:** Text HOME to 741741

- **SAMHSA National Helpline (Mental Health/Substance Use):** 1-800-662-HELP (4357)

- **International Readers:** Visit findahelpline.com for resources in your country

Final Prayer: A Prayer of Endurance

This prayer is not the end—it's the echo.
A quiet amen to a Gospel of Endurance.

God of fire and mercy, You saw him before I did.
You carried him when no one else could.

And even now, as his body grows tired, his spirit burns with a quiet
strength that humbles me.

He didn't ask for this story.
He just lived it—one breath, one prayer, one cracked joke at a time.

And through him, You taught me what it means to stay.

This isn't a gospel of ease.
It's a gospel of endurance.
Written in scar tissue.
Preached without a pulpit.
Lived in hospital rooms, war zones, and whispered forgiveness.

Thank You for giving him the strength to endure.
Thank You for the miracles I didn't recognize until years later.
And thank You—most of all—for not wasting a single wound.

Let me carry the page now, Lord.
Let my life echo his.

And may I too learn how to stay, how to love, how to endure.

Amen.

www.ingramcontent.com/pod-product-compliance
Lightning Source LLC
Chambersburg PA
CBHW030905120626
46554CB00001B/16